Necessity Entrepreneurs

Necessity Entrepreneurs

Microenterprise Education and Economic Development

Edited by

Jeremi Brewer

Brigham Young University, USA

Stephen W. Gibson

The Academy for Creating Enterprise, USA

Edward Elgar

Cheltenham, UK • Northampton, MA, USA

Published by
Edward Elgar Publishing Limited
The Lypiatts
15 Lansdown Road
Cheltenham
Glos GL50 2JA
UK

Edward Elgar Publishing, Inc.
William Pratt House
9 Dewey Court
Northampton
Massachusetts 01060
USA

A catalogue record for this book
is available from the British Library

Library of Congress Control Number: 2013954348

This book is available electronically in the ElgarOnline.com
Business Subject Collection, E-ISBN 978 1 78195 618 2

ISBN 978 1 78195 617 5

Typeset by Servis Filmsetting Ltd, Stockport, Cheshire
Printed and bound in Great Britain by T.J. International Ltd, Padstow

Contents

Figures

Tables

Contributors

Eva Balan-Vnuk is currently a PhD student at the Entrepreneurship, Commercialisation and Innovation Centre at the University of Adelaide, investigating social enterprise sustainability, and an alternative approach for identifying and developing collective strategies. She is a Visiting Research Fellow at the Entrepreneurship, Commercialisation and Innovation Centre at the University of Adelaide, Australia. Her research areas incorporate various aspects of entrepreneurship, in particular the strategy, resources, innovation capabilities, and evolution of small and medium enterprises. She has a particular interest in understanding how the application of business principles can aid the sustainability of social enterprises.

Jeremi Brewer is currently conducting his postdoctoral research at Brigham Young University where he is leading the Microenterprise Education Initiative (MEI) at the Ballard Center for Economic Self-Reliance in the Marriott School of Management. He received his Bachelor of Arts in Teaching English to Speakers of Other Languages (TESOL) at Brigham Young University, Hawaii and his PhD in the Hispanic Studies Department at Texas A&M University with an emphasis in Necessity Entrepreneurship Education, Culture, and Poverty.

Mark Coffey oversees Global Partnerships' (GP) social investment funds, directing both the capitalization of GP investment funds and the lending of capital to GP's microfinance and cooperative partners. Prior to his work at Global Partnerships, he served as President of ShoreBank Pacific, the first commercial bank in the United States with a focus on environmentally sustainable community development. Mark has more than 25 years of experience in banking and lending, including serving in executive roles at Homestead Capital, Bank of the Northwest, First Interstate Securities and First Interstate Bank of Texas. An active community member, Mark served as a member of the Board of Directors of BRAC Bank, a development bank known for its work with small business lending in Bangladesh, as a representative to the Board of BRAC Bank Afghanistan, and on the Board of Directors of XacBank, a microfinance bank in Mongolia. Mark is fluent in Spanish and has significant humanitarian volunteer and business experience in Latin America.

John C. Dencker is an Associate Professor in the School of Labor and Employment Relations at the University of Illinois at Urbana-Champaign. He joined the University of Illinois following a postdoctoral fellowship at the Max Planck Institute for Human Development in Berlin, Germany. During the 2011–2012 academic year, he was a visiting professor at the ESADE Business School in Barcelona, Spain. Dr. Dencker's research examines effects of corporate restructuring on the employment relationship, public policy programs designed to help the unemployed transition to self-employment (entrepreneurship), generational dynamics in the workplace, and causes and consequences of domestic and cross-border mergers and acquisitions. He has published his research in several leading journals such as the *Academy of Management Journal*, *Academy of Management Review*, *American Sociological Review*, *Administrative Science Quarterly*, *Industrial Relations*, and *Organization Science*. He serves on the editorial board of the *Academy of Management Journal* and *Administrative Science Quarterly*. Dr. Dencker was born in Elkhart, Kansas, USA in 1968. He received a BA in Economics and US History from Northwestern University in 1990, an MA in Sociology from Harvard University in 1995, and a PhD in Sociology from Harvard University in 1998.

Manjula Dissanyake is a Researcher in Innovation and Entrepreneurship at Entrepreneurship Commercialisation and Innovation Centre (ECIC), the University of Adelaide. Prior to starting his PhD candidature at the ECIC, he was a founding member with highly successful technology start-up companies, one of which was acquired by Symbol Technologies (now a Motorola Company) in 2002. Manjula has worked on innovative projects for leading clients in retail, banking and government sectors including for the Fortune 500. Manjula has co-authored granted US patents in the technology space mainly for the retail industry. He has served on numerous boards of universities and industry chambers including the American Chamber of Commerce. He has presented and chaired sessions at international conferences on Entrepreneurship. He obtained his Bachelors in Information Systems from Manchester Metropolitan University, UK with a First Class Honours and Masters in Advanced Computing from School of Computing University of Colombo, Sri Lanka. He has also obtained his executive management training from Stanford University, USA. He lives in Adelaide with his wife Mano and children Savin and Saheli.

W. Gibb Dyer is the O. Leslie Stone Professor of Entrepreneurship and the Academic Director of the Ballard Center for Economic Self-Reliance. Dr. Dyer is a recognized authority on family business and entrepreneurship and has been quoted in publications such as *Fortune*, *The Wall Street Journal*, *The New York Times*, and *Nation's Business*. In 2007 he was given the faculty teaching award from Brigham Young University's division of continuing education, and in 2008 was given the outstanding faculty award from the Marriott School at BYU. He was recently ranked one of the top 10 researchers in the world in the field of family business. He has published over 45 articles and seven books that have been cited over 4,000 times.

Stephen W. Gibson is Senior Entrepreneur-in-Residence, Center for Entrepreneurship and Technology, and a retired teaching professor at Brigham Young University, Marriott Business School. In 1999, he and his wife, Bette, founded the Academy for Creating Enterprise (ACE), in Cebu, the Philippines. This is a non-profit learning center which has taught 3,640 Filipinos and on their Mexico Campus, 1,700 young adult Mexicans how to start and grow microenterprises. Thousands have worked themselves out of poverty after attending the Academy. He has started nine businesses, including Barclays Oxygen Homecare with eight offices in six states. His primary interests include microfranchising, entrepreneurship and international development. Steve has written and co-edited a five-volume series entitled *Where There Are No Jobs*. His latest Edward Elgar co-edited book was in 2007, entitled *Microfranchising: Creating Wealth at the Bottom of the Pyramid*. He and his wife, Bette, reside in Provo, Utah.

Marc Gruber is Full Professor at the College of Management of Technology at EPFL where he holds the Chair of Entrepreneurship and Technology Commercialization (ENTC). Dr. Gruber joined EPFL in the fall of 2005 coming from the Munich School of Management, University of Munich, where he was the Vice-Director of the Institute of Innovation Research, Technology Management and Entrepreneurship (INNOtec) and manager of the ODEON Center for Entrepreneurship. He has held several visiting scholar posts at the Wharton School, University of Pennsylvania, where he conducts research on technology commercialization and entrepreneurial marketing. Dr. Gruber has published his research on entrepreneurship in several leading journals such as the *Academy of Management Journal*, *Management Science*, *Organization Science*, the *Journal of Business Venturing*, and *Entrepreneurship Theory & Practice*. In addition, he is the co-editor of a textbook on entrepreneurship and was a regular contributor to a weekly column on entrepreneurship in the 'Frankfurter Allgemeine Zeitung'. Dr. Gruber graduated in management from the University of St. Gallen in 1995 and received a PhD in Management from the same university in 2000.

John Hatch earned his Bachelor of Arts degree in History from Johns Hopkins University. In July 1962 Hatch joined the Peace Corps for a two-year tour of duty in Colombia. He returned home for graduate studies at the University of Wisconsin–Madison, obtaining a Master of Arts in Economic History (1970) and a PhD in Economic Development (1973). In between (1970–71) a Fulbright grant allowed him to spend two crop cycles as a hired laborer to 30 peasant farmers in Peru, documenting the power and wisdom of their traditional farming practices. The experience taught him deep respect for the subsistence skills of the poor. For the next 12 years he worked as a consultant in the design, management, and evaluation of mostly agricultural projects seeking to benefit the poor, eventually completing over 55 assignments in 28 countries of Latin America, Africa, and Asia. In 1984, Hatch created his own non-profit agency – the Foundation for International Community Assistance (FINCA), which has been referred to as the 'World Bank for the Poor' and a 'poverty vaccine for the planet' – is quite remarkable and even miraculous. FINCA currently operates village banking programs in 23 countries and since 1984 it has assisted over 1,000,000 families, lending over $360 million (in 2007) to the world's poorest families with a repayment rate of 98 percent, while also generating enough income to completely cover the operating costs of the field programs themselves. Moreover, there are now over 800 village banking programs worldwide in 60 countries created by about 30 other non-profit agencies.

Robert D. Hisrich received his BA from DePauw University, his MBA and PhD degrees from the University of Cincinnati, and honorary doctorate degrees from Chuvash State University (Russia) and the University of Miskolc (Hungary). Prior to joining Thunderbird, Dr. Hisrich held the A. Malachi Mixon, III Chaired Professor of Entrepreneurial Studies at the Weatherhead School of Management, Case Western Reserve University. Dr. Hisrich was a Fulbright Professor at the International Management Center in Budapest, Hungary in 1989. In 1990–91 he was again named a Fulbright Professor in Budapest at the Foundation for Small Enterprise Economic Development, where he also held the Alexander Hamilton Chair in Entrepreneurship. Dr. Hisrich has written over 300 articles on entrepreneurship, international business management, and venture capital, which have appeared in such journals as the *Academy of Management Review*, *California Management Review*, *Columbia Journal of World Business*, *Journal of Business Venturing*, *Sloan Management Review*, and *Small Business Economics*. He has served on the editorial boards of the *Journal of Business Venturing, Entrepreneurship Theory and Practice, Journal of Small Business Management*, and *Journal of International Business and Entrepreneurship*. Besides designing and delivering management and entrepreneurship programs to US and foreign businesses and governments, particularly in transition economies, Dr. Hisrich has instituted academic and training programs such as the university/industry training program in Hungary, a high school teachers' entrepreneurship training program in Russia, an Institute of International Entrepreneurship and Management in Russia, and an Entrepreneurship Center in Ukraine.

Claudine Kearney lectures and researches at University College Dublin. She completed her postdoctoral fellowship at Thunderbird School of Global Management, Arizona in 2010. She holds a PhD and MBS from the University College Dublin, Michael Smurfit Graduate Business School. Dr. Kearney's research pursuits are focused on entrepreneurship and innovation with special interests in antecedents and outcomes of corporate entrepreneurship in private and public sector organizations; entrepreneurship in large corporations, strategy, structure, and their impact on organizational performance; properties of emergence in early stage ventures. She has extensive experience lecturing undergraduate bachelor's degree programs and postgraduate MSc and MBA across the United States, Europe, and Asia and recently held a visiting professorship in entrepreneurship and strategy at the University of Groningen, the Netherlands. Dr. Kearney serves on editorial boards and has published numerous academic journal articles, books, book chapters, and conference papers.

Wendy A. Lindsay is a Lecturer in Entrepreneurship and Innovation, Online Program Coordinator at University of Adelaide. She received her MBA from Bond University and her PhD from the University of Adelaide.

Allan O'Connor is the Academic Director for Innovation and Entrepreneurship Post-Graduate programs at the Entrepreneurship Commercialisation and Innovation Centre (ECIC), the University of Adelaide, Australia. Entrepreneurship and innovation has been at the core of much of Allan's industry experience. Commencing his professional career in 1979 in mechanical engineering, Dr. O'Connor has worked primarily in the small and medium enterprise sector developing and introducing new products, entering new markets, and expanding sales and business opportunities in both established and new business environments. His qualifications in entrepreneurship include a Master in Enterprise Innovation and a PhD in the field of public policy for entrepreneurship education and economic development. Allan's research involves enquiry at the intersections between entrepreneurship and socio-economic development.

Foreword

Lawrence E. Harrison[1]

Although I have lived a half-century longer than he, Dr. Jeremi Brewer and I share a world-view that emphasizes (1) the goal of human progress as defined by the UN Universal Declaration of Human Rights: democratic governance; social justice, particularly with respect to the availability for all of health and education services; and an end to poverty; (2) the obligation of the beneficiaries of these three progressive conditions to help those who have not been as fortunate; and (3) the belief that culture matters—that at the root of underdevelopment lies a set of values, beliefs, and attitudes that block human progress.

I must mention that Dr. Brewer, who is conducting his research at Brigham Young University, is a member of the Church of Jesus Christ of Latter Day Saints – a Mormon – a religion that promotes the values of the UN Universal Declaration but also enables its young people to see first-hand the consequences of religions/cultures that fail to promote those values. (My new book, *Jews, Confucians, and Protestants: Cultural Capital and the End of Multiculturalism*, devotes half a chapter to Mormonism to the writing of which Dr. Brewer made a major contribution.)

Dr. Brewer and I also share work experience in Latin America. I worked for the US Agency for International Development (USAID) for 20 years, including assignments in four Latin American countries (Costa Rica, the Dominican Republic, Guatemala, and Nicaragua) and one African–American country, Haiti. Dr. Brewer focused on Latin America – primarily Mexico, Peru, and Brazil.

I went to my first assignment, Costa Rica, in 1964, believing that Latin Americans had essentially the same value system as we Americans. But by the time I left my second assignment, the Dominican Republic, in 1970, I had become convinced that there was a profound gap that separated essentially Anglo-Protestant American/Canadian culture from the essentially Ibero-Catholic Latin American value system.

Because of his experience in Latin America and the Philippines – so similar to Latin America after three centuries of Spanish rule – Dr. Brewer gravitated to the same conclusion that I had reached: that Latin America's problems were principally the consequence of a value system that suppressed creativity, trust, sense of responsibility, and sense of agency – in a word, entrepreneurship – the consequence of a value system that suppresses individual initiative.

In his capacity as a social-entrepreneur, Dr. Brewer's focus has historically been to institutionalize the Academy for Creating Enterprise (the Academy); a program founded in Cebu, the Philippines, in 1999 by Stephen W. Gibson (the co-editor of this volume), and a program that Dr. Brewer has since spread throughout Latin America, Asia, and West Africa. At its very core, the Academy is specifically designed to help Latter-day Saint necessity entrepreneurs compensate for the entrepreneurial shortcomings of progress-resistant cultures, where 'necessity entrepreneurs' abound. Since 1999, the Academy has training thousands of necessity entrepreneurs in developing countries through its religious-infused entrepreneurship curricula.

In the realm of academia, however, Dr. Brewer's pursuit is find scalable solutions for radical change among 'necessity entrepreneurs' regardless of their religion. His approach to achieve a global impact has been to launch and lead the Microenterprise Education Initiative (MEI) at Brigham Young University's Ballard Center for Economic Self-Reliance, housed in the Marriott School of Management. Through MEI, Dr. Brewer has partnered with research associates at Stanford University, Harvard University, and Mexico's Tecnológico de Monterrey in an effort to develop and provide entrepreneurship and leadership training to 'necessity entrepreneurs' throughout the world.

The fundamental question Dr. Brewer seeks to answer as an academic and social-entrepreneur is: Can a hands-on training approach to 'necessity entrepreneurs' provide them with the values, attitudes, and simple business skills necessary for success – all of which are alien to the culture in which they have reached adulthood. The recent criticism of Nobel Peace Prize winner Muhammad Yunus and his Grameen Bank in Bangladesh underscore this problem.

Consequently, as Dr. Brewer openly recognizes, this book should not be viewed as prescriptive. The contributions are, rather, a highly valuable effort of description and analysis aimed at assessing the value of the 'microenterprise' dimension of economic development.

NOTE

1. Lawrence E. Harrison is the author of *Underdevelopment is a State of Mind, Who Prospers?, The Pan-American Dream, The Central Liberal Truth*, and co-editor,

with Samuel Huntington, of *Culture Matters: How Values Shape Human Progress*. Between 1965 and 1981, he directed USAID missions in the Dominican Republic, Costa Rica, Guatemala, Haiti, and Nicaragua. Harrison was associated with Harvard University's Weatherhead Center for International Affairs for eight years during the period 1981–2001. His articles have appeared in *The New York Times*, *Washington Post*, *Wall Street Journal*, *Boston Globe*, *Atlantic Monthly*, *Foreign Policy*, and *The National Interest*, among other publications.

Acknowledgements

This first volume of the two-volume series was initially conceptualized by Stephen W. Gibson (founder of the Academy for Creating Enterprise) and Dr. Jeremi Brewer, Director of the Microenterprise Education Initiative (MEI) at Brigham Young University. However, this volume would not have been possible without the support and collaboration of Alan Sturmer (Edward Elgar Publishing) and Todd Manwaring (Director of Brigham Young University's Ballard Center for Economic Self-Reliance).

We are especially grateful to Matthew Taylor who has volunteered countless hours of work to make this book a reality. We also want to thank Jessica Pino for her dedication as a research assistant in the Ballard Center and for helping this book come to fruition. We would like to thank Dr. Marc Gruber and Dr. John Dencker for collaborating throughout this publication process and for hosting the 2013 Inaugural Necessity Entrepreneurship Conference. We must also thank Dr. Rebecca A. Brewer for her unwavering support and for being a source of wisdom and strength throughout the years. We would also like to thank Bette M. Gibson for her continued support and vision on the need for educating necessity entrepreneurs in developing nations.

Finally, we send our appreciation to each contributor of this volume for the time spent on preparing meaningful content that will surely shape the discourse of economic development throughout the world.

Introduction

Stephen W. Gibson and Jeremi Brewer

The field of necessity entrepreneurship is gaining traction in academia, as well as among international policy makers. This book comes to fruition just a few weeks after the Inaugural Necessity Entrepreneurship Conference, which was sponsored by the Ballard Center for Economic Self-Reliance in the Marriott School of Management at Brigham Young University, as well as the University of Illinois and the Kauffman Foundation. The primary purpose of the Necessity Entrepreneurship Conference was to provide thought leaders and policy makers from around the world with a platform that fostered theory creation and debate. Many of the chapters produced in this book were delivered, discussed, and debated during this conference.

This book is the first volume of a two volume book series dedicated to clarify who necessity entrepreneurs are and how microenterprise education can more fully help necessity entrepreneurs productively impact the economic development of their respective families, communities, and nations. The theory presented in this volume suggests that microenterprise education can – if presented in a culturally-specific curriculum – do a greater amount of good for necessity entrepreneurs than loaning them money without business education.

Jeremi Brewer

For the past 25 years I have watched the waves of microcredit rise and fall with each passing decade. Perhaps this is one of the greatest blessings of age: one can watch and reflect upon decades of time. In fact, I remember when we first started hearing how microcredit was surely the 'silver bullet' to help end poverty through small loans to the poor in remote areas. I remember donating to microcredit organizations that claimed to help raise the poor out of poverty. After many years, when I sold my business, I decided I would become more involved in the space of social-entrepreneurship: even if that meant sitting on a board of an institution that was lending money to the poor.

I had my reservations about lending money to the poor. I found myself asking questions to those involved in the space such as: If money alone solved the problems of poverty, then would the billions of dollars sent as foreign aid to impoverished nations from developed nations for a century, not have solved the problem a long time ago? Then there was the question about how the poor would deal with receiving a loan. After all, these are wonderfully hard-working people who historically had no access to money and who definitely had not received money-management training previously. It seemed to me that burdening them with debt to start or grow their businesses was simply not the most appropriate venue to help them succeed. The risk was just too high.

The more I became involved with NGOs seeking to help the poor through loans the more unsettled I became. I had made a half a dozen trips to the Philippines and would shake my head as I came home and think: giving money to individuals who have started a small income-generating activity out of necessity is not the best solution to the problem because they simply do not know to use the money to start or grow their microenterprise. Instead, what these necessity entrepreneurs really need is a basic, business education and a shift from a financial culture of poverty to a culture of financial success.

As of today, we all can see that microcredit has not universally eradicated poverty. Undoubtedly, there are many whose lives are better, but the masses of poor still remain. This is precisely why I offer microenterprise education as another tool and resource for the poor who are already involved in operating a small business. I am convinced that, if we can help microenterprise operators understand the most basic business principles and overcome the deeply seeded, multi-faceted challenges of culture (in other words, separating personal and business finances, fatalism, record keeping, formal/written agreements) we will see a significantly positive economic impact within developing nations.

Stephen W. Gibson

This volume has opened the door to, and laid the groundwork for, a more precise discussion on necessity entrepreneurship and economic development. In Chapter 1, Dr. Jeremi Brewer overviews the leading sources regarding necessity entrepreneurship in an effort to illustrate how necessity entrepreneurs can range from the young children of La Paz, Bolivia peddling their products in the streets to the college educated Filipino who simply has little access to formal employment. Dr. Brewer also proposes an innovative categorization of the various necessity entrepreneurs, suggesting that there are at least three categories of necessity entrepreneurs: (1) Low-performing (individuals with little to no formal education), (2) Mid-performing (individuals with some formal education) and finally (3) High-performing (individuals with college degrees).

In Chapter 2, Stephen Gibson shares his vision on how to better understand the needs of necessity entrepreneurs and how to help them prosper in their microenterprises by providing them with a culturally-based business curriculum that focuses on both external and internal factors for behavior change.

In Chapter 3, Dr. Gruber and Dr. Dencker empirically explain how necessity entrepreneurs (founders) lack the necessary business know-how for starting, operating, and growing a small business. Furthermore, they articulate that, once individuals have acquired more skills in a specific industry *or trade* they are much more likely to succeed in creating a sustainable microenterprise.

Chapter 4 is written by Dr. John Hatch, founder of FINCA. In his chapter, Dr. Hatch draws upon his 40 years of experience in the field of economic development and argues that the 'truest' necessity entrepreneurs throughout the world are not the highly educated, nor the moderately educated, but rather, illiterate women and mothers. And, in the spirit of seeking a brighter future for these illiterate mothers, Dr. Hatch suggests that, while the mothers may not be able to read or write, they have access to family capital (in other words, their children who can read and write) which enables them to have a higher chance of success with their microenterprise.

In Chapter 5, Mark Coffey proposes a hybrid of integrated non-financial services and lending for necessity entrepreneurs. Coffey also articulates the need for micro-finance initiatives (MFIs) to place far less attention on pure financial terms (such as increased cash flow, assets purchased and increased profits – all of which lead to improved standards of living) and more attention on the life-changing impact of the additional non-lending services that *could* be provided by MFIs. Coffey then addresses the current movement within the microfinance sector toward MFIs offering a hybrid of integrated non-financial services and traditional loan products to necessity entrepreneurs who, without such assistance, would perhaps never break out of poverty.

In Chapter 6, Dr. Robert Hisrich and Dr. Claudine Kearney build upon the theory offered by Joseph Schumpeter, in that entrepreneurship is as a major influence in driving economic growth and development. They articulate that, though Schumpeter predicted an increase in the number of entrepreneurs will result in an increase in economic growth, his theory has not been supported in the developing world where necessity entrepreneurs abound. Futhermore, Hisrich and Kearney focus their attention on the various bureaucratic barriers that necessity entrepreneurs face when starting/operating a microenterprise and how governments and policy makers could streamline such barriers.

In Chapter 7, Dr. Wendy A. Lindsay highlights the stark reality that necessity entrepreneurs face in developing nations, namely: they struggle to cause any type of significant impact on the economic development of their respective nations. She then explains how, from a policy perspective, it is important to understand the underlying entrepreneurial motivations for individuals if effective entrepreneurship encouragement and support programs are to be developed and implemented. Finally, she offers an empirical case of 287 South African necessity entrepreneurs who participated in a longitudinal (three year) training program. Ultimately, Lindsay concludes that a comprehensive entrepreneurial training program could enhance the entrepreneurial intentions and outcomes of nascent entrepreneurs motivated by necessity.

In Chapter 8, Dr. Gibb Dyer applies his family capital theory to the case of the necessity entrepreneur. In this chapter, Dyer explains how, while 'necessity entrepreneurs' often have greater difficultly gaining access to the resources they need, compared with those more experienced entrepreneurs who have established resource networks, most necessity entrepreneurs can access one form of capital that can help them succeed – family capital. 'Family capital' is the human, social, and financial resources that are available for individuals or groups as a result of family affiliation.

In Chapter 9, Dr. Allan O'Connor, Dr. Eva Balan-Vnuk, and Dr. Manjula Dissanyake analyze policies for entrepreneurship education in Sri Lanka, a country that exhibits a high level of necessity-based entrepreneurship. In their chapter, they address several important questions such as: How is entrepreneurship education policy used in practice to support the development of necessity-driven entrepreneurs in Sri Lanka? Will the empirical evidence from Sri Lanka shed light on whether government policy for entrepreneurship is socially skewed in necessity-based contexts? Can we expect that the alleviation of poverty and reduction of unemployment will dominate the entrepreneurship policy agenda or will a more enlightened approach recognize the importance of entrepreneurship in the knowledge and market sectors of the economy?

As is the case with most thought-provoking books, it is the desire of the co-editors that more questions and academic inquiries will result from this, the first of two volumes, addressing the great potential that microenterprise education has for the tens of millions of necessity entrepreneurs throughout the world. It is the vision of the co-editors of this book, as academics, policy makers, governments, and practitioners (NGO/NPO) join the growing discourse and movement regarding microenterprise education for necessity entrepreneurs, millions of individuals, families, employees, and communities will see a quantifiable and significant impact on the economic development of nations.

Jeremi Brewer
Stephen W. Gibson

1. Defining and classifying necessity entrepreneurs: a review of the literature

Jeremi Brewer

The Global Entrepreneurship Monitor (GEM) coined the terms 'necessity entrepreneurship' and 'necessity entrepreneur,' in 2001 (Block and Wagner, 2010). This chapter aims to demonstrate how the concept of 'necessity entrepreneurship' has been referred to by many individuals, but also how the term itself has yet to be fully integrated into the fields of entrepreneurship education, development, and poverty alleviation.

Sternberg and Wennekers (2005) took the concept of necessity entrepreneurship a step further by explaining that there exist two types of entrepreneurs around the world:

> In an effort to clarify the difference between the two types of entrepreneurs doing business, GEM categorized opportunity entrepreneurs and necessity entrepreneurs into two groups based on the motivation of the start-up. Opportunity entrepreneurs are viewed as entrepreneurs who start a business in order to pursue an opportunity, while necessity entrepreneurship is more need-based. (p. 161)

By clarifying that *motivation* is what separates necessity entrepreneurs from opportunity entrepreneurs, Sternberg and Wennekers (2005) add a significant perspective on how entrepreneurship differs between developed and developing nations. However, while both teams of researchers focused their attention on the role of necessity entrepreneurship in developed countries, neither applied the concept of necessity entrepreneurship to developing countries.

Building on the research of Sternberg and Wennekers (2005), Block and Wagner (2010) further explain why governments, policy makers, and development experts must comprehend the difference between necessity entrepreneurs and opportunity entrepreneurs:

> Understanding the distinction between necessity and opportunity entrepreneurship is important for two reasons: First, understanding why individuals

engage in entrepreneurship explains the steadiness of education and economics at the macro structure. Second, it directly impacts policy initiatives. In many industrialized countries, economic policy differs greatly between these two types of entrepreneurs. For example, in Germany, the state uses funds to promote entrepreneurship as a way out of unemployment and thereby (almost exclusively) supports necessity entrepreneurs. (p. 165)

Block and Wagner add important substance to the lean body of literature on necessity entrepreneurship. They clarify why individuals engage in entrepreneurship, and how that relates to the macro-level structure of their nation. Block and Wagner also demonstrate that by understanding necessity entrepreneurship, policy makers, development experts, and government officials will be better informed on how to create incentives for formal entrepreneurship, as well as the transition from unemployment to self-employment.

Even with these insights and advancements in the literature, Block and Wagner (2010) only investigate the role of necessity entrepreneurship in the context of developed nations. Thus, this investigation falls short of explaining the phenomenon of necessity entrepreneurship in developing nations. As Scott Hipsher (2010) explains: 'While formal business education and the media almost exclusively concentrate on the formal sector of the global economy, the reality is that most of the world's workers are informally employed' (p. 53).

The questions that beckon to be answered, therefore, are: (1) *Why* is most of the world's workforce informally employed, (2) *Who* is writing about them, and (3) *How* can we better serve this massive population?

SUPPLY AND DEMAND: BASIC ECONOMICS

The concept of necessity entrepreneurship in developing nations is easily understood by comparing Oscar Lewis' 'culture of poverty' typology[1] with Lawrence Harrison's and Samuel P. Huntington's *Culture Matters* (2010) 'progress-prone and progress-resistant' typologies (p. 287). First, Lewis explains how many individuals are *forced* into entrepreneurship because they have no other viable options for income and because they had no better opportunity than to take to the streets and peddle their products and services. In other words, there were simply not enough jobs available to them, and even when there were jobs available, the jobs paid so little that it made no financial sense to take them. This is the first half of the equation.

The second half of the equation is found in the Argentine culturalist Mariano Grondona's cultural typology of economic development

(Grondona, 2000), adapted by Harrison. Together, both Harrison and Grondona explain that the amount of support provided for entrepreneurs, in general, is virtually non-existent – which wreaks havoc on nations where the vast majority of their population is self-employed, necessity entrepreneurs working in the informal sector. Harrison further explains why the governments of developing nations view entrepreneurship as a hazardous, even destructive concept – hence they are 'progress-resistant cultures.' Their legal structures and policies are not formed with the intent to foster entrepreneurship in their nations; consequently, a lack of interest in innovation and job-creation undermines the overall economic structure (see Tables 1.1 and 1.2).

The equation is uncomplicated: when the government of a nation does not invest in microenterprise education for its citizens – assuming that the nation's culture does not inculcate its citizens with progressive values, beliefs, and attitudes – then it produces an under-qualified and under-prepared citizenry. This problem is further exacerbated by a generalized lack of investment in innovation, industry, and job creation. The result is chronic economic underdevelopment and an overwhelming number of necessity entrepreneurs. Such is the case in nearly every developing nation.

DAVID BESANKO AND RONALD BRAEUTIGAM

Borrowing the basic economic precept that commerce depends on supply and demand, business management Professor David Besanko and economics Professor Ronald Braeutigam of Northwestern University offer a convincing formula that can be used to explain why necessity entrepreneurs abound in developing nations:

> The four basic rules of economics are:
> 1. If demand increases and supply remains unchanged, then it leads to higher equilibrium price and quantity.
> 2. If demand decreases and supply remains unchanged, then it leads to lower equilibrium price and quantity.
> 3. If supply increases and demand remains unchanged, then it leads to lower equilibrium price and higher quantity.
> 4. If supply decreases and demand remains unchanged, then it leads to higher price and lower quantity. (Besanko and Braeutigam, 2007, p. 33)

As Besanko and Braeutigam (2007) point out, when the macroeconomic infrastructure of a nation does not create (or nurture the creation of) a sufficient number of jobs, the citizens of that nation are forced to rely on their own ingenuity and talents to make a living. In short, they become

Necessity entrepreneurs

Table 1.1 Harrison's 25-factor typology of 'Progress-Prone' and 'Progress-Resistant' cultures

Factor	Progress-Prone Culture	Progress-Resistant Culture
Worldview		
1. Religion	Nurtures rationality, achievement; promotes material pursuits; focus on this world; pragmatism	Nurtures irrationality; inhibits material pursuit; focus on other world, utopianism
2. Destiny	I can influence my destiny for the better	Fatalism, resignation, sorcery
3. Time orientation	Future focus promotes planning, punctuality, deferred gratification	Present or past focus discourages planning, punctuality, saving
4. Wealth	Product of human activity is wealth expandable (positive sum)	What exists (zero sum) is wealth; not expandable
5. Knowledge	Practical, verifiable; facts matter	Abstract, theoretical, cosmological, not verifiable
Values/Virtues		
6. Ethical code	Rigorous within realistic norms; feeds trust	Elastic, wide gap twixt utopian norms and behavior = mistrust
7. Lesser virtues	A job well done, tidiness, courtesy, punctuality matter	Lesser virtues unimportant
8. Education	Indispensable; promotes autonomy, heterodoxy, dissent, creativity	Less priority; promotes dependency, orthodoxy
9. Work and achievement	Live to work: work leads to wealth	Work to live: work does not lead to wealth; work is for the poor
10. Frugality and prosperity	The mother of investment	Threat to equality because those who save get rich, provoking envy
11. Entrepreneurship derives connections	Investment and creativity	Rent-seeking: income from government
12. Risk propensity	Moderate	Low
13. Competition	Leads to excellence	Is a sign of aggression, and a threat to equality – and privilege
14. Innovation	Open; rapid adaptation to innovation	Suspicious; slow adaptation to innovation

ity entrepreneurs_5

Table 1.1   (continued)

Factor	Progress-Prone Culture	Progress-Resistant Culture
15. Advancement	Based on merit, connections	Based on family and/or patron connections
Social Behavior		
16. Rule of law and corruption	Reasonably law-abiding; corruption is prosecuted	Money, connections matter; corruption is tolerated
17. Radius of trust identification and trust	Stronger identification with broader society	Stronger identification with the narrow community
18. Family	The idea of 'family' extends; fortress to broader society	The family is a fortress against the broader society
19. Association (social capital)	Trust, breeds cooperation, affiliation, participation, anomie	Mistrust breeds extreme individualism
20. The individual/ the group	Emphasizes the individual but not excessively	Emphasizes the collectivity
21. Authority	Dispersed: checks and balances, unfettered, often consensus	Centralized: arbitrary
22. Role of elites	Responsibility to society	Power and rent seeking; exploitative
23. Church–state relationship	Secularized; wall between church and state	Religion plays major role in civic sphere
24. Gender relationships	If gender equality not a reality, at least not inconsistent with value system	Women subordinate to men in most dimensions of life
25. Fertility	Number of children should depend on the family's capacity to raise and educate them	Children are gifts of God; they are an economic asset

necessity entrepreneurs. As Hipsher (2010) reports, 'the primary motivator to become entrepreneurs was *survival and not the dream of wealth*, since finding paid employment was challenging' (p. 51). Thus, hundreds of millions of necessity entrepreneurs create microenterprises (small businesses) around the world just so that they can survive.

Table 1.2 A comparison: 'Culture of Poverty' and 'Progress-Resistant Culture' typologies

Factor	Culture of Poverty (Lewis)	Progress-Resistant Culture (Harrison)
Worldview		
1. Religion	100% of Lewis' informants are Catholics; focus on heaven; God = control of all	Nurtures irrationality; inhibits material pursuit; focus on afterlife; utopianism
2. Destiny	Mysterious hand moves all things; we have no control; that which must happen, will happen	Fatalism, resignation, sorcery
3. Time orientation	Past = important; punctuality = unimportant; gratification not deferred	Present or past focus discourages planning, punctuality, saving
4. Wealth	Wealth = evil; wealth = pride; wealth = corruption	What exists (zero sum) is wealth; not expandable
5. Knowledge	Facts not available; cannot trust what government says, locally oriented and focused	Abstract, theoretical, cosmological, not verifiable
Values/Virtues		
6. Ethical code	No clear line of right/wrong; idealistic; suspicion of others	Elastic, wide gap twixt utopian norms and behavior = mistrust
7. Lesser virtues	Public courtesy = important; cleanliness = unimportant	Lesser virtues unimportant (cleanliness = unimportant)
8. Education	Important; hard to access; requires money/resources; desirable	Less priority; promotes dependency, orthodoxy
Economic Behavior		
9. Work and achievement	Work is scarce; no jobs available; capitalism is evil; illegal immigration is preferred to legal immigration	Work to live: work does not lead to wealth; work is for the poor
10. Frugality and prosperity	Saving brings on illness; no control over tomorrow, spend today; saving impossible, expenses too high	A threat to equality because those who save will get rich, provoking envy
11. Entrepreneurship derives connections	There are no jobs; no other options to make money than starting own business; will most likely fail, but will have enough for food	Rent-seeking: income from government; legal structure does not support start-ups
12. Risk propensity	No other choice; take risks or die; gambling is good option	Low

Table 1.2 (continued)

Factor	Culture of Poverty (Lewis)	Progress-Resistant Culture (Harrison)
13. Competition	Leads to destruction of others; to be avoided; creates enemies	Is a sign of aggression, and a threat to equality – and privilege
14. Innovation	Mistrust of new ideas and new government policies	Suspicious; slow adaptation to innovation
15. Advancement	Only with *palancas* (connections); family name important	Based on family and/or patron connections
Social Behavior		
16. Rule of law and corruption	Mistrust; use systems locally; corruption is expected/the norm	Money, connections matter; corruption is tolerated
17. Radius of trust Identification and trust	Immediate family = trust, but not with money; neighbors used but not trusted; narrow community; rich cannot be trusted	Stronger identification with the narrow community
18. Family	Family = blood relatives; high divorce rates; matrifocal families headed by women; neighbors expected to help; infidelity expected/accepted by women	The family is a fortress against the broader society
19. Association (social capital)	Most people cannot be trusted; family first; help others in need	Mistrust breeds extreme individualism
20. The individual/ the group	Collectivity emphasized; help all in need; reduce suffering of others; sacrifice personal progress to help those in need	Emphasizes the collectivity
21. Authority	Centralized, *machismo*, patriarchal	Centralized: arbitrary
22. Role of elites	Elites = unrighteous, prideful; not to be trusted; exploit the poor, have an obligation to help poor	Power and rent seeking; exploitative
23. Church–state relationship	Religion must play a role in every decision; God is always watching; '*Dios ante todo*' (God before all)	Religion plays major role in civic sphere
24. Gender relationships	*Machismo*; male-dominant, men govern homes	Women subordinate to men in most dimensions of life
25. Fertility	Children are inheritance of God	Children are gifts of God

Table 1.3   Adjectives and nouns used to denote underground enterprise[2]

	Words Denoting Underground Enterprise			
Adjectives	Black	Cash-in-hand	Clandestine	Concealed
	Dual	Everyday	Ghetto	Grey
	Hidden	Invisible	Irregular	Marginal
	Moonlight	Non-observed	Non-official	Occult
	Other	Parallel	Peripheral	Unregulated
	Precarious	Second	Shadow	Submerged
	Subterranean	Twilight	Underground	Unexposed
	Unobserved	Untaxed	Underwater	
Nouns	Activity	Business	Economic activity	Economy
	Employment	Enterprise	Firms	Industry
	Sector	Work		

Note: Extension of Williams (2004, Table 1.1).

COLIN C. WILLIAMS

In his seminal book *The Hidden Enterprise: Entrepreneurship in the Underground Economy* (2006), Colin Williams, Professor of Public Policy in the School of Management at the University of Sheffield, provides an extensive overview of the various terms that academics have used regarding necessity entrepreneurs in developing nations. To help exemplify the myriad of words used to describe this 'underground' economy, Williams (2006) employs the use of certain adjectives and nouns as a demonstration of the vast, yet 'hidden,' economic engine created by necessity entrepreneurs (see Table 1.3).

Most importantly, Williams' table shows that the term *necessity entrepreneur* has yet to be adopted by academics focusing on economics, poverty, or development policy.

In addition to combining the most popular terms used by academics, Williams explains that he has written in an effort to fill the void found in the literature on the 'hidden enterprise culture around the world' by offering an in-depth analysis of what has, and has not, been discussed/ written regarding the hundreds of millions of individuals who are pushed into entrepreneurship. His thesis is straightforward: governments and citizens worldwide are aware that there exists a vast, but 'hidden enterprise culture,' which has yet to be fully understood (p. 4). Furthermore, his purpose has been to demonstrate how 'those studying entrepreneurship and those studying the underground economy have widely omitted to explore how they are interrelated' (p. 7).

Williams explains that another major motivation for his research was to differentiate his subjects, who participate in the massive underground economy around the world, from the traditional opportunity entrepreneurs who have been extensively researched:

> Until now, the entrepreneur has been predominately represented by academic textbooks, the media, and government as some sort of superhero figure and ideal-type that lesser mortals can only dream of emulating, while enterprise culture has been depicted as a risk-taking society that always plays by the rules. Here, however, *I will expose how such an uncontaminated*, wholesome, and legitimate representation of entrepreneurship and enterprise culture is wholly out of keeping with the lived experience, as the practices of the Jasons of this world so clearly display. (Williams, 2006, p. 4)

Williams is trying to differentiate *opportunity* entrepreneurship from *necessity* entrepreneurship, and he accomplishes this by comparing 'the Jasons' of this world (an individual in his book who was forced into selling items in the streets of Bolivia) to the hundreds of millions of necessity entrepreneurs who are forced to peddle products in the streets in order to feed their families. The term 'necessity entrepreneurs' would more adequately describe what Williams is trying to explain.

For further clarification, Williams explicitly defines who the individuals involved in the 'underground economy' are and what they tend to do in their businesses. His purpose was to debunk the commonly held beliefs that necessity entrepreneurs participate in illegal and immoral transactions:

> For those who might assume that drug dealers, those selling stolen goods, and so forth are being discussed, this definition explicitly denotes that the only criminality about underground work is the fact that the production and sale of the goods and services are not registered for tax, social security, and/or labour law purposes. Underground workers are here defined as those engaged in the production and sale of goods and services that are unregistered by, or hidden from, the state for tax, social security, and/or labour law purposes but which are legal in all other respects. The underground economy, that is, covers only work where the means are illegitimate, not the ends (goods and services) themselves. As such, underground workers are engaged in either: the evasion of direct (that is income tax) and/or indirect (for example VAT, excise duties) taxes; benefit fraud where the officially registered unemployed work while claiming benefits; or the avoidance of labour legislation, including employers' insurance contributions, minimum wage agreements or certain safety and other standards in the workplace. (Williams, 2006, p. 5)

Williams' distinction of the legal means implemented by necessity entrepreneurs, as well as his definition of the 'hidden' entrepreneur, clarifies who the subjects of his research are and what they do to survive.

HERNANDO DE SOTO

Hernando de Soto, one of the most popular Latin American economists of
the twenty-first century and a staunch activist against the 'culture matters'
thesis, supports Williams' (2006) claim that the majority of necessity
entrepreneurs are not involved in (producing or selling) illegal products
and services. Rather, their businesses do not abide by government regulations. De Soto (2000) refers to these businesses as 'extra-legal' activities
performed by individuals in developing nations who, because of the
imbalanced supply and demand of employment, find their own solutions
to survive. The concept of 'extra-legal' activities approaches the sentiment
of necessity entrepreneurship.

For De Soto (2000), individuals born and living in developing nations,
especially in Latin America, are forced to participate in 'extra-legal' business practices because they have no other viable alternatives for survival;
there are not enough jobs provided by the economy, and the jobs that are
available are so low-paying that it makes no sense for the citizens of that
nation to work for another person when they can sell their own products
and services in the streets and make equal or more money. Additionally,
De Soto places the majority of the blame on the world-view of the governments running developing nations.

Like Harrison, De Soto (2000) holds the sociopolitical structure of a
country responsible for development. For example, De Soto (2000) decries
the world-view of the various governments of Hispanic America, and
especially the government of his native country, Peru, for creating and
implementing dysfunctional, obtuse, and backward legal structures that
do not foster or nurture formal entrepreneurship. De Soto (2000) postu-
lates that Hispanic America remains chronically developing (poor), not
because there is a lack of active entrepreneurs or natural resources; rather,
Hispanic America is chronically developing because the 'extra-legal'
(necessity) entrepreneurs do not follow government regulations and formally register their businesses. However, De Soto (2000) is quick to defend
the abundant 'extra-legal' activity in developing nations by blaming the
cumbersome, arbitrary, and absurd laws and regulations created and
enforced by the governments of developing nations.

In an effort to justify his thesis, and to illustrate just how arbitrary and
absurd the legal structures of 'progress-resistant' governments can be,
De Soto (2000) uses a personal object lesson to reiterate why the 'extra-
legal' entrepreneurs in developing nations have absolutely no motivation,
reason, or incentive to formally register their businesses with their governments. In his book, *The Mystery of Capital: Why Capitalism Triumphs in
the West and Fails Everywhere Else*, De Soto (2000) experiences first-hand

the absurdities faced by 'extra-legal' entrepreneurs in various nations by starting his own business:

> My team and I opened a small garment workshop as an experiment in meeting the requirements for a new, and entirely legal, business. Although the shop was organized to operate with only one worker, it took 289 days and legal costs 31 times the minimum monthly wage to register the business. To obtain authority to build a house on state-owned land took 6 years and 11 months, and 207 administrative steps in 52 governmental offices. Obtaining a legal title to the land took 728 steps. Someone in the Philippines who wants to formalize informal urban property must follow 168 steps over a period of 13–25 years. Someone in Egypt who wants to obtain access to desert land for construction purposes must follow 77 steps with 31 different governmental entities over a period of 6 to 14 years. In Haiti, it takes 111 steps and 4,112 days to obtain a five-year lease contract. (De Soto 2000, pp. 19–20)

Illogical and extensively cumbersome legal bureaucracy is De Soto's explanation for how governments impede the progress of entrepreneurs in developing nations around the world. His example further supports Harrison's sociopolitical typology of how governments fail to foster entrepreneurship and clearly demonstrates that many of the poorest nations in the world have government structures that make formal entrepreneurship unachievable. De Soto (2000) argues that, in order for formal entrepreneurship to take root in developing nations, the governments of those nations must overhaul their microenterprise (small business) regulations, as well as help individuals obtain rights to their land and property. For De Soto, *government matters*.

De Soto must be commended for writing in defense of the 'extra-legal' entrepreneurs. His work provides a first-hand perspective on the challenges and difficulties that hundreds of millions of necessity entrepreneurs living in developing nations face each and every day. His personal example also testifies to the chasm between governments and citizens in developing nations.

CHI HUANG

Social entrepreneur and graduate of Harvard's School of Medicine, Chi Huang understands necessity entrepreneurs. In his book *When Invisible Children Sing*, Huang (2006) sheds substantial light on the day-to-day realities faced by poor Bolivian youth who are forced to survive in the streets:

Look at them. Poverty can cause mothers to abandon their own children, fathers to beat their sons and daughters. Poverty can lead to alcoholism. Some of these children have been molested by their own blood and kin. They are running away from the worst things imaginable. (p. 110)

For Huang's informants, poverty is a vicious, but terribly real, cycle. Many children, as young as five years old, are forced to choose between living at home, where they will experience physical or sexual abuse, and living in the street.

Though he never defines his informants as necessity entrepreneurs, Huang describes how various *external factors* force his informants to move to the streets and, consequently, how they are left with no alternative other than entrepreneurship. The following excerpts are a detailed exhibition of the realities lived by necessity entrepreneurs in Bolivia:

Informant:	'I need to earn money!'
Huang:	'How do you earn money?'
Informant:	'I sell stuff!'
Huang:	'What kind of stuff?'
Informant:	'Just stuff. Chino. Just give me five Bolivianos!'
Huang:	As you can see, we are located in the downtown area, not far from the old cathedral of San Francisco and the grand city square known as Plaza San Francisco, where the *campesina* women set up shop and the street children sell drinks and shine shoes. (p. 8)
Huang:	I walk down the cobblestone steps of the hospital. On the hospital veranda women sell candy, soft drinks, toys, and trinkets. (p. 89)
Huang:	Hundreds of wooden stands sell thousands of imitation goods. Foreigners are rarely seen around these crowded alleyways. (p. 80)
Huang:	'Where is Pedro now?'
Informant:	'Oh he sells gum in the streets by the hospital and then goes to an adolescent boy's home at nights.' (p. 201)
Huang:	Most of the street children have finished working for the day – peddling gum or drinks, washing cars or windows, or singing on the bus. (p. 214)
Informant:	Up Tile Street is where prostitutes sell their bodies. . ..
Huang:	I tell her how she could earn more money selling gum or soda in the street instead of her body – and yes, the juxtaposition of these three 'items' now seems normal to me. (p. 59)
Informant:	'Ten Bolivianos for the blessing. This is what we charge.'
Huang:	'Since when do we sell God?'
Informant:	'The priest needs to feed himself, you know. He is supported by offerings.' (p. 188)

Gum, drinks, cards, trinkets, toys, priesthood blessings, and sex are the 'stuff' that the street children represented in Huang's ethnography are forced to sell. They have no other options. They are, without question, the lowest-performing level of necessity entrepreneurs we see in the streets around the globe.

JOSEPH MUÑOZ

Joseph Muñoz, Professor of International Business at Milikin University and founder of Muñoz and Associates, a firm that facilitates business development, marketing, and finance in emerging markets, investigates the inner workings of microenterprises in developed and developing nations. In his book *Contemporary Microenterprise: Concepts and Cases*, Muñoz (2010) focuses on the microenterprises created by necessity entrepreneurs:

> The tough global environment requires small and medium-sized enterprises, private corporations, and even governments to re-examine existing models and seek out viable operational forms. Countries that experienced financial crises have seen a multitude of hungry and unemployed entrepreneurs coming up with inventive business models to feed themselves and their families. The models created were lean, market-responsive, required minimal capital, and were profitable. With tough economic times, countries around the world are seeing the emergence of microenterprises. (p. 3)

Though he does not refer to these microenterprisers as necessity entrepreneurs, he does explain that the fundamental motivation for starting their small businesses was necessity. Therefore, the term 'necessity entrepreneur' aptly describes these individuals.

Muñoz is right: hungry and unemployed entrepreneurs are coming up with inventive business models to feed themselves and their families. Consequently, individuals either are unable to find employment, or their employment does not pay them enough money to cover necessary expenses. This is necessity entrepreneurship at its very core. His book adds a significant voice to the field of necessity entrepreneurship by compiling various definitions and categorizations for the different types of microenterprises launched by necessity entrepreneurs.

The following is a succinct categorization of the various characterizations employed by leading authorities on microenterprises, as compiled by Muñoz (2010):

Micro entrepreneurs

- Micro entrepreneurs (persons engaged in the practice) find it challenging to seek employment through regular channels, and tend to create their own jobs by starting a small business enterprise. This may be a full-time or part-time arrangement.
- In emerging nations, this sector is largely composed of women with families, the physically challenged, and residents in rural communities.

- Most individuals with an entrepreneurial drive and motivation can operate a microenterprise.
- Male entrepreneurs tend to act immediately upon stimulus (need) and use multiple information sources; female entrepreneurs wait for about one or two years and rely more on informal channels such as family, friends, and acquaintances.

Microenterprises

- The combined terms 'micro' and 'enterprise' suggest that microenterprises are fairly small business operations. Many of them have gross sales of under $25,000 a year.
- Microenterprises are viewed as ventures that are owner-managed, having few employees and limited capital.
- Microenterprises typically have fewer than ten employees, and more commonly fewer than five.
- The majority of microenterprises are operated from home (Muñoz, 2010, p. 4).

These categorizations provide the field of necessity entrepreneurship with a working terminology that can be used to describe the conditions wherein different microenterprises have been created, for the most part, by necessity entrepreneurs.

Most of the microenterprises created by necessity entrepreneurs fail because their owners/operators are under-prepared, under-qualified, and ignorant with respect to the most basic business skills. These necessity entrepreneurs lack the necessary skill set and know-how to launch, grow, and harvest a business. And, finally, though Muñoz maintains that 'most individuals with an entrepreneurial drive and motivation can operate a microenterprise,' he fails to recognize that the greater part of these microenterprises tend to employ fewer than three people, pay little (if any) taxes, or grow their businesses into larger enterprises (p. 5). Thus, while they may appear to operate a business, the vast majority are living day-to-day, trying to survive. These are the necessity entrepreneurs who would benefit significantly from simple and specific business training.

FRED NEWA

In response to Muñoz' (2010) position, Fred Newa, Professor in Strategic Management and international business at the United States International University in Kenya, explains to what extent the microenterprises created by necessity entrepreneurs affect the economies of developing nations/ regions. In writing about Africa, and specifically Kenya, Newa (2010) cites the following data:

> Micro and small enterprises/enterprisers (MSEs) have been cited as a major contributor to poverty reduction in developing countries (p. 89). According to the World Bank, between one-third and three-quarters of total employment in most developing countries is in the informal sector is relevant in Africa, United Nations data indicated that informal employment in the region accounted for 25 percent of the total African labor force and 65 percent of the urban labor force. MSEs constitute 96 percent of all businesses in the country – approximately 1.6 million enterprises – and contribute to 20 percent of Kenya's GDP. (p. 93)

Microenterprises, which are the innovations and creations of individuals pushed into entrepreneurship, are a critical component of developing economies. As Mai Thi Thanh Thai and Ho Thuy Ngoc (2010) suggest, when explaining the role of microenterprises in Vietnam (another chronically developing nation): 'Microenterprises [are] the backbone of the country's socio-economic system' (p. 47).

MICHAEL TROILO

Michael Troilo, Professor of International Business at Tulsa, conducted a case study to demonstrate that progress-resistant governments are found not only in Latin America, but also in nations like Vietnam. In his case study, Troilo (2010) compares and contrasts the legal procedures of the United States with the legal procedures of Vietnam through the experiences of two entrepreneurs: France Au and Duc Pham. Both of these men are of Vietnamese descent: France Au, who was born and raised in Kansas, moved to Vietnam with the hopes of launching a small movie café; and Duc Pham, who was born and raised in Vietnam, moved to Tulsa, Oklahoma and launched a small real estate firm.

Through his case study, Troilo (2010) elucidates the major differences experienced by France Au in Vietnam and Duc Pham – who was not a US citizen – in the United States. Neither Duc nor France Au was forced into entrepreneurship. Instead, each desired to take the risk and launch his respective business. In the end, Duc was able to open his real estate firm by securing a business loan in Tulsa and purchasing different properties with his line of credit. All of the necessary paperwork took Duc less than five days to obtain, sign, and secure. France Au, conversely, was forced to shut down his business after only a few months of breaking even. France Au attributes the failure of his café to the following conditions:

1. **Lack of Government Clarity**: It took France Au six months to get the necessary paperwork; the regulations enforced by the government were not clearly stipulated at the time of opening his business.
2. **Government Dishonesty**: France Au was unable to keep his suppliers honest; they lacked consistency and quality of product, and they charged for products he never received. France Au also found out that a competitor paid the police; several government agencies arrived without notice to inspect his location, and he was required to pay the same fine three separate times to three separate agencies.
3. **Thievery**: France Au was robbed by his employees, his neighbors, and the government; he was forced to pay bribes to get paperwork through the government offices; he was required to pay the police to keep himself and his business protected.

France Au learned the hard way: the Vietnamese government – at both the micro- and macro-level – rejects clarity and transparency, and fosters thievery. Even with great credit in the United States, France Au was unable to secure a loan for his business. He had to fund his business himself.

In contrast to France Au's situation, Duc experienced none of these issues; when Duc opened his business, after securing a loan from a local bank in Oklahoma and registering his corporation with the local government office, he was given step-by-step instructions on how to proceed. His suppliers were willing to provide him with the necessary products for his business, just as they did with his competitors. These case studies show the difference in Third World and First World governments and their support, or lack thereof, of microenterprises.

MUHAMMAD YUNUS

Nobel Peace Prize winner Muhammad Yunus has led the fight against poverty for several decades. Through his efforts, Yunus has provided hundreds of millions of dollars through microcredit loans to millions of people living in poverty around the world. In his book *Banker to the Poor: Micro-Lending and the Battle Against World Poverty*, Yunus (2007) writes the following:

> In many Third World Countries, the overwhelming majority of people make a living through self-employment. Not knowing where to fit these individuals into their analytical framework, economists lump them in a catchall category

called the 'informal sector.' But the informal sector really represents the people's own effort to create their own jobs. I prefer to call it the 'people's economy.' In the absence of economists' support, organizations like Grameen[3] must step into the breach. (p. 184)

The 'breach' that Yunus speaks of refers to the fact that the poor in developing nations are unable to secure loans, much like Troilo's (2010) case study demonstrated. For Yunus, helping the poor gain access to financial capital was of utmost importance. Money, however, constitutes an external factor.

CATEGORIZATION OF NECESSITY ENTREPRENEURS

To date, no formal classification, hierarchy, or categorization of necessity entrepreneurship is found in the literature, and by default, nearly all necessity entrepreneurs have been clumped together (Newa, 2010, p. 88). As Neck and Nelson (1987) explain, 'over 50 different definitions in 75 countries' have 'adopted diverse classifications, depending on its purpose and stage of development of microbusinesses' (p. 101). This shows the overwhelming challenges that arise when trying to compare and contrast necessity entrepreneurs around the globe. Thus, in the spirit of innovation, and with a desire to initiate and facilitate a cohesive discourse on necessity entrepreneurship and necessity entrepreneurs in the academic field, I propose the following highly simplified categorization of necessity entrepreneurs: (1) Low-performing, (2) Mid-performing, and (3) High-performing.

Low-performing

When Oscar Lewis described the lives of his informants, he wrote of how they devised their own ways to survive each day by selling homemade trinkets or crafts in the streets. They had no official office or shop. Seldom had they received a formal education beyond a few years in primary school. They had no business administration training. They did, however, have to survive. They were forced to engineer their own survival. They are the citizens who were forced to construct a survival strategy, or coping mechanism (Leacock, 1971, pp. 10–12). These are the individuals described by Huang earlier in this chapter.

Some examples of low-performing necessity entrepreneurs found in Lewis' research are the children of the families who, with clown-painted faces and balloons stuffed in their pockets, juggle balls to entertain individuals sitting in their cars waiting at the stop lights in Mexico City. They are the old men and women who are found pushing rusty wheelbarrows down the streets, collecting scraps of metal for recycling. They are the adolescents cooking tacos at home and selling them house to house or on the street corner, just to survive.

Rarely do low-performing necessity entrepreneurs have more than a few years of primary education. They never have employees. They never formally register their businesses. If they do not work today, then they do not eat today. In colloquial terms, the low-performing entrepreneurs are referred to as 'street vendors,' 'peddlers,' 'hustlers,' or 'beggars.'

Mid-performing

Mid-performing necessity entrepreneurs have varying levels of education – anywhere from a few years of primary school to a high school diploma – but they tend to have less education than high-performing necessity entrepreneurs. They live in nations where job opportunities are scarce. When there are jobs, the pay is so low that they have no ambition to stay. Prior to launching their ventures, mid-performing necessity entrepreneurs may have a short strategy session of how they want their business to be. They may have a small locale or office, which tends to be in their private domicile or residence. They tend not to register their enterprise formally with the government. They normally have only family members as employees, if any at all. The majority of mid-performing necessity entrepreneurs are self-employed and have debts with friends and family members who lent them money to launch their venture.

High-performing

High-performing necessity entrepreneurs are plentiful in developing nations. They tend to have higher levels of education, usually beyond a high school level. They formally register their businesses with the government. They usually have an accountant and pay taxes. They tend to have more than three employees, not limited to family members. They have an office or locale, whether at their home or a rented/owned space near their place of residence. They tend to have a larger initial capital investment, which is usually granted to them from a microcredit or banking institution. Thus, the majority of high-performing necessity entrepreneurs carry heavy burdens of debt.

Necessity entrepreneurs abound in developing nations. Nevertheless, despite their level of necessity, they are forced to use their own intelligence and combat their conditions through enterprise innovation. In order to survive, and to make sure they feed their families, they are forced to buy, make, or trade something of value. Necessity entrepreneurs should not be confused with criminals or individuals engaged in illegal activities. They do, however, tend to lack the necessary skills and economic know-how – even though they are involved in business activities every day.

Necessity entrepreneurs tend to form part of the informal economy – the world's largest economic sector. Nevertheless, they are truncated, or stuck. And, contrary to popular belief, what they lack is knowledge of strategies for business growth, *not* the resources to progress. Finally, in spite of having capital and credit available to them, and notwithstanding their legal business-owning status, they lack the cultural habits to grow profitable businesses.

CONCLUSION

Necessity entrepreneurs are not lazy, dumb, or less capable than opportunity entrepreneurs. Historically, necessity entrepreneurs have less access to social, cultural, and financial capital, but these are not limitations that justify generational poverty as Yunus and others suggest. Instead, the vast majority of necessity entrepreneurs merely lack access to transparent and simple governmental policies for formal business creation. They lack the *knowledge of how* to start and grow their small income-generating activity. And, they lack the culture of business success. They lack the awareness of how to *do* what needs to be done to succeed. These, and many other reasons, are why hundreds of millions of necessity entrepreneurs throughout the world are not creating successful microenterprises and why the informal sector employs the enormous majority of citizens in developing nations. The solution is not to bring in massive companies for jobs, but rather, to bring basic education to those who are already involved in operating a microenterprise – for small businesses are the backbone of every society around the globe.

The positive solution to the overwhelming sadness we see with necessity entrepreneurs eking out a living, however, is that policy makers, governments, and educators could implement simple adjustments for their citizens to acquire a new culture of business and financial success. Governments could stop handing out free food and money, and start providing their citizens with the necessary resources, clarity of law, incentives, and tools for starting and growing their already existing microenterprises. This is a solution that would help hundreds of millions of individuals operating microenterprises throughout Latin America, Africa, Asia, the United States, or Europe.

Present-day realities, however, indicate that the external factors thesis answers only half of the equation. It does not, however, explain why the formally (legally) registered microbusinesses created by necessity entrepreneurs are also failing all around the world. While external factors do indeed force individuals into business, there are tens of millions of necessity entrepreneurs who have overcome the cumbersome bureaucratic barriers, registered their microenterprise, and paid taxes, but who are still falling short of success. Thus, we must acknowledge that the 'external factors' thesis only addresses half of the equation; the other half of the equation is answered by the 'culture matters' thesis.

Much has been written about changing the external factors that limit, impede, and cause the necessity entrepreneurs in developing nations to fail in their microenterprises. Very little, however, has been researched or understood about *what* the hundreds of millions of necessity entrepreneurs around the world are actually doing *inside* their businesses that causes them to continue as *micro*enterprises. That is to say, very little is known about the businesses practices – *the business culture* – that necessity entrepreneurs implement. Could it be that, in addition to the challenging external factors mentioned, the necessity entrepreneurs of developing nations with microenterprises are failing because of their innate progress-resistant culture? Is it possible that necessity entrepreneurs continue to fail because their core value system – or culture – discourages competition, ambition, growth, integrity, honesty, a future orientation of time, goal setting, contractual agreements, or record keeping, all of which are necessary practices to succeed in business? Could it be that these internal factors are what cause hundreds of millions of legally recognized necessity entrepreneurs to fail in their microenterprises?

These are the questions that very few scholars have taken into consideration when researching the microenterprises created by necessity entrepreneurs. And, these are the specific questions that have inspired the research of this chapter. The time has come to stop looking solely at external factors and start looking within the businesses created by necessity entrepreneurs, for there are millions of individuals who do not have formally registered businesses, but who are selling legal products and rendering legal services. *Internal factors* are crucial to focus on in order to explain why the microenterprises created by necessity entrepreneurs continue to fail. *Internal factors* are what affect the ways in which necessity entrepreneurs do business: the way they think about business, how they view competition, and the way they gauge (or do not) ambition and growth. When investigating the culture of the individual running a business, we must analyze how necessity entrepreneurs participate in business practices and interact with each other.

NOTES

1. Oscar Lewis never created a typology from his works. Instead, I created this typology after synthesizing Lewis' completed works.
2. Extension of Williams (2006, Table 1.1).
3. Grameen Bank was founded by Yunus. It started in Bangladesh and it is an organization dedicated to lending small amounts of capital to the poor without requiring training or collateral.

REFERENCES

Besanko, D. and Braeutigam, R. (2007). *Microeconomics.* Chester, MD: Von Hoffman.

Block, J., and Wagner, M. (2010). Necessity and opportunity entrepreneurs in Germany: Characteristics and earnings differentials. *Schmalenbach Business Review (SBR)*, *62*(2), 154–174.

De Soto, H. (2000). *The mystery of capital: Why capitalism triumphs in the west and fails everywhere else.* New York, NY: Basic Books.

Grondona, Mariano (2000). In Harrison, L. and Huntington, S.P. (eds) (2000). *Culture matters: How values shape human progress.* New York, NY: Basic Books.

Harrison, L. (2000). In Harrison, L. and Huntington, S.P. (eds) (2000). *Culture matters: How values shape human progress.* New York, NY: Basic Books.

Harrison, L. and Huntington, S.P. (eds) (2000). *Culture matters: How values shape human progress.* New York, NY: Basic Books.

Hipsher, S. (2010). Theoretical view on microenterprise entrepreneurial motivators. In Muñoz, J.M.S. (ed.), *Contemporary microenterprise: Concepts and cases* (pp. 49–61). Cheltenham, UK and Northampton, MA, USA: Edward Elgar Publishing.

Huang, C.C. (2006). *When invisible children sing.* Carol Stream, IL: Tyndale House.

Leacock, E. (1971). *The culture of poverty: A critique.* New York, NY: Simon and Schuster.

Muñoz, J.M.S. (ed.) (2010). *Contemporary microenterprise: Concepts and cases.* Cheltenham, UK and Northampton, MA, USA: Edward Elgar Publishing.

Neck, P.A. and Nelson, R.E. (1987). *Small enterprises development: Policies and programs.* Geneva, Switzerland: International Labour Organization.

Newa, F. (2010). Microfinance and the growth of micro and small enterprises (MSEs) in Sub-Saharan Africa: The case of Faulu Kenya. In Muñoz, J.M.S. (ed.), *Contemporary microenterprise: Concepts and cases* (pp. 87–101). Cheltenham, UK and Northampton, MA, USA: Edward Elgar Publishing.

Sternberg, R. and Wennekers, S. (2005). Determinants and effects of new business creation using global entrepreneurship monitor data. *Small Business Economics*, *24*, 193–203.

Thai, M.T.T. and Ngoc, H.T. (2010). Microentrepreneurship in a transitional economy: Evidence from Vietnam. In Muñoz, J.M.S. (ed.), *Contemporary micro-enterprise: Concepts and cases* (pp. 32–49). Cheltenham, UK and Northampton, MA, USA: Edward Elgar Publishing.

Troilo, M. (2010). Microenterprise start-up: A cross national comparison. In Muñoz, J.M.S. (ed.), *Contemporary microenterprise: Concepts and cases* (pp. 9–20). Cheltenham, UK and Northampton, MA, USA: Edward Elgar Publishing.

Williams, C.C. (2004). *Cash-in-hand work: The underground sector and hidden economy of favours.* Basingstoke: Palgrave Macmillan.

Williams, C. (2006). *The hidden enterprise culture: Entrepreneurship in the underground economy* (p. 4). Cheltenham, UK and Northampton, MA, USA: Edward Elgar Publishing.

Yunus, M. (2007). *Banker to the poor: Micro-lending and the battle against world poverty.* New York, NY: Perseus.

2. Understanding and helping the necessity entrepreneur prosper

Stephen W. Gibson

I remember the first necessity entrepreneur I ever met – unfortunately, perhaps I should say *failed* necessity entrepreneur. This single experience marked a turning point in my life, motivating me to undertake a quest that has now lasted 14 years and touched the lives of many people, with no end in sight.

I was on my third week-long volunteer trip in the Philippines when I first got to know Arlene, a 24-year-old Filipina living in humble rural circumstances in northern Luzon. No doubt once hopeful for the future, she now seemed depressed and downtrodden, and for good reason. About a year before I met her, Arlene had suffered a terrible accident while doing volunteer humanitarian work on Manila's crowded and noisy streets. The *jeepney* she was riding in was rear-ended by a truck, and Arlene's mangled legs had to be amputated, leaving her wheelchair-bound for life.

Arlene's volunteer organization felt an obligation to help her financially. They sent out an American husband-and-wife team to build some shelves on her small porch, so she could run a little grocery store or *sari-sari* store, as such businesses are called in the Philippines. The couple painted the shelves green and stocked them with canned goods and non-perishable food. Arlene would be able to run the store from her wheelchair, and her merchandise would help supply her small rural village of 30 homes. Most of all, the couple hoped that the store would enable Arlene to escape poverty and move toward self-reliance.

When I accompanied this humanitarian couple on a follow-up visit to Arlene, we found her green shelves bare and her purse empty. What had happened? Where were all the foodstuffs that the couple had delivered just a month before?

As we spoke with Arlene, we formed a picture of what had gone wrong. Neighbors had come to her store, selected the merchandise they wanted, taken it, and promised to pay for it the next day. Arlene believed them, but the next day never came. In addition, her mother needed food from the *sari-sari* store to feed Arlene's young brothers and sisters, so Arlene had let her take products as well, without paying for them, of course.

Soon, Arlene had no merchandise left to sell. Great intentions had gone astray; hopes and dreams of self-reliance were gone. No wonder Arlene looked so depressed – she had added another big failure to her downward spiral of hopelessness. How different things might have been if the well-meaning couple could have given Arlene just a little business training, some basic rules of thumb for how to achieve success in retail. Without such training, donating merchandise or even supplying money provides little lasting support to people like Arlene and hundreds of millions of other necessity entrepreneurs around the world.

This experience with Arlene deeply affected me, capturing both my compassion and my imagination. I felt driven to find out more about who these impoverished people are, what makes them tick, and what is required for them to rise out of poverty and become self-sufficient and perhaps even prosperous. I wanted to find out what, beyond mere hand-outs, was already being done for these people, and I wanted to explore whether there were any avenues through which my wife, Bette, and I could personally play a role in helping them.

While I cannot tell you what ultimately happened in Arlene's life, I can tell you what Bette and I have learned and what we have accomplished so far on our quest to assist some of the world's necessity entrepreneurs. To date, this quest has helped improve the lives of nearly 6,000 people in developing nations, as well as the lives of their families, their neighbors, and, in many cases, their paid employees and the employees' families.

UNDERSTANDING THE NECESSITY ENTREPRENEUR

By most definitions, entrepreneurs are people who start new businesses. Entrepreneurs invent or adapt a business concept, risk their time and money to establish the business, and strive to operate it and expand it for maximum profit. In ideal circumstances, what motivates an entrepreneur is spotting a dynamic opportunity to introduce a new product or service or to open a new market. When such 'opportunity entrepreneurs' prove successful, they make significant contributions to the economy by purchasing from suppliers, expanding their business locations, hiring hundreds or thousands of employees, and paying taxes.

On the other hand, particularly in developing countries, many entrepreneurs – no doubt hundreds of millions worldwide – start businesses not to capitalize on a perceived opportunity but simply because they have no other option. For these 'necessity entrepreneurs,' the local job market does not work because they do not have the right education or the right connections, and many times there simply are not enough jobs to go around. According to social-innovation journalist David Bornstein (2004), 'The majority of the world's poor are not employed in factories; they are self-employed – as peasant farmers, rural peddlers, urban hawkers, and small producers, usually involved in agriculture and small trade in the world's vast "informal economy"' (p. 156). Authors James W. Lucas and Warner P. Woodworth (1999) wrote, 'Traditional economists have tended to overlook the informal sector, assuming it to be only a short-term substitute for people during a crisis, such as a factory layoff. But the reality is that in the urban Third World, the informal sector is neither small nor temporary. Rather, it is a central aspect of national survival for many nations, ranging from 20 to 60 percent of total national GNPs' (p. 36). In the Philippines, where I have done most of my work in this field, analysts estimate that 93 percent of all businesses are microenterprises run by necessity entrepreneurs. Many consider themselves fortunate if they earn enough profit in a day to feed their family one meal that evening.

With little or no business training or experience, necessity entrepreneurs are prone to make costly mistakes that prevent their businesses from succeeding, which keep them stuck in the multigenerational cycle of poverty. Driven by desperation, they make up their business models on the fly as circumstances allow, often selling goods or services from a blanket, table, cart, or stall. And yet an organization like USAID, which puts out a 120-page 'Entrepreneurship Toolkit' to train its employees on how to promote entrepreneurship in developing countries, readily admits that 'the focus of this toolkit is centered on opportunity entrepreneurship,' rather than on necessity entrepreneurs, which number in the hundreds of millions in developing countries (USAID, 2011, p. 7). Further, external forces – such as civil unrest, government intervention, natural disasters, unscrupulous landlords, organized crime, and corrupt police – often interrupt the efforts of necessity entrepreneurs or even wipe out their fragile microbusinesses. In some cultures, people's attitudes, values, norms, and beliefs work against the fundamental business practices that lead to success, as shown in the story of Arlene and her empty green shelves. Many necessity entrepreneurs either do not recognize cultural attitudes as a cause of failure or do not know how to resist the cultural pressures – even if they realize that giving away their inventory is not good for business, many would still rather help others than say no, even if it means personal and business failure. As a result, their learning curve is often steep and painful, with damage done to their family, their marriage stability, and their own self-esteem and self-actualization. Ultimately, if they keep giving in to counterproductive cultural mores, their businesses will die.

As I have traveled in places like the Philippines, Mexico, and Brazil and collected second-hand observations from around the world, I have noticed patterns among necessity entrepreneurs that reflect a culture of poverty, as opposed to a culture of success:

- They tend to work very hard but not very smart. They are motivated to work 14-hour-plus days by the need to feed their families, and they do not have much time or energy left over to think about how they could improve their business – and even if they did, they do not have a source for learning proven business principles.
- They are focused only on today. With pressing needs at home, this is understandable. However, this hand-to-mouth focus causes them to miss out on business strategies such as analysing past results, planning for future growth, or seeking out new customers.
- Many are extremely generous with their business inventory, equipment, and proceeds. They do not understand that if they are less generous in the beginning, they can build a business that will enable them to become more generous in the future to their family members and friends.
- They typically do not think of their microbusiness as a long-term endeavor. They see it as a stopgap measure until they get a full-time job, marry into money, win the lottery, or otherwise experience good fortune. As a result, they do not feel motivated to build – or even consider the idea of building – a permanent asset with a solid business model and foundation. As author Adrian Slywotzky (2002) wrote, 'To succeed in business, you have to have a genuine, honest-to-goodness interest in profitability. And most people do not. That's all there is to it' (p. 57).
- They tend to copy each other rather than differentiate their businesses. If their neighbor succeeds in a particular line of business, they start selling the same product, and soon the local market gets oversaturated and prices drop.
- Many of them frequently change their business focus, going from one microenterprise to another, much like a bee going from flower to flower, instead of building up momentum in one area of focus. In contrast, management guru Jim Collins (2001) compares improving a business to rotating a massive, heavy flywheel. At first, you have to push hard for a long time with little result. With consistent, sustained effort, however, the flywheel gradually builds up speed. 'There was no single defining action, no grand program, no one killer innova-

tion, no solitary lucky break, no wrenching revolution' that got the wheel spinning, Collins (2001) writes. Momentum 'comes about by a cumulative process – step by step, action by action, decision by decision, turn by turn of the flywheel' (p. 165).

- As sole operators, they often do not make time to keep records or even see the point in doing so. They are comfortable keeping their knowledge of their business all in their head. Consequently, they do not have the data they need to make good business decisions. Even something as simple as a written inventory control system is beyond the operational prowess of many. In addition, they typically do not acquire licenses or pay taxes, which further destabilizes the local economy.

- Many overvalue personal relationships, emphasizing trust and loyalty to a fault. For example, if a long-time supplier raises prices, some will preserve the relationship by continuing to buy from that supplier rather than find a cheaper supplier. Some will not fire family members or employees even when the person is hurting their business, such as by stealing.

For further comparison of the culture of success versus the culture of poverty, see Table 2.1.

By clinging to limiting cultural attitudes, many necessity entrepreneurs fail to produce all the income they could for themselves and their families, let alone grow their businesses – and of course, many fail altogether. When asked what they need to become successful or perhaps even rise to the level of an opportunity entrepreneur, many would say, 'I need more capital.' But providing more capital to someone who cannot or will not use it effectively often simply allows them to fail at a higher level, lengthening out the business death cycle in a manner not unlike giving blood transfusions to a patient with an open artery. As reported in Rowland's (1991) article in *The New York Times*, 'Most small business failures . . . are attributed to management deficiencies rather than to capital or market problems' (as cited in Kuehl and Lambing, 1993, p. 17).

To take a broader view, informal economies driven by necessity entrepreneurship can improve only when individuals are willing to take risks and buck the culture and are taught basic business principles. When individuals resist this kind of change, the entire system stays crippled. Unless individuals get out of their comfort zones and grow, the economies of their communities and nations do not prosper. In extreme cases, dysfunctional cultures resemble crabs trapped in a coffee can – when one crab begins to climb up the side, the others pull him back down. Another metaphor for this cultural mentality is the tall poppy syndrome – when someone

Table 2.1 Typology of microenterprise development

Culture of success	Culture of poverty
I define my own destiny	I have no control over what happens to me – it's God's will
I plan for the future	I worry only about today
I strive for individual growth and success	I want to stay on the same level as others in my community
I can trust employees and others	I distrust anyone except family
I keep records	I can remember everything about my business
I keep my business separate from my family	My business and family are one entity
I run a cash-only business	I extend credit to family, neighbors, and friends
I negotiate with multiple suppliers for the best price	I stay loyal to one supplier
I focus on a single business	I run many businesses at once
I keep strict hours	I open when convenient and close often
I take responsibility for what happens	I feel that circumstances are beyond my control
I value time and punctuality	When I get there is on time
I keep promises	I do what's best for myself
I build my business as an asset	My business is temporary until something better comes along
I plow profits back into the business	I take out all revenue daily
I identify opportunities	I copy my neighbor's business
I want to become wealthy	If God wanted me to be rich, I would have been born wealthy
My individual creativity leads to success	I must have government connections to succeed
I am goal oriented	'Whatever will be will be, come what may'
I feel a sense of urgency	'Mañana, mañana, mañana is good enough for me'
I strive to make my business thrive	Survival is my primary motivation
I work to improve my family's living conditions	I cannot do much to improve our circumstances
If I make wise business decisions, I can succeed	I will succeed if someone gives me more capital
I must work smart at building my business	If I work long enough hours I will succeed
I hire and train accomplished people	I hire my family because I can trust them
If I compete, I can be very successful	I do not want to appear bigger or better than others

demonstrates more merit, talent, or achievement than the average person, the others resent it and cut him or her down. Economic historian David Landes (2000) recounts a Russian joke: 'Peasant Ivan is jealous of neighbor Boris because Boris has a goat. A fairy comes along and offers Ivan a single wish. What does he wish for? That Boris's goat should drop dead' (p. 39).

Those of us who want to help necessity entrepreneurs do not want them to abandon the positive, unique aspects of their culture. However, we do want to help them identify and change the cultural issues that are holding them back from progressing in their businesses. As religious leader Dallin H. Oaks (2012) says, helping people grow and prosper often involves teaching them to 'give up any personal or family traditions or practices that are contrary' to a culture of progress and success (A Distinctive Way of Life section, para. 2).

So the question is, how can we help shorten the learning curve for necessity entrepreneurs and help them behave more like opportunity entrepreneurs – or at a minimum, help them grow their microenterprises into a flourishing business that they can pass on to the next generation to further grow the family asset? We need to help them produce income at a faster rate, grow their businesses, and hire employees, so they can make their world a better place.

HELPING THE NECESSITY ENTREPRENEUR

In order for necessity entrepreneurs to move into the formal economy, achieve self-reliance, and help their communities prosper, they must somehow grow beyond day-to-day subsistence and start earning enough revenue to reinvest in their businesses and develop assets that increase in value. While there's certainly a need for wealthy nations to provide food, medicine, clothing, and shelter to suffering people, this kind of temporary relief does not generally help necessity entrepreneurs – rather, it often undercuts their efforts when visiting do-gooders give away the same goods that local necessity entrepreneurs are trying to sell. When well-meaning Americans bring over bales of free clothing, such generosity can put the community's clothing shop out of business. It's wonderful when a visiting team of dentists provides free dental care to poor people who would otherwise never be able to afford it – in doing so, however, they might inadvertently draw business away from any local dentists practicing in the vicinity.

One approach to helping necessity entrepreneurs is microcredit, a movement that has expanded and evolved in recent years and is accomplishing much good. The philosophy of microcredit is to provide not handouts but small loans so that poor people can expand their microbusinesses by acquiring additional merchandise or equipment and paying for other business needs. However, according to their report from the Mercatus Center at George Mason University, Cowen et al. (2008) said that 'Most microcredit lenders will not lend money for startups: they issue loans only if a borrower's business is already up and running – if the borrower already has a track record as a business person' (p. 3). Microcredit organizations train their borrowers primarily on how to make sure they pay back their loans, not on how to make their businesses more successful. Success is measured within the microcredit industry by the rate of loan repayment, not by how much more profitable the borrower becomes. According to Muhammad Yunus, the 2006 Nobel Peace Prize winner who is generally regarded as the father of microcredit, most microcredit organizations do not teach business skills to their borrowers for two reasons: such training is time-intensive and costly, and when training is provided and the business fails, borrowers tend to blame the lender rather than themselves – creating ill will and leaving unpaid loans (personal communication, May 1998).

Yes, microcredit provides capital to necessity entrepreneurs at a discounted rate, as opposed to loan sharks or 'five-sixers,' aggressive lenders in the Philippines who loan 500 pesos in the morning and demand repayment of 600 pesos that evening. However, as I have written previously:

> Although many microenterprises that were started with microcredit loans have prospered and transformed lifestyles for the people who run them, they seldom move beyond the ability to provide a somewhat meager income for the borrower. In 1998, a group of university students interviewed microcredit borrowers about the status and size of their microenterprise. Of 381 interviewees, only a very small percentage had grown their microenterprises to the point where they had hired a non-family employee; only one had a non-cottage business, several employees, and multiple locations in multiple villages. Although the rest of the interviewees had improved their standard of living, they were still very small by comparison. (Gibson, 2007, p. 21)

Clearly, something deeper and more fundamental is needed to empower these people, so they can parlay their efforts and their capital – whether borrowed or earned – with maximum effectiveness. In my experience, what necessity entrepreneurs need more than anything else is microenterprise education, which teaches universal, proven business skills that can help people develop or improve a business and turn it into a successful venture that provides significantly more income. This training is designed for impoverished people who are willing to put in disciplined effort to learn sound business principles and apply them in microenterprises. Microenterprise education aims not only to help necessity entrepreneurs better understand business basics but also to actually transform their attitudes and practices, including the counterproductive behaviors often imposed by local cultures. The goal is to help them start small but think big. Without microenterprise education, most necessity entrepreneurs will never permanently rise above a subsistence level, even if they receive numerous microcredit loans.

Although microenterprise education is fairly new, dozens of NGOs are already engaged in this approach. For my wife Bette and me, our life circumstances have enabled us to help blaze a more entrepreneurial-minded trail in microenterprise education. After twenty years of entrepreneurial pursuits in the fields of employment recruiting and home oxygen supply, we had reached the point where we'd acquired enough means and experience to begin a new phase of our lives. We were inspired by the philosophy of Andrew Carnegie (1933), who challenged the successful individual to live moderately and then 'consider all surplus revenues which come to him simply as trust funds, which he is called upon to administer in the manner which, in his judgment, is best calculated to produce the most beneficial results for the community – the man of wealth thus becoming the mere trustee and agent for his poorer brethren' (p. 333). With this new sense of mission, I started volunteering at Brigham Young University's Center for Entrepreneurship in Provo, Utah, where I soon became a faculty member. At BYU, I met a professor and author named Warner P. Woodworth, who opened my eyes to our opportunity and responsibility to help the poor internationally.

Fired up with purpose, I began traveling to the Philippines to provide volunteer assistance. As I worked with Filipinos, I found myself developing a personal philosophy for helping the poor. I was struck by a statement made by a past leader of my religious faith, who taught that our charity is most effective when we 'put the poor in a way to help themselves so that in turn they may help others' (Smith, 1907, pp. 831–833). Because of my entrepreneurial background, this concept clicked with me. My business experience had taught me to seek a quick return on my investments, and I wanted to achieve similar results with my philanthropic endeavors. I wanted to use my resources to help people learn to help themselves in the fastest time possible, as well as empower them to help others. I did not want to repeatedly invest over a long period of time in people who lacked the desire, the will, the discipline, or the ability to help themselves. In short, I wanted to focus on helping disadvantaged people who demonstrated real entrepreneurial potential. I have come to see this as a form of social entrepreneurship – in other words, identifying a social problem, innovating a solution, and organizing the resources needed to help individuals develop their own capacity to solve their problems, with help from well-designed and effectively taught business principles.

I soon realized that the best way to get the quickest return would be to provide business education to breadwinners, not only so they could better provide for their spouse and children but also so they could train and perhaps even employ other people, in addition to family members. In this way, I could spread my investment throughout a family and a community, potentially improving the lives of thousands of people. As we consulted with others, Bette and I decided to develop a curriculum to teach entrepreneurship to ambitious young people in places like the Philippines. Bette has an extensive background in education, so she was an ideal partner for this undertaking.

In November 1999, we founded the Academy for Creating Enterprise, a non-profit organization for teaching microenterprise business principles to poor people living in Third World countries. We packed up 13 suitcases full of clothing, training materials, and 15 used laptops that we were able to purchase for $150 apiece. Upon our arrival in Cebu, the Philippines, we rented a large house with 12 bedrooms, two kitchens, and a spacious living room that we turned into a training room, intending to use this facility to house and train up to 30 students at a time from all over the Philippines. We began reaching out through church channels to identify suitable students. In January 2000, our first group of 27 eager participants, ages 21 to 35, arrived for an eight-week course of study. Each student paid $50 and their own transportation costs, an amount that was often not easy for them to raise – however, part of our philosophy was that people place a higher value on something for which they have to sacrifice. We then covered the remaining expenses with our own funds and donations from others. We realized that the cost was high – and it has since, by the way, dropped to nearly half the original amount. But when we compared the cost to a charitable effort such as an orphanage, where it costs considerably more to house and feed a child for 16 years or more, we felt confident that this investment would yield far better long-term results than anything else we could do.

After that first successful eight-week session, Bette and I worked and lived in the Philippines for a total of 19 months. In addition to educating hundreds of students, we trained local Academy graduates as our replacements before returning home to Provo to run the Academy from there. Over the past 14 years, the Academy has taught nearly 5,000 students in Brazil, Mexico, and the Philippines about how to create profitable businesses. In addition, Academy curriculum has been taught by others in numerous countries throughout the developing world.

METHODS AND RESULTS OF MICROENTERPRISE EDUCATION

The Academy for Creating Enterprise provides young men and women with the necessary hope, motivation, education, and practice needed to plan, start, grow, and continuously improve microenterprise businesses. The principles we teach are simple yet critical to doing well in business, even if the business is nothing more than selling fresh fruit or running an Internet café. Our curriculum teaches students about discipline, patience, self-improvement, hard work, goal setting, honesty, and helping others. In addition, the course disrupts common cultural paradigms that can keep necessity entrepreneurs from becoming prosperous (Gibson, 1999). As students become immersed in learning how to recognize opportunities for economic gain, they get excited for the future because they can finally see a realistic reason for hope. This changed mindset is one of the most life-altering economic outcomes among our graduates.

Beyond traditional methods such as lectures and reading assignments, the Academy also employs several additional styles of teaching, including the discovery method, experiential training, practical application, and case studies.

We use the discovery method to introduce the core of our curriculum: 25 vital principles that we call the rules of thumb (see Table 2.2). These simple phrases, usually six words or less, encapsulate basic business concepts for operating a microenterprise profitably. However, our instructors do not simply spoon-feed these rules to the students. Through the discovery method, which emphasizes asking students strategic questions and using case studies rather than simply giving them the answers, instructors guide the students to essentially come up with the rules of thumb themselves. In other words, each Academy class recreates the 25 rules of thumb seemingly from scratch. In contrast with rote learning, this approach engages the students more deeply, teaches them critical-thinking skills, and gives them a sense of ownership of their new hard-won knowledge. In individual mentoring sessions held years after graduation, we find that business owners can often self-diagnose their business's shortcomings by citing the memorized Rules of Thumb.

Another way the Academy teaches is through experiential training. In addition to attending classes, the students spend time practicing income-generating activities through a trade-up exercise. Inspired by the experience of Kyle MacDonald, a Canadian blogger who started with a red paperclip, made 14 trades over the course of a year, and ended up with a house, we give students a small item, such as an egg, a marshmallow, or even a rock, and then we set them loose in the community (One Red

Table 2.2   The 25 rules of thumb

Rule	Explanation
1. Sell What the Market Will Buy	Solving a critical, recurring problem is the best way to create a business.
2. Practice Separate Entities	Keep personal and business money separate.
3. Start Small, Think Big	Learn basics when small and less costly. Then grow.
4. Be Nice Later	Do not give your product, services, or business capital away to friends and relatives.
5. Keep Good Records	Success comes from beating yesterday's sales and profit records.
6. Pay Yourself a Livable Salary	This eliminates taking all the cash out of the business for living expenses.
7. Buy Low, Sell High	The bigger the difference, the greater the potential profit.
8. Do not Eat Your Inventory	Consuming inventory or seed capital will quickly kill your business.
9. Use Multiple Suppliers	Negotiating with several suppliers for the best price is critical to success.
10. Buy on Credit, Sell for Cash	Selling products before payment to suppliers increases cash flow.
11. Purchase in Bulk	Suppliers usually sell products cheaper if purchased in volume.
12. Use Suggestive Selling	Suggest to each customer other items they might like or need.
13. Increase Sales, Decrease Costs	As the gap grows bigger, net profits also grow bigger.
14. Turn Your Inventory Often	Profit is made every time inventory is priced right and sold.
15. Value Your Customers	Keeping them coming back and buying more is a key to success.
16. Differentiate Your Business	Give customers a reason to return; better, cheaper, faster.
17. Hire Slow, Fire Fast	Screen potential employees carefully. Terminate bad hires quickly.
18. Inspect More, Expect Less	Consistent performance comes from inspecting, not expecting.
19. Have Written Agreements with Partners, Suppliers, Landlords and Employees	The dullest pencil is better than the sharpest memory.
20. Work on Your Business 10 Hours a Day, Five and a Half Days a Week	Anything less is a hobby.

Table 2.2   (continued)

Rule	Explanation
21. Practice Kaizen	Kaizen means continual improvement. This is vital to income growth.
22. Make a Profit Every Day	If a work day goes by without profit, it's a loss.
23. Work *on* Your Business, Not Just *in* Your Business	Stand back and watch, then fix immediately.
24. Write Daily/Weekly Business Goals	Stretching for more will move business forward faster.
25. Focus, Focus, Focus	A concentrated effort on one venture pays huge returns.

Paperclip, 2006). By searching for opportunities and negotiating, they trade their small items for progressively more valuable assets. One student went out with an egg and came back with a live chicken, thus answering the age-old question of which comes first, the chicken or the egg. This exercise helps students start thinking more like entrepreneurs who strive to identify economic opportunities and increase the value of their assets. At our academy in Mexico, where students currently pay $310 USD to attend a five-week course, the goal is for them to earn back their fee through this exercise, so they will have seed money available for starting a business after graduation. During 2012, about 60 percent of Academy students successfully earned back their fee while taking the course, together raising a total of $96,500 USD.[1]

One of the best ways to help students internalize new concepts is to provide opportunities for practical application. The Academy does this in several ways. One effective approach involves taking students out into the microbusiness community to visit local microenterprises and talk with owners about what they have learned so far at the Academy. At the same time, the students observe real microenterprises in operation, finding out more about what works and what does not work. It's powerful for students, even after the second week, to rub shoulders with real necessity entrepreneurs and witness first-hand that it's possible to run profitable businesses on a micro scale, as well as observe why knowing the rules of thumb is so important.

Case studies have long been a vital component of business education, allowing instructors to simulate real business situations in the classroom so that students can wrestle with concepts and search for solutions. At the Academy, our facilitators, mentors, coaches, teachers, and discussion leaders use microenterprise case studies to help students think through issues and problems, struggle with conflicting facts, and use their knowledge to form educated conclusions. The case studies are real, country-specific, and personal, and students work on them in groups. Not only do case studies help students apply abstract theories and principles to practical situations, but the students seem to really enjoy them – after all, it is human nature to engage with good stories and learn from them. We have seen countless students become energized and motivated as they realize how applying simple and universal principles can help them solve a case study's complex underlying problems. They develop new analytical skills that they can use to create their own successful microenterprises.

Once a student graduates from the Academy, we provide several channels through which they can stay involved and benefit from ongoing training, networking, and support. During their Academy experience, students are grouped into teams according to the geographic proximity of their home towns, which encourages connections and partnership opportunities after graduation. The Academy's alumni chapters – now numbering more than 100 around the world – provide considerable support and opportunities to graduates. In recent years, we have been moving these chapters away from a Rotary Club-style model and more toward behavior-modification learning centers like Weight Watchers or Alcoholics Anonymous, where ongoing, personalized peer groups can analyze local businesses and learn together. Inspired by Napoleon Hill's (1960) concept of the 'Master Mind' – which he defines as 'coordination of knowledge and effort, in a spirit of harmony, between two or more people, for the attainment of a definite purpose' – the alumni meet to tell their stories, reinforce one another, focus on local problems and solutions, and work together on case studies and other training materials provided by the Academy on a monthly basis (Hill, 1960, pp. 168–169). During a recent meeting of experienced Academy alumni, a survey found that the attending individuals employed an average of 4.6 employees in their own businesses.

Allow me to share a couple of examples of real people whose lives changed as a result of their Academy training. Not long after graduating from the Academy's eight-week course in the Philippines, Jonith Blancaver visited a stationery store near his old high school. As he shopped, he overheard some students asking whether the store offered photocopying services. The clerk replied that not only was that service unavailable in this store, but she did not know of any such service anywhere in town.

Sensing an opportunity, Jonith contacted a member of his church who sold photocopiers and arranged to borrow a machine. He then rented a small space in the stationery store across the street from the high school, promising to pay the rent at the end of the month. The store owner was kind enough to also sell him some copier paper on credit.

After a few initial hurdles, Jonith's photocopying business began gaining traction as he applied the Academy's rules of thumb. By the end of the first month, he had earned enough money to pay his rent, make a first payment on the photocopier, cover his other expenses, and pay himself a small salary. He now owns three copiers and a printing business that services local schools and businesses. He has also purchased a travel franchise, opened a small special-education school, and owns an Internet café.

Another inspiring example is Julie Durano, who lives on the island of Mindanao in the Philippines. Her story illustrates not only successful bootstrap entrepreneurship but also resilience in the face of natural disaster. A certified midwife, Julie was considering going overseas to work when a previous employer encouraged her to open her own birthing center. After attending the Academy, Julie launched her first birthing facility in Moncayo and soon opened another branch in the Compostela Valley.

Up until December 2012, everything went well for Julie as she applied the Academy's rules of thumb and grew her business. She was able to employ three midwives and one certified nurse. In 2010, Julie won an entrepreneurial award, and she used the prize money to upgrade her equipment, including better patient beds, computers, an infant heartbeat monitor, and more. In 2011, she purchased a van to use as an ambulance, which helped her get more patients. With three wards and one air-conditioned private room for patients who could afford it, each branch was delivering about 25 babies a month.

Tragedy struck in December 2012 when tropical storm Pablo swept through the area, destroying approximately 7.1 billion pesos' worth of infrastructure, crops, and property. During this storm, a flash flood completely wiped out Julie's Mancayo birthing center, and floodwaters reached the ceiling of her Compostela Valley center. All her equipment was destroyed, and the van was damaged.

Despite this almost-complete loss, Julie kept applying one of the key principles she'd learned at the Academy: never give up. She was able to convert a TV into a computer monitor, purchase additional second-hand equipment, and repair the beds and the van. Three months after the storm, she reopened her Compostela Valley birthing center and began rebuilding her business. Julie is now looking into moving the center to higher ground, and she's exploring the possibility of opening some mobile birthing facilities.

In 2008, Dr. Ronald M. Miller took ten students to the Philippines to conduct a study of how 353 Academy graduates compared with a control group of 344 non-graduates of similar demographics and socio-economic status. As shown in Figure 2.1, Academy graduates owned nearly twice

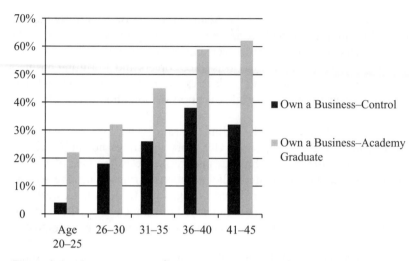

Figure 2.1   Business ownership comparison: control group versus treated group

as many businesses as the control group – fresh out of training, roughly 30 percent of graduates owned businesses, while eight years later, roughly 60 percent of graduates owned businesses. In addition, Academy graduates brought in significantly more gross revenue through their businesses. According to Dr. Miller, 'In terms of a social return on investment (SROI), the money donated to the Academy is yielding a very high return. In fact, statistically they are receiving a discounted SROI return of 17.3 times what they provided to the Academy and a non-discounted SROI return of 14 times their original investment' (Miller, 2008, p. 7). In terms of quality of life, Academy graduates possessed more laptop computers, were more likely to be the principal owner of their residence, had better roofing and flooring in their homes, and were more likely to own land and have family health insurance.

When microenterprise students begin taking control of their own futures, they are transformed by the application of their new knowledge and thrilled as they start realizing their financial potential. While it's true that only some people are ready to change and many others are not, in my experience, and based on the Academy's empirical evidence, microenterprise education is the single most promising way to help the world's necessity entrepreneurs (this is in stark contrast to what Hisrich and Kearney; see Chapter 6). We can help many more of the world's impoverished people become not only self-reliant but also able to lift others around them. This is our opportunity, and I personally believe it's our duty.

NOTE

1. Data provided by Jeremi Brewer, PhD, Executive director, The Academy for Creating Enterprise (AcademiaMexico.org), and postdoctoral research fellow, Marriott School of Management, Ballard Center for Self-Reliance, Brigham Young University.

REFERENCES

Bornstein, D. (2004). *How to change the world: Social entrepreneurs and the power of new ideas.* New York, NY: Oxford University Press.

Carnegie, A. (1920). *The autobiography of Andrew Carnegie and the gospel of wealth.* New York, NY: Houghton Mifflin Company.

Carnegie, A. (1933). *The gospel of wealth: And other timely essays.* New York, NY: Doubleday, Page & Company.

Collins, J. (2001). *Good to great,* New York, NY: Harper Collins Publishers.

Cowen, T., Boudreaux, K. and Sacks, D. (2008). Managing expectations for microcredit. *Mercatus on Policy,* 24 (August), Mercatus Center, George Mason University.

Gibson, S.W. (1999). *Where there are no jobs: The microenterprise handbook* (Vols 1–5, 6 forthcoming). Provo, UT: The Academy for Creating Enterprise.

Gibson, S.W. (2007). Microfranchising: The next step on the developmental ladder. In J. Fairbourne, S.W. Gibson and W.G. Dyer (eds), *Microfranchising: Creating wealth at the bottom of the pyramid* (pp. 17–42). Cheltenham, UK and Northampton, MA, USA: Edward Elgar Publishing.

Hill, N. (1960). *Think and grow rich* (Revised edition). New York, NY: Ballantine Books.

Kuehl, C.R., and Lambing, P.A. (1993). *Small business: Planning and management.* Hinsdale, IL: Dryden Press.

Landes, D. (2000). Culture makes almost all the difference. In L.E. Harrison and S.P. Huntington (eds), *Culture matters* (pp. 2–13). New York, NY: Basic Books.

Lucas, J.W., and Woodworth, W.P. (1999). *Working toward Zion.* Salt Lake City, UT: Aspen Books.

Miller, R.M. (2008). *Assessment report for The Academy for Creating Enterprise* (Unpublished). Cebu, Philippines.

Oaks, D.H. (2012). The gospel culture. *Liahona* (March), Retrieved from https://www.lds.org/liahona/2012/03/the-gospel-culture.

One Red Paperclip ABC 20/20. (2006). Video file (14 July). Retrieved from http://www.youtube.com/watch?v=BE8b02EdZvw.

Slywotzky, A. (2002). *The art of profitability.* New York, NY: Warner Books.

Smith, J.F. (1907). The message of the Latter-day Saints on relief for the poor. *Improvement Era, 10*(10), 831–833.

USAID (2011). *The entrepreneurship toolkit: Successful approaches to fostering entrepreneurship.* Washington, DC: Weidemann Associates.

3. Towards an improved understanding of knowledge requirements in entrepreneurship: an empirical investigation of founder and opportunity characteristics

Marc Gruber and John C. Dencker

INTRODUCTION

This chapter sheds light on two main factors driving the founding process of new organizations – the founder and the opportunity that is being exploited – in order to increase understanding of the heterogeneity encountered in entrepreneurship and, in particular, in those instances when people become entrepreneurs 'out of necessity.' As we will see, both the heterogeneity in terms of founder human capital endowments and in the opportunities being exploited will affect processes and outcomes in entrepreneurship, which in turn allows us to draw conclusions about the knowledge requirements that founders need to meet in order to become successful in entrepreneurship.

From a theoretical perspective, our discussion builds on entrepreneurship, organization, and human capital theories, as those theoretical bases allow covering both the founder and the opportunity side of the entrepreneurial process. Readers familiar with the entrepreneurship literature will recognize that our discussion is shaped by ideas that are core to the concept of the 'individual-opportunity nexus' (Venkataraman, 1997; Shane, 2003) in entrepreneurship theory. From an empirical perspective, the findings reported and discussed in this chapter stem from a large-scale empirical study that was conducted in Munich, Germany, in 2005, that focused on the process and outcomes of entrepreneurship by formerly unemployed people. Specifically, the results are based on econometric analysis of more than 450 new firms founded by the unemployed. Some of the main findings have been reported in individual research studies (Dencker, Gruber and Shah, 2009a, 2009b; Dencker and Gruber, 2012), yet to date have not been subject to a comprehensive discussion nor an evaluation that is focused on knowledge requirements that have to be met by different types of founders. These insights will help us to derive empirically-grounded suggestions to entrepreneurs as well as government agencies seeking to improve or create programs to support the unemployed transition into entrepreneurship.

ENTREPRENEURSHIP BY THE UNEMPLOYED

One of the most visible types of entrepreneurship can be found in high-technology sectors, as ventures in technology domains tend to have a strong growth potential and, if successful, create significant amounts of wealth for their owners (Roberts, 1991; Gruber, MacMillan and Thompson, 2008). Much less visible are the many new firms that are created by unemployed individuals. National statistics indicate that firms founded by the unemployed account for up to 62 percent of new firm foundings in Germany, 30 percent in Sweden, and 15 percent in Austria (SCB, 1994; Institut für Mittelstandsforschung, 2005). Although such firms are typically less glamorous than high-technology start-ups and receive less coverage in the popular press, their survival rates are impressive. Based on a number of empirical studies, including our own research, we have evidence indicating that about 12–15 percent of firms founded by the unemployed fail within the first three years after founding (Wiessner, 1998; Hinz and Jungbauer-Gans, 1999; Institut für Mittelstandsforschung, 2005). Firms created by the unemployed thus have slightly higher survival chances than other populations of newly created firms. For example, in their broader sample of firms in the Munich area, Brüderl, Preisendörfer and Ziegler (1992) indicate a 37 percent failure rate after five years. In addition, Watson and Everett (1996) provide a review of studies across countries to show that failure rates of new firms typically range between 30 percent and 60 percent after five years.

Samples comprising firms founded by the unemployed also tend to be more representative of the majority of new firms created in an economy than, for instance, samples comprising venture capital-backed start-ups. Yet, this also means that firms founded by the unemployed are fairly heterogeneous – they are founded by individuals with different types and different levels of human capital, in different industry settings, and with differing prospects of success. Hence, in order to offer effective support to unemployed individuals in their transition to self-employment, policy

makers as well as agents providing training and consulting to these
founders have to deal with the heterogeneity encountered in the domain.
For example, founders in the sample that we study had education levels
ranging from less than high school to PhD degree. In addition, the types
of firms in our sample were very diverse, involving businesses such as
consulting, advertising, floral shops, restaurants, graphic design, and
African drum sales (see Dencker et al., 2009b for a more inclusive list of
firm types).

In the following, we shed light on this heterogeneity in founders and the
opportunities that they exploit by (1) providing descriptive evidence on the
characteristics of people who create new firms from unemployment and
of their firms (opportunities), and by (2) discussing multivariate findings
gleaned from our earlier studies. We will use this rich evidence to point out
key knowledge requirements of founders seeking to establish their firms as
a means to get out of unemployment.

RESEARCH CONTEXT

Our empirical analysis is based on a sample of formerly unemployed
individuals who were supported by a policy program in their transition to
entrepreneurship. This program is similar to those at the state and local
levels in the US and in many countries across Europe (Blanchflower,
2004), as discussed in Volume II of this Necessity Entrepreneur book
series (see Haas and Vogel, 2013). In these programs, founders typically
receive limited financial assistance to help launch their new firms.

The unemployed individuals in our sample received 'bridging allowances' ('Überbrückungsgeld') from a branch of the German Federal
Employment Agency (FEA) serving the Munich region. The bridging
allowances took the form of a monthly stipend that is equivalent in
amount to the unemployment check they would have received had they
not founded a firm (Wiessner, 2000). Notably, these funds did not require
repayment, and on average provided founders with 1,000 Euros (monthly)
for a six month period in order to help offset the founder's social security
and living expenses. Anyone who had received unemployment pay for
at least four weeks was eligible to apply for funding. Before releasing its
funding, the FEA asked for a business plan outlining the unemployed
person's business idea and a statement from an expert (for example,
from a banker or tax consultant) attesting that the proposed firm was
economically viable and sustainable. Unlike in many other domains in
entrepreneurship (for example, venture capital funding), the threshold for
assessing economic viability was low, defined as providing firm founders

with an adequate income with which to support themselves (Wiessner, 2000).

The data used for our analysis were collected through a survey instrument that we distributed in 2005 to the 2001 cohort of such founders in Munich, Germany. Importantly, the sample thus includes founders still operating their businesses in 2005, as well as those founders whose firms had failed. Thus, we are able to include full information for founders whose firms failed at any time from inception to the date of the survey. The survey instrument was mailed to all of the 1,892 members of the 2001 cohort of funding recipients. A total of 456 responses were received, resulting in a response rate of 24.1 percent based on the size of the full cohort, or 31.4 percent based on the number of individuals who received the survey. This response rate is generally in line with or even higher than those rates reported in other empirical studies addressing business owners and top managers (Sarkar, Echambadi and Harrison, 2001; Simonin, 1997).

For our empirical analyzes, we combined the survey data with third party data from the Centre for European Economic Research (ZEW) capturing the average employment size as well as the credit risk ratings of newly founded firms in Germany at the fine-grained five-digit industry code level for each of the three business years covered in our study (cf. Dencker et al., 2009b; Dencker and Gruber, 2012). For example, the five-digit industry codes in Germany include detailed economic activity groupings such as 'Offices for Editorial Services,' 'Retail Sales in Photography,' 'Floor Laying and Pasting,' 'Retail Sales of Second-hand Goods in Stores,' and 'Cleaning of Polluted Soil and Recultivation of Damaged Areas.'

EMPIRICAL EVIDENCE: THE MUNICH FOUNDER STUDY

To improve understanding of the knowledge requirements that the unemployed should meet in order to improve their chances for successful entrepreneurship, we look at empirical evidence offered by the Munich Founder Study.

Descriptive Evidence

The descriptive evidence presented below is based on information obtained from a total of 456 founders who had previously been unemployed. As discussed elsewhere (Dencker et al., 2009a), our sample is representative of the entire 2001 cohort of funding recipients, along key dimensions such as age, sex, education level, initial monetary investment in the firm, and area of the business activity. Of the founders in our sample, about 60 percent are male, and 84 percent had founded the new firm by themselves, that is, without founding partner(s). On average, founders starting their firms from unemployment were about 45 years old, and possessed 16 years of work experience (maximum of 43 years).

Following the notion that the unemployed face increasing levels of 'necessity entrepreneurship' the longer they are unemployed before starting their firms, we examined a number of human capital and firm (opportunity) characteristics in relation to the length of founders' unemployment spells. The average unemployment spell prior to new firm creation lasted for about six months; as can be seen in Figure 3.1, about 15 percent of founders were unemployed for more than 12 months prior to creating their new firms. In other words, it seems that self-employment was not necessarily the 'last resort' for the majority of founders in our sample – especially in the case of founders who launched their firms within the first two months of becoming unemployed.

Focusing on founder characteristics, our data shows that founders who had been unemployed for a longer time before embarking on their entrepreneurial career tend to be older: specifically, founders who started their firms within a month of becoming self-employed had an average age of about 40 years, whereas those who were unemployed for about a year were about 47 years, and those who were unemployed for more than 12 months about 52 years.

Figure 3.1 also offers detailed insights on the length of the unemployment spell and the founders' educational endowments. We differentiate between five main types of educational degrees that founders can obtain in the German education system: secondary education ('Hauptschule,' 'Mittlere Reife'), vocational training, master-craftsman certificate, university degree and PhD degree. Even a casual glance at Figure 3.1 reveals that the unemployed who create new firms tend to be highly educated, as many possess a university degree/PhD degree. Interestingly, there seems to be a slight trend that people with lower educational degrees decide on a self-employed career at a relatively earlier stage during their unemployment spell. In other words, this evidence suggests that the more educated individuals among the unemployed search for alternative options (salaried employment) for a longer time before deciding to launch their own firms because their chances of finding salaried employment are greater than for people with lower levels of education.

Focusing on firm (opportunity) characteristics, Figure 3.2 shows the types of firms that were created by the unemployed with increasing duration of their unemployment spell. We differentiate between three primary types of firms – free occupations, trade businesses and craft businesses.

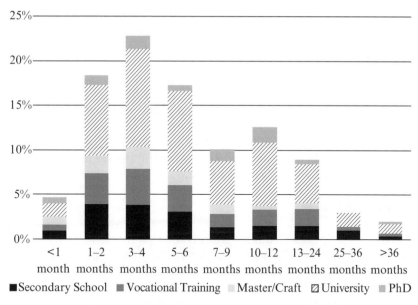

Figure 3.1   Unemployment duration and the founder's education

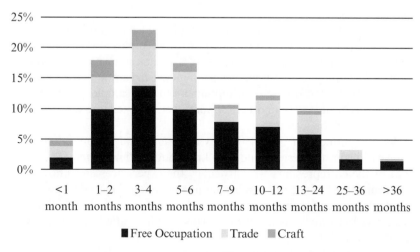

Figure 3.2   Unemployment duration and the type of firm created

One clearly sees that free occupations are the primary types of businesses founded by the unemployed, independent of the length of their preceding unemployment spell. Similarly, trade activities seem to be popular types of firms to be founded by the unemployed throughout, whereas craft businesses tend to be launched in the earlier stages of unemployment spells. This latter finding not only corresponds to an observation that could already be made in Figure 3.1, namely that people with master-craftsman certificates engage in entrepreneurial activities at earlier stages. This correspondence is of an inter-temporal, path-dependent nature, given that only people who had obtained master-craftsman certificates are in a position to launch businesses operating in the crafts.

Multivariate Evidence

To date, we have examined three critical outcomes for the formerly unemployed founders in our Munich Founder Study: survival rates (Dencker et al., 2009a), job creation (for others in addition to the founder) (Dencker et al., 2009b), and revenue generation (Dencker and Gruber, 2012). Below, we summarize each of these studies in turn, focusing on the key founder and opportunity characteristics that influence these different outcomes.

Survival rates
In our research, individual characteristics played a strong role in influencing survival rates of the firms founded by the unemployed (Dencker et al., 2009a). For instance, survival rates were declining in increasing duration of prior unemployment, but increasing in increasing amount of education. Thus, the most 'need-based' entrepreneurs in our sample generally had lower levels of success than other founders, yet, as noted, the survival rates were quite high on average.

We also found that two of the key human capital factors influencing these survival rates were the industry knowledge and management experience of the entrepreneurs. In particular, the experiences and knowledge that founders obtained prior to becoming unemployed played a key role in their entrepreneurial endeavors, allowing individuals who had high levels of such skills to create longer-lasting firms than individuals who had lower levels of such skills.

We also found that beyond the given pre-entry knowledge endowments of founders, learning had a significant effect on survival chances of the nascent firms. Specifically, our evidence indicates that founders who adapted their product lines to better reflect product demand after creating the new organization increased the likelihood that their firms survived.

Such adaptation requires founders to understand market signals, interpret financial data and to initiate those types of change in their organizations that address the identified problems. From a policy perspective, this evidence suggests that programs which assist founders in their learning and which offer training in critical business skills can be seen as meaningful additions to the financial support schemes offered by unemployment agencies.

Our evidence also indicates that adaptation of the new business is more important than pre-entry business planning for the firm's survival, and that the founder's pre-entry knowledge is a key endowment that shapes planning and adaptation activities. Specifically, our results indicate that founders who planned their new businesses extensively prior to founding their firms experienced diminished survival chances relative to founders who did not engage in extensive planning. In other words, although learning activities thus play a key role in the success of newly founded firms, we nevertheless found that many founders were reluctant to adapt to market changes, and instead tended to stick to their initial business plans. In addition, we uncovered that founders who engage in extensive business planning efforts prior to opening their new venture have lower rates of survival than founders who did not engage in extensive planning – with the survival chances lowest for founders who possess low levels of knowledge in management and of the industry.

Job creation for others in addition to the founder
In another study (Dencker et al., 2009b), we considered job creation for others in start-up firms, that is, for people who are employed in a new firm in addition to the founder. From a practical perspective, this dependent measure is of twofold relevance – first, it helps to understand the knowledge requirements of founders establishing firms with varying labor requirements; second, it helps government agencies to assess and predict the spillover effects of the public policy program in terms of creating jobs for others. Creating jobs is a high priority for almost any government around the world.

We shed new light on the job creation challenge by showing how characteristics of the founder and the opportunity characteristics of the business (in other words, the labor requirements of the opportunity in the form of the average number of jobs that a founder needs to create in order to run his/her firm effectively) influence job creation in newly founded firms. While, for instance, consultancies can be run with no employees, founders establishing restaurants need to hire additional staff to become operational. Although the effects of the labor requirements associated with an entrepreneurial opportunity may seem straightforward, prior

investigations have not accounted for opportunity and founder characteristics in estimating job creation outcomes.

Importantly, our empirical results show that there is a key second level to
firms founded by the unemployed: not only do they create employment for
themselves but they also create employment for others. For instance, the
founders in our sample created jobs for 498 other individuals, namely, 150
full-time positions, 44 part-time positions, 98 mini-jobs, and 206 freelance
jobs. These numbers are often overlooked, yet are meaningful from a public
policy perspective, as they help to understand the effectiveness of programs
seeking to reduce unemployment. Since many of the firms in our sample
could be run by just the founder (for example, consulting firms of various
types, graphic design, personal training, and so on), the impact of the job
creators in the sample is impressive. Moreover, even though these founders
created relatively fewer jobs than the general population of founders did,
when we account for their relatively low levels of investment capital, these
differences in job creation rates shrink considerably. In addition, although
the most 'need-based' entrepreneurs created fewer jobs than other founders
in the sample, the difference in magnitude was not substantial, suggesting
that even individuals who have been unemployed for long periods of time
can generate employment for others in the firms that they found.

We also found that the knowledge and experience that the founder
brings to the new firm creation process has an important effect on job
creation. For example, the empirical analysis indicates that the greater
a founder's knowledge of different business areas (for example, marketing, IT), the fewer the number of employees he/she will hire to help run
the firm's operations. By contrast, founders with leadership experience
create more jobs for others at a base level than those without such experience, allowing them to capitalize on their skills in leading and managing
employees. However, relative to founders without leadership experience,
they will hire fewer people once the labor requirements of a business
opportunity increase, as they are better leaders and can divide up tasks in
a more effective manner between the employees.

Overall, our job creation study highlights the critical role that the
opportunity plays in affecting the ability of founders to use their skills and
knowledge effectively – thus providing important evidence regarding the
individual-opportunity nexus framework (Shane, 2003; Venkataraman,
1997). Yet, it also highlights that this interaction does not always have a
uniform effect on outcomes (in that while high levels of leadership lead to
higher rates of job creation, a higher level of other types of skills does not
always lead to a higher number of jobs created by the founder). Finally, it
also has key implications for the types of knowledge and skills required to
exploit opportunities with different levels of labor requirements.

Revenues

In a more recent article (Dencker and Gruber, 2012) we assess how characteristics of the opportunity, in the form of its riskiness, interact with founder knowledge and experience to affect revenue generation. As in our other research, we find that human capital characteristics play a non-trivial role in the success of entrepreneurial endeavors of the formerly unemployed. For example, revenues are generally increasing in increasing levels of managerial experience, and decreasing in increasing time spent in unemployment prior to founding a firm. Yet, equally important in this regard is the nature of the opportunity being exploited. In particular, our findings not only show that opportunities influence new firm performance, but also that opportunity characteristics contextualize the effectiveness of founder knowledge, leading to key differences between managerial and industry experience in affecting the performance of nascent firms.

In order to measure the potential of an entrepreneurial endeavor, we use a variable that captures the industry-specific risk rating of the opportunity being exploited (*opportunity riskiness*) (cf. Stinchcombe, 1965; Shane, 2012). This is a heuristic device that can help scholars to both approximate the average value of an opportunity in a particular setting and to disentangle opportunity and founder effects. We find that as the risk of the opportunity increases, performance is increasing in increasing levels of managerial experience. However, founder industry experience does not provide such returns. Rather, as the risk of the opportunity increases, returns to high levels of industry experience grow at a much slower rate than do returns to low levels of managerial experience. In effect, the results offer strong support for the claim that the riskiness of the opportunity plays a key role in affecting the performance of start-up firms, above and beyond effects of founder characteristics.

Outcomes in the entrepreneurship process trace back to the relevance of a given type of experience in the choice of business opportunities, as founders with industry experience are more likely to stay on the industry path they chose prior to becoming self-employed, while founders with managerial experience have a greater range of opportunities to potentially exploit. Moreover, although founders with managerial experience tend to choose riskier opportunities, this selection effect does not alter the key findings in our study (for example, the individual-opportunity nexus patterns hold when controlling for selection on the riskiness of the opportunity).

Combined with other research in the Munich Founder Study, the aforementioned empirical insights suggest that the early decisions in new firm creation typically have a major, path-dependent, influence on the future development of the firm. Specifically, as Gruber (2010) shows, the human capital endowment of firm founders influence their consideration of alternative solutions in terms of the product-market to which the new firm seeks to cater.

Summary of Key Results from the Munich Founder Study

Taken together, the findings from our ongoing research stream indicate that there are several different types of knowledge that founders need to possess in order to become successful, and that there is considerable variation in how the nature of the opportunity influences outcomes in interaction with individual characteristics. In this vein, our results speak to a significant debate about whether it is the jockey (in other words, entrepreneur) or the horse (in other words, the opportunity) that is more important for achieving success (for example, MacMillan, Siegel and Subba Narasimha, 1985; Kaplan, Sensoy and Strömberg, 2009). Hence, it seems that this recurrent debate might better be phrased as which 'jockey' is best suited to ride which particular 'horse.' In other words, founder knowledge endowments and opportunity characteristics interact to shape outcomes in entrepreneurship and, in particular, determine the success chances of formerly unemployed founders.

Building on this point, our ongoing research also generates insights into the role of the founder's pre-entry knowledge endowments on performance outcomes (Brüderl et al., 1992; Burton and Beckman, 2007; Fern, Cardinal and O'Neill, 2012). A key reason for the lack of consistency in existing findings is the complexity in the relationship between founder's pre-entry knowledge and new firm performance. Existing studies tend to focus on the knowledge of founders while neglecting heterogeneity in their opportunities, and often do not consider that the opportunity can contextualize the ability of the founder to maximize the returns to her knowledge, and do so in ways that are not immediately obvious from assumptions in extant theoretical accounts. In short, by conceptually and empirically disentangling these core constructs, we demonstrate that the value of managerial experience and of industry experience is relative to the type of business opportunity being exploited.

IMPLICATIONS FOR ENTREPRENEURSHIP AND PUBLIC POLICY

By highlighting the heterogeneity in founder knowledge endowments and in opportunity characteristics, our findings have implications for potential entrepreneurs as well as for governments seeking to design or improve programs to support the unemployed transition into entrepreneurship.

Clearly, knowledge and learning are critical for becoming a successful self-employed person. In terms of survival rates, founders need to be aware of how far they can move beyond their existing knowledge and experience set when pursuing a business opportunity. If the opportunity is highly attractive, they may consider partnering with individuals who have extensive knowledge about – and/or experience in – the industry in which they seek to create their firms. In addition, founders need to be wary of the benefits that business planning handbooks typically promise. Oftentimes, too much planning can lead to paralysis by over-analysis and a stubborn resistance to engage in organizational change, thereby reducing the likelihood of success of an entrepreneurial endeavor.

In terms of job creation and revenue generation, our results highlight that potential entrepreneurs should have a detailed understanding of the opportunity they are seeking to exploit, and to be aware of both the labor requirements and the risk of their opportunities, and how these two exogenous factors interact with their own skills, knowledge, and abilities. For instance, the labor requirements of business opportunities in different sectors (detailed industries) are highly varied, and founders need to be aware of those differences, so that they can appropriately judge the challenges lying ahead of them. Moreover, founders lacking breadth of knowledge (expertise) across areas needed to successfully exploit a business need to be aware that they may need to hire more employees than would founders with extensive knowledge breadth. In addition, the findings on revenue generation indicate that founders with industry experience will not necessarily be as successful exploiting opportunities with a higher industry-specific risk profile than founders with managerial knowledge. Nevertheless, founders who have obtained high levels of industry experience in low-risk industries might need to resist the siren call of establishing firms in high-risk industries, as they are more likely to be successful if they continue along the path they are on, rather than seeking alternative avenues to explore.

Finally, our results also have interesting implications for public policy programs, particularly for government agencies seeking to reduce unemployment. Entrepreneurship offers the possibility of self-employment to all individuals and, thus, allows a broad range of participation in the economy (Bosma and Levie, 2010). The firms we studied were created under the auspices of a government program supporting the transition from unemployment to entrepreneurship. New firm creation by the unemployed is a fairly common phenomenon across many countries, as the statistics cited in the introduction indicated. One of the core findings that should be of interest to government agencies is the relevance of human capital as well as opportunities in achieving entrepreneurial outcomes. In the national programs we studied in relation to our ongoing research, however, there was a particular emphasis on human capital characteristics of the entrepreneur, whereas the nature and characteristics of the opportunities exploited by the entrepreneurs were typically assessed only in terms of the ability to offer a subsistence income to the entrepreneur.

These observations indicate several vantage points from which program offices could augment their services and, ultimately, the effectiveness of their programs. Taking into account opportunity characteristics, program offices could offer additional funding to those entrepreneurs who launch ventures with greater labor requirements. From a non-financial resource perspective, they could also help facilitate the filling of the required positions. For example, agencies may create a searchable database of unemployed individuals that allows founders to identify employees with the required skill set. By making the search for employees more efficient and effective, founders can devote more time to other tasks required in the new firm creation process. In addition, such a policy could have positive externalities, as it would limit the degree to which an individual's skills atrophy due to being unemployed.

Along these lines, agencies could also provide training on hiring processes, payroll and benefits administration, and government requirements related to hiring to founders starting larger firms. Such assistance would be valuable since the management of these activities is likely to be new to most founders and could distract significantly from revenue-creating activities (Cook, 1999; Klaas, McClendon and Gainey, 2000). Administrators could also provide motivational support to founders. For instance, because hiring other people leads to additional responsibilities for the founder, the agency might provide encouragement by pointing founders to research such as ours that highlights that people like them were able to cope with pressures of firm creation and successfully generate employment for others.

Looking at our findings on revenue generation, agencies should advise founders exploiting riskier opportunities to proceed with caution, and could perhaps intervene in ways to increase chances of entrepreneurial success. For instance, they could offer tailored training programs to founders who lack the requisite skills and knowledge to exploit an opportunity with a given risk profile.

Taken together, this discussion highlights a number of options that governments around the world can pursue in order to help founders who are pushed into entrepreneurship by the circumstances that they face, and do so in a way that not only improves their lives, but also of the lives of others.

CONCLUSION

Entrepreneurship is a critical way for individuals to fulfill their needs, and pursue their visions, dreams and desires. It offers everyone the chance of self-employment and allows broad participation in the economy – an element that is of particular relevance to unemployed persons who seek to reintegrate into the economy. As our findings indicate, the founder cannot be separated from the opportunity he or she exploits. Entrepreneurs as well as government agencies should thus consider that outcomes in this arena depend in important ways on the match between founder skills and the opportunity structure for entrepreneurship.

REFERENCES

Blanchflower, D.G. (2004). Self-employment: More may not be better. Working Paper, Hanover, NH, Dartmouth College.

Bosma, N.J. and Levie, J. (2010). *Global entrepreneurship monitor 2009, Global report*. Babson Park, MA: Babson College.

Brüderl, J., Preisendörfer, P. and Ziegler R. (1992). Survival chances of newly founded business organizations. *American Sociological Review, 57*(2), 227–242.

Burton, M.D. and Beckman, C.M. (2007). Leaving a legacy: Position imprints and successor turnover in young firms. *American Sociological Review, 72*, 239–266.

Cook, M.F. (1999). *Outsourcing human resource functions*. New York, NY: American Management Association.

Dencker, J.C. and Gruber, M. (2012). The effects of opportunities and founder experience on new firm performance. Working Paper, University of Illinois at Urbana-Champaign and EPFL.

Dencker, J.C., Gruber, M. and Shah, S.K. (2009a). Pre-entry knowledge, learning, and the survival of new firms. *Organization Science, 20*, 516–537.

Dencker, J.C., Gruber, M. and Shah, S.K. (2009b). Individual and opportunity factors influencing job creation in new firms. *Academy of Management Journal, 52*, 1125–1147.

Fern M., Cardinal, L. and O'Neill, H.M. (2012). The genesis of strategy in new ventures: Escaping the constraints of founder and team knowledge. *Strategic Management Journal, 33*, 427–447.

Gruber, M. (2010). Exploring the origins of organizational paths: Empirical evidence from newly founded firms. *Journal of Management, 5*, 1143–1167.

Gruber, M., MacMillan, I.C. and Thompson, J.D. (2008). Look before you leap: Market opportunity identification in emerging technology firms. *Management Science, 54*, 1652–1665.

Haas, M. and Vogel, P. (2013) in J. Brewer and S. Gibson (eds) *Necessity entrepreneurship: Microenterprise education and economic development*. Cheltenham, UK and Northampton, MA, USA: Edward Elgar Publishing.

Hinz, T. and Jungbauer-Gans, M. (1999). Starting a business after unemployment: Characteristics and chances of success. *Entrepreneurship Regional Development, 11*, 317–333.

Institut für Mittelstandsforschung (2005). *Statistik zu gründungen aus der arbeitslosigkeit.* www.ifm-bonn.org.

Kaplan, S.N., Sensoy, B.A. and Strömberg, P. (2009). Should investors bet on the jockey or the horse? Evidence from the evolution of firms from early business plans to public companies. *Journal of Finance, 64,* 75–114.

Klaas, B.S., McClendon, J. and Gainey, T.W. (2000). Managing HR in the small and medium enterprise: The impact of professional employer organizations. *Entrepreneurship: Theory and Practice, 25*(1), 107–124.

MacMillan, I.C., Siegel, R. and Subba Narasimha, P.N. (1985). Criteria used by venture capitalists to evaluate new venture proposals. *Journal of Business Venturing, 1,* 119–128.

Roberts, E.B. (1991). *Entrepreneurs in high technology.* New York, NY: Oxford University Press.

Sarkar, M.B., Echambadi, R. and Harrison, J.S. (2001). Alliance entrepreneurship and firm market performance. *Strategic Management Journal, 22,* 701–711.

SCB (1994). *Nyföretagandet i Sverige 1992 och 1993* (New Firm Formation in Sweden in 1992 and 1993). Örebro, Sweden: SCB Publishing Unit.

Shane, S. (2003). *A general theory of entrepreneurship: The individual–opportunity nexus.* Cheltenham, UK, and Northampton, MA, USA: Edward Elgar.

Shane, S. (2012). Delivering on the promise of entrepreneurship as a field of research. *Academy of Management Review, 37,* 10–20.

Simonin, B.L. (1997). The importance of collaborative know-how: An empirical test of the learning organization. *Academy of Management Journal, 40,* 1150–1174.

Stinchcombe, A.L. (1965). Social structure and organizations. In J.G. March (ed.), *Handbook of organizations* (pp. 153–193). Chicago, IL: Rand McNally.

Venkataraman, S. (1997). The distinctive domain of entrepreneurship research: An editor's perspective. In J. Katz and R. Brockhaus (eds), *Advances in entrepreneurship, firm emergence, and growth* (pp. 119–138). Greenwich, CT: JAI Press.

Watson, J. and Everett, J.E. (1996). Do small businesses have high failure rates? Evidence from Australian retailers. *Journal of Small Business Management, 34,* 45–62.

Wiessner, F. (1998). Das überbrückungsgeld als instrument der arbeitsmarktpolitik-eine zwischenbilanz. *Mitteilungen aus der Arbeitsmarkt- und Berufsforschung, 1,* 123–142.

Wiessner, F. (2000). Erfolgsfaktoren von existenzgründungen aus der arbeitslosigkeit. *Mitteilungen aus der Arbeitsmarkt- und Berufsforschung, 33,* 518–532.

4. Necessity entrepreneurs: transforming illiterate mothers into businesswomen

John Hatch

INTRODUCTION

This chapter begins with an attempt to place my own brackets on the definition of who is a 'necessity entrepreneur'. This catchy term attracts me precisely because it brings together two strong and value-laden terms – one inclusive, one potentially exclusive – that for many would seem contradictory. Does 'necessity' explicitly include those persons or households who are considered 'poor', 'very poor', or even 'destitute'? Does the term 'entrepreneur' presume a minimum level of skills, education, or personality traits whose absence would disqualify an illiterate mother from acting entrepreneurially and running a sustainable business? These questions acquire added significance when we consider that the global microfinance move – despite its poverty-alleviation rhetoric – has generally failed to focus its attention and resources on serving the 'bottom billion', the roughly one-fifth of the human family that lives on less than \$1/day.[1] And the face that best represents this terribly disadvantaged and neglected sector is that of an illiterate mother and sole breadwinner for three or more dependents, who has lost or been abandoned by her husband.

Even a term like \$1/day greatly over-simplifies the plight of the poorest. In the first place, as Collins, Morduch, Rutherford and Ruthven (2009) have so convincingly documented in their study *Portfolios of the Poor* the meager incomes the poorest *do* manage to earn are remarkably unstable, seasonal, and unreliable from week to week. But beyond income, the poorest households usually manifest additional and very serious baseline liabilities such as illiteracy, malnutrition, chronic illness, physical or age-related disability, virtual homelessness, low self-esteem, social marginalization, and other kinds of 'brokenness' – all characteristics that many microfinance practitioners would argue disqualifies or disables them from being able to take advantage of entrepreneurial training and micro-finance services.

I would argue the exact opposite. The fact that the poorest families manage to stay alive, smooth out erratic income flows, set aside emergency savings, scrounge many free resources, engage in grueling manual labor, find food and prepare meals, walk long distances to obtain water, cope with sickness and disease, build and maintain their own shelters, and still display enough stamina to keep working and providing day after day, is *prima facie* evidence that the poor can be remarkably resilient, resourceful, and successful managers of the one business that matters most – day-to-day survival. Indeed, most of the world's better-educated and better-resourced entrepreneurs would not last a month if forced to live under conditions faced by the poorest, for whom the penalty for failure is starvation and death. Does this not also qualify even the most destitute beggar as an 'entrepreneur', defined by Webster as 'one who organizes, manages, and *assumes the risks* [italics mine] of a business or enterprise' (Entrepreneur, 2013). Thus, such people deserve to be included in the definition of 'necessity entrepreneurs'. But once we include the poorest, we're left with what feels like a 'mission impossible'. Hence the reason for the sub-title of this chapter, which triggers not one but two questions: first, how *can* an illiterate mother transform herself into a businesswoman? And second, what do we 'outsiders' need to learn – need to do – to facilitate this transformation?

Obviously I would not pose these questions if I did not think they can be answered. I believe that with application of the right attitudes, the right principles, and the right strategies, we 'outsiders' can facilitate the transformation of illiterate mothers into businesswomen. Some of my recommendations will go beyond the transformation itself to justify why the poor and poorest should be given far higher priority in development assistance programs, why they should be treated not just as passive beneficiaries but as prime movers, and why they should be full participants in the design, management, and evaluation of any project created to assist them. I am sure such bottom-up beliefs will sound absurd to many academicians, consultants, and foreign aid bureaucrats, who seem to conduct their business as if they had a monopoly on development expertise and a God-given mandate requiring every project initiative be designed from the top-down. To go against all that makes me an iconoclast. So I feel it is important for me to at least describe how I came up with some of my ideas, and to do that I need to share with the reader some of my personal background.

THE EDUCATION OF A BOTTOM-UP DEVELOPMENT MAVERICK

My development career began in 1965 when, as a newly-minted Peace Corps Volunteer in Colombia, South America, I had my first and arguably my most important lesson about poverty. Walking down the trail from my lodging one morning I encountered a naked 2-year-old black boy. His hair was tinged red, his belly was bloated, and he was squatting over a puddle of diarrhea he had just left in the middle of the trail. The evidence for chronic malnutrition and a severe risk of dehydration could not have been more obvious. I should have taken the boy by the hand, walked him to his parent's shack nearby, and made sure he had a caretaker who understood his immediate need for liquids (even a Coca Cola would have helped). But I did not. I had a bus to catch, I was in a hurry. So I chose not to get involved, walked around the boy, and continued on to my business beyond the village. Two days later a small crowd of my neighbors came to the boy's shack carrying a little white coffin in which they would carry the little boy's body to the church and then the cemetery. That was when I learned that poverty kills. I also learned that indifference to poverty – my indifference to an obviously malnourished child – also kills. The guilt of this experience so deeply affected me that I would later seek a career in economic development so I could do everything in my power to reduce infant malnutrition in the world. For in those days, UNICEF was reporting global infant mortality at about 60 million per year.

Following a two-year follow-up stint with the Peace Corps in Peru, my commitment to fight infant mortality induced me in 1967 to pursue a doctorate in development economics at the University of Wisconsin. Three years later, while completing a Fulbright field research grant for my doctoral dissertation, I spent two crop cycles in coastal desert Peru working as a farm laborer for 30 subsistence corn farmers, all illiterates. These illiterates were literally brimming with sophisticated, effective, but utterly low-cost traditional technology, and they generously shared it with me down to the minutest detail. Not surprisingly, the most important lessons came when I stopped asking my academic questions and silently embraced the grunting, sweaty regimen of exhausting manual labor. Only then it was my 'barefoot professors' who broke the silence to spout commentary about their farming strategies, their hopes and dreams for their families, and offer endless coaching tips to help their hapless gringo student become more proficient – with shovel and machete – at planting, hilling, weeding, irrigating, harvesting, threshing, husking, and grinding the corn that sustained their lives. Illustrated with 80 pen-and-ink illustrations, my doctoral thesis – *The Corn Farmers of Motupe* (1987) – would become a textbook for a subsistence technology class at the University of Wisconsin. More importantly, from this research adventure I gained tremendous respect for the poor and for their endless insights and practical wisdom. These lessons would later nurture ten years of international consulting (55 assignments in 15 countries) during which I became a strenuous advocate of 'bottom-up development' – guided by the principles of respecting and consulting the poor – and thereby ending, as I phrased it, the 'outsiders' monopoly' in the design, management, and evaluation of the projects intended to benefit the poor. To my astonishment, few of my consulting clients were interested in giving the poor any voice whatsoever. Eventually, I decided I would have to create my own non-profit foundation to insure that I could put into practice what I was preaching.

It finally it came to pass that during a flight to Bolivia in 1983 – and fueled by two double bourbons – I had an 'epiphany' during which Spirit and I created a new model called 'village banking'. Bolivia was in the midst of a drought and banking crisis, crops had failed, famine threatened, and the US Agency for International Development (USAID) was anxious to get cash assistance into the hands of hungry farmers, who in turn were needed to keep producing the food needed for hungry voters in the cities. A rapid cash-delivery model was called for. The day following my epiphany I presented my villager banking idea to the USAID mission in Bolivia. Within 24 hours the agency gave my consulting firm – Rural Development Services (RDS) – a grant (in Bolivian pesos) equal to $1 million USD, while obligating me (over the next two years) to put my own skin in the game (called a 'counterpart contribution') for the amount of $250,000. To fund the latter I would eventually have to organize a non-profit foundation. Nine months later the Foundation for International Community Assistance (FINCA) was born. Its explicit purpose was to provide financial services (credit and savings) to the rural poor.

This first village banking model in Bolivia was breathtakingly audacious. Each village bank consisted of 50 household heads, represented by a three-person management committee of trusted local leaders. Each village banker was authorized to receive a cash loan of $50, repayable in one year (following the harvest) and bore an interest rate of 1 percent per month. Each borrower was handed his cash, then certified his/her commitment by placing a fingerprint (all were illiterate) beside their name on a handwritten loan document scribed on the spot by a literate local resident and dictated by an RDS staffer. The cash was drawn from sacks of Bolivian banknotes carried by the RDS organizing team in their Jeep Cherokee. The start-up of each 'bank' usually lasted no more than two hours, and a single organizing team with a vehicle could launch and fund three village banks per day. RDS deployed five organizing teams, each serving one of the five main geographical regions of the country. Until the money ran out 17 months later, RDS (eventually FINCA) had created village banks in 433 rural villages and distributed sub-loans benefiting 17,000 families. In our first year we had more clients than the Agricultural Bank of Bolivia.[2] I was the project's only American, handling overall project planning, fundraising, vehicle procurement, and report writing from FINCA's office in the bedroom of my apartment in New York. All supervisors, and senior managers were Bolivians, the in-country director was a Quechua-speaking Peruvian (my partner in RDS),[3] and for field staff we recruited 50 Quechua-speaking farmers to routinely visit FINCA's village bank operations scattered around the country. This Bolivia project generated many lessons, most noteworthy of all were (1) trusting the village banks to manage themselves (we achieved an overall loan repayment of 98 percent); (2) teaching and then trusting village bank members to keep their own records of loan use, income and expenditure (even illiterates did so, using literate children as scribes); (3) discovering that women borrowers were more enterprising (managing diverse income-generating activities) and were more strategic in their use of loan funds (distributed to multiple short- and medium-term uses) than men (who shot their wad in a single purchase of fertilizer); (4) women proved to be better savers and money managers than men; and (5) all borrowing families understood that keeping all of their school-age children in school was their highest priority, thus creating their family's best chance – over two generations – of an eventual escape from poverty.

Over the next 30 years (1987–2007), FINCA extended its operations to 23 countries in Latin America, Africa, Eastern Europe, and Central Asia. It presently serves a collective clientele of about one million families. Meanwhile, FINCA's village banking methodology – which eventually evolved into a women-only loan program – has been widely shared with other microfinance institutions (MFI), thus resulting in the methodology's application (with different variations and adaptations) to over 800 programs worldwide and collectively serving an estimated clientele of 10 million families. During this period FINCA became one of the best-managed (and dare I say 'profitable'?) MFIs in the world. FINCA has evolved into a network of commercial banking institutions (with a share capital structure) that is currently attracting tens of millions of investment capital to finance the growth of existing as well as new country programs. But this bold expansion came about because financial objectives were prioritized at the expense of the original mission of serving the poorest. As FINCA's founder I railed for years against this 'mission drift' but was never able to reverse it.

Then, in 2011, a miracle occurred. At a FINCA board meeting that

year a director observed that nearly 100 percent of total meeting time
was devoted to discussions of financial issues, but almost zero time was
spent discussing FINCA's social mission. To remedy the imbalance,
this same director presented a motion that FINCA creates a new board
committee, to be known as the Social Performance Audit Committee
(SPAC). The motion was approved unanimously. And since then at
every FINCA board meeting the SPAC is allocated 1–2 hours to discuss
social performance issues. In turn, this board mandate has jolted FINCA
senior management into a flurry of activity to (1) develop an agency-wide
definition of social performance, (2) define different levels of poverty, (3)
create instruments that target severely poor clients, (4) integrate social
performance variables into client loan applications, (5) open a comprehensive dialogue with FINCA field programs about social performance
and to establish country-specific targets, and (6) conduct action research
on potential new social projects – collectively known as 'FINCA-Plus' –
involving agriculture, education, housing, health insurance, solar panels,
potable water and other initiatives. So now for the first time in over two
decades of spectacular growth on the financial services side – mostly focusing on the not-so-poor and non-poor clients – the objective of extending
FINCA services to the poor and poorest has finally been embraced once
more. Which brings us, dear reader, back to the topic of this chapter:
how to best extend financial services (including entrepreneurial training) to the poorest families, and how to transform illiterate mothers into
businesswomen.

As I write these lines I am recently returned from a FINCA consultancy
in Tanzania to design a program strategy for extending FINCA loans,
savings, business training, and other social services to families living in
extreme poverty. This consultancy involved interviews with 40 of the
poorest families we could find. It was arduous research conducted in
oppressive heat and humidity, on location amid our respondents' squalid
living conditions, and I found the experience as physically demanding as
my adventures as a farm laborer in Peru in the 1970s. But the insights from
these interviews were both amazing and humbling. Much of this learning
was germane to the topic of this chapter and will be shared in the following
pages.

As a consumer advisory, I once again remind the reader of my biases. I
reject the assumption that there are families too poor to be eligible for, or
benefit from, microfinance and entrepreneurial training services. I reject
the companion assumptions that providing such services to the poorest
is 'too expensive', 'too complicated', 'too time-consuming' and would
thus represent an irrational investment of the MFI's scarce financial and
staff resources. These untested assumptions are simply pretexts for not

changing the way things are currently done. They are excuses for continuing to favor clients who are the less-poor or non-poor families who do not need to be convinced to take out a loan, who already vociferously clamor for the financial services the MFI currently offers, and who are also located in neighborhoods that are easier to reach by public transport and require less walking by MFI field officers. And finally, regarding the term 'necessity entrepreneurs', I believe that the most perfect expression of a *necessity entrepreneur* is a woman, most likely illiterate, and the single breadwinner for a family gripped in severe poverty. She might not be the easiest or least expensive client to motivate, train, or mentor, but she will be the 'client in greatest need'. She might not have the numeracy and literacy skills to create a business plan or keep books, but one of her children might. She might not have the self-confidence to begin to save, or take out small loans or grow her business, but with the companionship and mentoring of a trusted neighbor her efforts might thrive. If we can figure out how to help the very poorest, the most vulnerable, the most 'broken' of necessity entrepreneurs, we can help any and all necessity entrepreneurs.

STAGE 1: STABILIZING 'BROKENNESS'

Despite its wide prevalence, severe poverty is not normal. It is a state of 'brokenness'. Nobody willingly desires to be severely poor, to risk starvation, to be unable to buy medicine, to live in a makeshift shanty. Whether by their own fault, or bad luck, or circumstances beyond their control, families fall into destitution because they have been broken by events they never intended. A perfectly normal and viable family loses everything in a flood, earthquake, fire, drought, or other 'act of God'. A husband and principal breadwinner dies suddenly, or leaves for a distant location to find work and never returns. A mother, who never went to school and is totally illiterate, tries to find work locally but finds she is 'unemployable'. A single mother in her anguished search for support may beget a child with a man who promises to support her, but is once again abandoned and ends up with one more fatherless child to support. A mother, her spouse, or one of her children is diagnosed with a chronic disease (like AIDS) or physical disability and suddenly much of the cash income raised by the household must now be spent on purchases of medicines and medical services. A 60-year-old mother struggles to support her invalid husband, but with failing eyesight and energy she is too old to be employed; and then her son or daughter dies of AIDs, leaving the grandparents with orphans to raise. A large rural family loses its farm in a flood, earthquake, or political unrest and must move to a city slum. Such tragedies happen all the time

– all common examples of tier 1 families living in severe poverty at the bottom of the income pyramid.

And why should we care? *Because severe poverty kills.* In fact, it's the greatest killer of children in the world. Even with all the progress of medical science in recent decades, over 9 million children under five years of age still die each year worldwide from chronic malnutrition and hunger-related diseases – the victims of severe poverty. They simply represent a population too large to ignore, and like the Nazi Holocaust, we have a moral obligation not to ignore it. Thus the first challenge we outsiders need to face in assisting the poorest *necessity entrepreneur* is that we first must try to understand the particular kind of brokenness that has driven this potential client into severe poverty. We then have to identify what specific interventions are needed, if any, just to help keep this would-be entrepreneur and her family alive. At the very least we need to keep her situation from deteriorating, help stabilize the conditions that are pulling her family down, and 'buy' time or space for her to pause long enough to consider positive 'next steps' that will at least marginally improve her life. No wonder so many microfinance institutions shun this level of outreach! It's painful, it's time-consuming, and it's hard! But even beyond that, a mother who is exhausted, malnourished, worried to death about her family, and depressed about the future – what energy does she have left to entertain the thought of starting a business and taking on the responsibility of repaying a loan? At this stage the challenge seems impossible. One fast possible response is a simple cash gift to meet the most basic needs of the endangered household and buy time for other longer-term solutions.

'BAREFOOT CONSULTANTS'

In the world of financial services many practitioners have a knee-jerk reaction against gifts of cash as a stabilizing first intervention for assisting the poor. These practitioners worry about creating client dependency on outsiders, undermining self-help motivation, and even the possibility of the money being totally 'wasted' on non-income-generating uses like food, medicine, and paying off the bill at the grocers. To get around these objections, in Tanzania a FINCA-sponsored consultancy involving myself and a British team decided to disguise the cash gift as a payment-for-information. The idea was to compensate respondents for the time they spent being interviewed by our team, as well as covering possible future follow-up interviews. We went one step further and gave them the distinctive title of 'barefoot consultants' (*washauri peku peku* in Swahili). These consultants would have the important research purpose of providing information about how they spent their cash payments, thus providing us insights into their spending priorities, needs, and choices, including (hopefully) efforts to start a tiny business or other income-generating activity. Unfortunately, the results and lessons from this approach will not be available for this chapter, but I include it here as a respectful way to deliver stabilizing cash liquidity to the poor and at the same time create a compact that allows the poor to teach us what we need to know about their lives in order to create subsequent interventions and services that meet their need.

Theoretically the information yield of the cash-payment approach could be amplified by leaving with each respondent a ruled notebook (like primary school children use) plus a ball-point pen, so her family can keep a diary of income, expenditures and other 'events' related to their use of the cash grant (as well as other family income). Of course, most mothers are illiterate and could not keep the diary themselves, but any family with a child who has learned to read and write in elementary school (or a neighbor's child, for that matter) could serve as a scribe for the illiterate respondent. I know this note-keeping strategy is feasible because I have personally tested it with hundreds of poor households in Peru, Bolivia, El Salvador, Guatemala, and Mexico. The accuracy of the data recorded is not particularly important; rather the notebook entries are useful in stimulating discussions between the respondent and researcher concerning steps taken, lessons learned, and possible next steps. An additional benefit is that the notebook provides school children with a chance to practice the literacy and numeracy skills they have learned in school. As will be seen further on in this chapter, using children as scribes can play a critically important role in their mothers' transformation toward becoming a businesswomen.

LOCAL MENTORS: ANOTHER PRACTICAL WAY OF ADDRESSING BROKENNESS

For simplicity, let us call the broken respondent our 'client' and ourselves – the would-be change agents – as 'outsiders' or simply 'we' or 'us'. As we have seen, In the case of a severe life-threatening situation, the fastest stopgap response might be for the outsider to offer the client a modest cash gift to 'tide her over' for a few days or weeks to buy food or medicine or pay off a debt at the grocery store. Alternatively, we might offer the use of a project vehicle to get the client and her threatened family member to a clinic. Such a gesture will buy good will for future visits and interventions. It might also assuage the outsider's helplessness and guilt. But it is only a temporary action, not a solution.

To my way of thinking, the guiding principle for addressing brokenness is *not* to gallop off and identify external sources of emergency supplies of food and medicine. I believe a more humane and practical way to treat the client is to use her brokenness as a pretext for building a *local* support strategy for ameliorating that brokenness. Thus, the outsider might ask: 'Among your nearest neighbors, has anyone ever helped you in any way?' If the answer is positive, we write down names and pay this person or persons a visit. If the answer is negative, we ask, 'Who among your neighbors would you most trust to help you?' If the answer is again negative, we select the closest neighbor whose house suggests she might be significantly better off, or alternatively, the closest neighbor who might already be a micro-finance client – for example, a member of a FINCA village bank – and pay her a visit. For simplicity we will call this neighbor a 'potential mentor'. After describing our role and institutional affiliation, the outsider can proceed to explain that s/he represents a microfinance or other development program whose social mission is to make sure every location they assist becomes a 'poverty-free' community. We might employ a slogan like 'Leave Nobody Behind'. We might then ask if the potential mentor knows of any very poor neighbor who needs help or, coaching, or even a small act of charity (food, clothing, and so on). Hopefully this neighbor will designate the already-visited client; if not, a new client might be identified for future visitation. The conversation might expand to details of the client's brokenness, ending with a query as to whether the potential mentor would accompany the outsider for a client visit. Such a visit would explore ideas for what possible assistance might be mobilized from the potential mentor herself, from elsewhere in the community, and beyond – with the outsider's agency offering to match resources raised locally. Once local assistance has been identified, we would engage the potential mentor in discussing the possibility of her becoming a part-time mentor for, say, one hour per week, to provide ongoing assistance or companionship to the poor community resident who is her neighbor. In exchange for this service the potential mentor might receive some kind of compensation – for example, a 1 percent/month reduction in the interest rate on her FINCA loan for every client she is mentoring. In any given village multiple local potential mentors could be encouraged.

It is obvious from the above description that addressing brokenness is too detailed, exacting, and time-consuming to be conducted by an MFI's existing field staff. To force this responsibility on already over-burdened staff would be a mistake, because it would inevitably distract staff from their financial service supervision duties, which could result in increased loan delinquency or even declining client outreach. But by recruiting local mentors we incorporate a new source of expertise, leaders who are more familiar with their own communities (and their resources) than MFI employees, with the critical added value that the mentor's services will be much less expensive. At the same time the mentor is likely to be more highly motivated than an MFI employee – perhaps because being of service to a neighbor makes her feel better about herself or satisfies a sense of community or class responsibility (*noblesse oblige*), or knowing she is helping to create and live in a poverty-free neighborhood. In the case of FINCA, with field programs in 22 countries and over a million clients, even if only one experienced client in a hundred became a mentor, this could create – worldwide – an army of 10,000 additional motivators and facilitators explicitly dedicated to expanding microfinance-linked social project interventions to the very poorest households.

STAGE 2: INTEREST-FREE LOANS

One of the most important insights gathered from my recent Tanzania consultancy was that, without exception, every one of the respondents I interviewed was scared to death of taking out a FINCA loan because of the interest rate charged. The interest rate itself did not seem to matter; rather it was the fact that interest (*riba* in Swahili) of *any* kind was feared. Admittedly, these were Muslim women who knew that the Koran forbids charging interest. However, interest free loans – called 'help' (*msaada* in Swahili) – are commonly used by all respondents with great frequency. Tiny, tiny loans of cash, food, and clothing were exchanged weekly or even daily. These were needed to help a family smooth income instability, cover shortfalls in grocery purchases and so on, and were normally repaid within a few days or a week. My respondents commonly gave *msaada* as often as they received it. It was how neighbors help each other out. Indeed, *msaada* has a savings function as well. One possibly safer way to save a surplus (other than a hiding place at home) is to lend it to neighbors, thus creating the obligation to return this money when it is requested.

This works fine for meeting subsistence consumption needs, but it's not enough to finance a small start-up business – like a food/beverage stand (*génge* in Swahili) – which some respondents already had. From this they would seek a larger msaada called a *mkopo*, but still interest-free. So when I informed respondents that they might qualify for an interest-free trial loan from FINCA – called a *mkopowa mayaridio* in Swahili – they definitely became interested.

An interest-free 'trial loan' becomes a natural next step for a now-stabilized client, particularly if a local mentor relationship has been established to coach the client in different ways to set up an income-generating small business. We know that trial or interest-free loans can be very effective because they have already been tried by other microfinance institutions. The Grameen Bank in Bangladesh has made such tiny interest-free loans to some 30,000 beggars. The loans are used to purchase simple merchandise like candy, gum, cigarettes, ribbons, and so on, which the beggar sells while she conducts her begging rounds. These sales give the poor client a 'taste' of earning additional income, practicing the task of recycling her modest working capital, and learning the discipline needed to both meet her loan repayment obligations while also setting aside minuscule saving deposits. In turn, these experiences nurture a growth in self-worth. From the viewpoint of the sponsoring MFI, mini-loans represent nearly zero risk because (1) they are so small to begin with, and (2) these loans do not have to be closely monitored by the MFI's normal field staff if a local mentor has agreed to coach the client.

Other MFIs such as BRAC in Bangladesh, and Heifer International, have not even begun with mini-loans in cash but rather with technical assistance (coaching) and resource grants-in-kind – in the form of animals – to help indigent clients launch income-generating livestock operations. In the case of Heifer, the animals are provided in a quasi-credit arrangement with the expectation that a pair of offspring from the gifted animals will be on-granted to another indigent recipient, creating a virtuous cycle of 'paying it forward'.

THE CHALLENGE OF PLATEAUING MICRO BUSINESSES

'Trial loans' are a starter-project. They build confidence and grow business skills and discipline. But unless loan sizes grow significantly – and the business grows also – such starter loans do not offer much of a long-term 'lift' for a family seeking to escape poverty. At some point real loans are needed – $100, $200, and beyond. I like to think of both 'brokenness' interventions (stage 1) and 'trial loans' (stage 2) as forming a two-stage ramp that leads the client up to a point where she is ready and able to grab hold of the lowest rung of the credit ladder – say $100. Once the client can get to the first rung, she has a structure that allows her to climb to higher and higher rungs as her abilities and loan history allow. In my opinion, the image of a 'ladder of credit access' provides the client with a reassuring symbol for a way out of poverty. But can we take it for granted that the client will continue her climb? And if so, how far?

Ten years before my retirement in 2006, I was in charge of running FINCA's impact evaluation activities. We developed an efficient impact evaluation instrument called FCAT (FINCA client assessment tool), sent a dozen two-person teams of research interns to the field each summer to interview about 300 clients per country, thus conducting about 3,600 client interviews over ten country programs each summer. From these exercises at least two widespread major findings emerged. The first finding was that, on average, new clients just entering FINCA programs were better off (higher daily per-capita expenditures) than clients who had been in the program several years – a clear sign of mission drift away from the poorest. The second finding was that clients who had been in the program several years (usually after about 20 months) stopped growing their businesses and/or either reduced the amount of their loans or began to use an increasing share of their loans for non-business purposes. This phenomenon of plateauing business growth appeared to affect about eight out of every ten clients, while the non-plateauing clients keep on vigorously growing their businesses and borrowing ever-larger loans for that purpose. Why the plateau in business growth? Further analysis showed a strong correlation between a plateaued business and clients with little or no education. In contrast, the superstars of business growth (and borrowing) were either (1) literate or (2) had one or more children who had completed elementary school and in some cases one or more years of high school, in other words, the family had one or more members who were solidly literate and numerate and could keep records.

These findings have important relevance to the topic of this book and this chapter. We micro-finance practitioners strongly believe that creating a growing and profitable family business is an important, if not indispensable, tool in lifting a low-income household out of poverty. However, most of us assume (seldom based on hard proof) that if a client continues to borrow ever-larger loans (1) she is investing most of those loans in her business, (2) her business is thus growing, and (3) she has a growing loan repayment capacity as well. But my research evidence shows our growth assumptions are mostly validated only by our non-poor households (those who are literate and numerate), *not* by the poorest and least educated ones.

Let us put ourselves inside the head of a client who has little education and does not have literate/numerate family members to help her. She lacks the self-confidence of better-educated colleagues. She is unfamiliar with keeping business records. If given rudimentary business training she does not have the rapid writing skills to keep notes and must depend almost entirely on her memory. By her fourth or fifth loan she has grown her business to a level that she alone can personally manage during the equivalent of an 8-hour day. Yet to sell more she would need additional workers. To use her children for selling would possibly distract them from their schooling. If she used non-family labor, how would she supervise them? How would she know when they were cheating or stealing? Or if they kept their own records how would she check their validity? Furthermore, the longer she stays in business the more competition she finds in the marketplace. Her profit margins are shrinking, yet with every additional and larger loan her repayment burden grows. And the market itself shifts wildly from season to season, day to day, even hour to hour, which results in wide changes in number of clients and their demand for her products. What if she or a family member gets sick and she must temporarily close her business? What if her home, or family, or the market itself is damaged by a fire or flood or other natural or man-made disaster, leaving her unable to meet one or more loan payment installments? Suddenly she would be a delinquent, owing more money than she can pay, and would not this destroy both her business as well as her reputation in the community? We can imagine her thinking: 'Who needs these headaches? The present size of my business is just large enough to support me and my family. When I am old and my children are gone and they fail to take care of me, I know at my present level I can still survive with this same little old business I have now'.

THREE FALLACIES OF THE 'CREDIT LADDER'

For a mother who is illiterate, to get past the impasse of the plateaued business is not only complicated but also time-consuming and increasingly risky. In the first place most MFIs do not even recognize this problem, and when they do their field workers usually lack the time and patience to deal with it. This is especially true when those employees receive performance bonuses based on number of clients served, total portfolio supervised, and high loan recovery rates – all incentives that push field staff toward recruiting better-educated and less-poor clients, both initially (because they are easier to work with in the first place) as well as later when they seek to replace clients who have dropped out or plateaued.

I mentioned earlier that the purpose of the 'test loan' was to move a severely poor client up the entry ramp until she can reach the first rung of the 'credit ladder'; that once at the first rung the client now had the capacity and self-confidence to climb higher and higher. This view implies that climbing the credit ladder is virtually synonymous with the client lifting herself and her family out of poverty. But the reality of plateauing business growth suggests a different outcome, namely: that most clients only climb one or two rungs up the credit ladder and then stop, usually at a level well below what they might require to generate enough income to lift their families from severe to moderate poverty, or from moderate poverty to just above the poverty line into lower middle income. So the automatic functioning of the credit ladder is a dangerous fallacy. A second and related fallacy is that it is the mother – our client, business owner, and credit-ladder climber – who bears the exclusive responsibility for lifting her family out of poverty. A third fallacy is the expectation that this climb can be successfully completed within a few years – three? Five? Ten?

All of these fallacies are dangerously incorrect, and because we entertain them the potential of microfinance to lift the poor out of poverty tends to be enormously over-rated and exaggerated by MFIs. The truth is, for a family to lift itself out of poverty, this effort involves a process that is far more complicated, riskier, slower, and involves more actors – and actions – than we outsiders would like to admit. Microfinance itself is a very young movement with barely four decades of experience, and while we practitioners think we know a lot, our depth of learning is still quite shallow and our learning curve quite steep. During our first quarter-century we practitioners have learned a great deal about how to provide millions of low-income clients with efficient financial services. In fact, today the movement's collective service outreach now exceeds 140 million families. Including family members/dependents this represents about one-tenth of the population of the earth! But remarkably we practitioners have barely scratched the surface of what we need to know about the phenomenon we call poverty, its causes and effects, risks and dilemmas; indeed, the very definition and description of poverty changes from one country and continent to another. It is ironic that we 'outsiders' worry so much about what our clients need to learn to succeed, yet our biggest constraint in helping them is that we know so little about them. And like when I was a farm laborer in Peru, I did not really start learning until I stopped talking and became a good listener. We need to 'hang out' with these clients, hear their stories, and understand their priorities, their greatest fears. Before we can offer better products and services, we first have to be much better listeners.

MOTHERS AS THE WORLD'S GREATEST PHILANTHROPISTS

From the earliest days of FINCA, we quickly learned to offer our financial services primarily (if not exclusively) to women clients, in other words, female heads-of-households. We believed in the following inspiring adage: 'support the mother and you benefit the entire family'. At the time I did not fully understand the power of this principle. I favored working with mothers because I believed they were more trustworthy as borrowers, more strategic in their use of loan capital, and more vital to the well-being of children. I believed that if we empowered these mothers with access to credit, their improved income from self-employment would enable them to finance the nutrition, health, and sanitation improvements needed to gradually eliminate the principal causes of infant mortality. I think this expectation has been dramatically fulfilled in the last quarter-century. When I was in the Peace Corps in the early 1960s, UNICEF was reporting an estimated global infant mortality of 60 million children per year. By 2012 that mortality had declined to 7 million! Obviously, this success story can partly or mostly be attributed to wide-scale improvements in public health systems throughout the developing world; but I also believe the rapid worldwide expansion of microfinance programs that targeted mothers also played a major role.

However, this dramatic quarter-century decline in global infant mortality tends to distract us from the key factor, lesson, or insight that most explains and justifies micro loans to mothers. It is simply this: *self-employed mothers are the world's greatest philanthropists.* From the gross weekly sales/profits of her business, the mother first sets aside sufficient income to meet her weekly/monthly loan installment + interest + savings. Next, she sets aside enough income to sustain (or possibly expand slightly) the weekly working capital required by her self-employment business. Once these set-asides have been made, the balance is her *net profit.* And here's the point: *virtually every penny* of this net profit will be spent by the mother not just to benefit her family but more specifically to benefit *her children.* The MFI who lends her money will first define this mother by her type of business – as the owner of a fruit stand, a seamstress, a seller of lottery tickets, a goat-walker, and so on – but from her own perspective the real business of this mother is to *invest in her children.* Her true purpose in life is to keep her children alive, keep them healthy, keep them fed, and – most important of all – *keep them in school.*

THE KEY IS EDUCATION

As referenced earlier, one of the salient findings of FINCA's client research was that virtually all respondents, whether literate or illiterate, had managed to keep all of their school-age children in school – at least through 5–6 years of primary education. This is enough to guarantee basic literacy and numeracy skills, which in turn qualifies a young adult to be an 'employee' versus a minimum wage laborer. The difference is that the former stands to earn about $5/day more than the latter. Over a year's labor calendar of 300 days, the literate employee would generate about $1,500 more income than the illiterate. Should a child manage to complete high school, the differential might rise as high as $10–$15/day ($3,000 to $4,500 per year). Unfortunately, for a child to attend high school is an unaffordable luxury for most low-income families. Why? Because throughout the developing world elementary schools will be found within easy walking distance of the poorest slums and villages, while high schools usually are located in market towns and in the elite districts of cities – in other words, much more distant. This means that a student from a poor family would need to spend $2–$4/day in transportation costs to attend the nearest high school, in addition to tuition, uniforms, textbooks, and other costs. But even though most of the children of the poor drop out of school after finishing primary education, by achieving basic literacy and numeracy these primary school graduates represent the potential for adding a significant additional source of income for their families – significant because one literate breadwinner can bring in twice as much income as an illiterate one. A family with only one breadwinner (the mother) would be considered very poor. A family with two breadwinners (one literate) would reach the level of not-so-poor. A family with three breadwinners (two literate) would reach the level of lower-middle income. Thus a mother's sacrifices and investments to educate her children can be seen as very strategic, rational, and essential if her family is to lift itself out of poverty.

ON THE THRESHOLD OF TRAINING IN ENTREPRENEURSHIP

With the above understandings in place it is now easier to see that for an extremely poor family to sustainably lift itself out of poverty, the female head-of-household – even with access to business loans – is unlikely to accomplish this task by herself. First, to even get started she may require the patient guidance and companionship of a neighbor – a mentor. Second, she may also require temporary gifts of food, medicines, and clothing to help stabilize her 'brokenness'. Third, she may next need to gain experience and self-confidence by taking out a small interest-free 'test loan' so she can attempt a small start-up business while learning the discipline of meeting periodic savings and loan-repayment installments. Fourth, she might then try her hand at taking out a modestly larger interest-bearing loan and launching a micro business capable of generating $2–$3 per day in net profits. Fifth, with this enhanced cash flow she will continue to invest in the education of her children while also gradually growing her business until her comfort level is reached and her business plateaus. But at this point – provided she herself is functionally illiterate, and none of her children have yet achieved basic literacy and numeracy – her progress is likely to come to a halt.

The scene changes as one or more of the children of the head-of-household begin to master basic reading, writing, and arithmetic. This is the moment when a child with 4–5 years of schooling can begin to assist his mother in her business by *becoming her scribe* – by keeping simple accounts of income and expenses, by helping her with selling 1–2 hours a day, and (on weekends and holidays) by helping to peddling her products door-to-door. This kind of collaboration has a double benefit: (1) it gives the child a vehicle for practicing skills learned in the classroom, and (2) it enables his mother to attend entrepreneurship training classes that enhance the productivity and profitability of her business endeavors, present and future.

So, for our female head-of-household to truly break through her business plateau – in other words, for her to truly become a 'businesswoman' capable of generating sufficient income to lift her family above the poverty line – she needs not only additional loan capital but higher-level business skills that only her literate children are in a position to help her learn, but which are not taught in school. For example, she needs to learn the importance of business record-keeping, analysis of market demand,[4] business planning; cash-flow analysis, cost analysis to determine mark-up and price, frequency of working capital rotation; inventory management, and so on. Acquiring and applying these skills involve literacy and numeracy, which are clearly the province of the next (recently schooled) generation, and in turn will require their active participation as students and scribes in entrepreneurship classes attended by their mothers.

AND IT'S NOT ONLY FOR MOTHERS

This is also where the MFI can create simplified business training classes for young adults who are the sons and daughters of current clients. These classes might be organized around different curriculums, for example: (1) skills that focus on starting a new business or strengthening an existing one; (2) skills that train young adults to start different kinds of micro-franchising businesses; and (3) skills that help young adults research employment opportunities, prepare resumés, and interview for jobs. Students with the best class performances might also qualify for special awards like a business loan of their own, or consideration as a candidate for recruitment into the ranks of the MFI's field staff. In programs where clients belong to village banks, centers, or solidarity groups, FINCA over the years has allowed many young adults (usually literate daughters of members) to serve as assistants/scribes to group members who are illiterate. Following a policy of 'drinking from our own well' FINCA has subsequently recruited many of these young adults for field staff positions. Among my fondest hopes is that, in every country where FINCA has a program, it will become that country's largest employer of the sons and daughters of our clients – who were born into poverty but became active participants in the struggle to overcome it.

A CLOSING APOLOGY AND SUMMARY

At this point I owe my readers an apology. I have brought our illiterate mother to the door of the entrepreneurial classroom. To become a businesswoman in her own right she needs to open the door and enter this classroom. But for her to understand, apply, or otherwise derive any benefit from this opportunity – please mark this well – *she MUST attend these classes accompanied by her literate son or daughter, acting as her scribe*. Even if our illiterate mother is unable to fully understand the class content, what matters is that her scribe – her literate son or daughter – *will* understand and *will* help her apply the principles learned to the family business. Furthermore, even if the mother decides to plateau her business and refuses to budge, her literate son or daughter *will* be able to apply the entrepreneurship skills taught in the classroom to become a businessman or businesswoman themselves. Thus, for the transformation we have been discussing in this chapter to take place, it might take two generations rather than one. Thus, from the MFI's point of view, it is the child-scribe, not the mother, who is the most important student in the classroom.

Despite my doctorate in economics, I have never taken a course in business or basic accounting. I could not possibly teach a class in entrepreneurship. And I would never pretend to suggest the required topics and course materials for such a class. I leave those topics to other authors and chapters of this book. What I *do* know is how to respect poor people, how to honor their wisdom, how to move them towards ever-greater self-reliance, and how to mobilize the talents of their literate children in a two-generational enterprise to escape poverty.

This said, I will close by attempting to summarize the main principles, strategies, and recommendations contained in this chapter.

1. The perfect candidate for a 'necessity' entrepreneur is an illiterate low-income mother who is a single head of household supporting

    several children in school, one or more of whom is literate and numerate (or soon will be).

2. Before this necessity entrepreneur is ready for business training, she first needs to pass through three prior stages: (1) stabilization of her 'brokenness' and (2) experience with an interest-free trial loan, and (3) a small interest-bearing loan.

3. In the first stage she may need a cash advance, not as a gift but as payment for information as an advisor/consultant willing to educate outsiders with insights into her family's special handicaps, obligations, and priorities.

4. Both in the first stage and the second, the necessity entrepreneur can benefit immensely from the companionship and coaching of a neighbor willing to serve as her mentor.

5. The necessity entrepreneur should not be viewed a single individual entrepreneur but as an entrepreneurial team consisting of herself, her literate child, and possibly a neighbor who serves as her mentor.

6. Trust the poor. Do not underestimate their skills, wisdom, and resourcefulness. As outsiders we cannot pretend to know how best to help them if we have not learned how to listen to their stories and to capture their insights.

7. A family's climb out of poverty requires the participation of two generations. In this struggle, no investment is more important and more cost-effective than keeping a child in school, at least until they can read and write.

8. Severe poverty kills. It kills directly via infant mortality caused by malnutrition and hunger-related diseases. It kills indirectly via illiteracy, which robs children of their future employability and dreams. Sooner or later, it also kills through the indifference of society at large.

9. Do not buy in to the 'outsiders' monopoly'. Top-down design of development programs seldom works and ultimately results in ultra-expensive failures. Allow the poor to fully participate in the design, management, and evaluations of programs designed to help them. This will usually yield the most inexpensive and most successful solutions.

10. If you want your MFI to bring its financial and social objectives into balance, so it can re-focus more energy and resources on serving very poor clients (the 'bottom billion'), this initiative needs to start with your board of directors. Create within the board a Social Performance Audit Committee, and watch – from senior management to lowest field worker – how quickly your institution responds.

NOTES

1. While this number is widely used by development practitioners, the media, and the public at large, there still remains a lot of conflict about its precise meaning, how it is calculated, and its practical applicability. It usually is referenced as 'one international dollar' or PPP dollar adjusted to reflect purchasing power parity in order to facilitate comparisons between countries. PPP calculations are complicated, rely on seldom up-to-date market basket estimates, and are little understood by field staff, much less the clients themselves. A $1/day is difficult to apply consistently between urban and less-monetized rural settings.
2. I am not certain I can prove this, but I believe the FINCA village banking program in Bolivia also holds the world record for fastest and largest microfinance program start-up ever attempted.
3. His name was Aquiles Lanao, an accountant and auditor by profession, with a Zapata mustache and a loud, garrulous, good-humored personality. He was like a father to me, my friend and business partner from 1962 until the present, a relationship of over 50 years. He was the perfect country director – charismatic, respectful, detail oriented and tireless – and without his leadership our Bolivia start-up could easily have failed.
4. To my mind, this single topic is the most important of all. We outsiders tend to overlook that when we encourage the poor to start a business, that start-up will usually occur in a neighborhood where almost everybody else is also poor. When I asked one woman with a tiny grocery stand in Tanzania why her business only offered a half-dozen products for sale, and her stock for each one did not exceed a half-dozen as well, she explained: 'My daily sales seldom exceed 1,600 shillings ($1 USD). Nobody has money around here. I live off the road. Few people walk past my store. I would love to sell more but to whom?'.

REFERENCES

Collins, D., Morduch, J., Rutherford, S. and Ruthven, O. (2009). *Portfolios of the poor: How the world's poor live on $2 a day.* Princeton, NJ: Princeton University Press.

Entrepreneur (2013). In Merriam-Webster.com. Retrieved 31 March 2013, from http://www.merriam-webster.com/dictionary/entrepreneur.

Hatch, J.K. (1974). Corn farmers of Motupe: A study of traditional farming practices in northern coastal Peru (Doctoral dissertation). Retrieved from ProQuest (7422123).

5. Toward a hybrid of integrated non-financial services and lending

Mark Coffey[1]

INTRODUCTION

For the past decade Global Partnerships has been inviting necessity entrepreneurs from Latin America to speak at its annual Business of Hope fundraiser in Seattle. Originally, the vast majority of these speeches concentrated exclusively on the benefits of receiving a micro loan to either establish a microenterprise or to invest in an ongoing concern. Annual praise was given to the impact the cash had on businesses and livelihoods in pure financial terms such as increased cash flow, assets purchased and increased profits, which all led to improved standards of living. As the years passed, however, a shift in the focus of the speeches became more and more apparent. Speakers began emphasizing the life-changing impact of the additional non-lending services provided by microfinance institutions (MFIs):[2] business education modules, the technical assistance advice, and health care classes and services. In one speaker's case these services not only changed her life. They actually saved it.

The keynote speaker in 2010 was Edelma Altamiro from Nicaragua. A few years earlier Edelma joined a local village bank created by a local MFI and secured a loan to invest in a clothing resale business. Edelma spoke passionately about how the credit and support from the MFI had provided her with the confidence to run the business and the expertise to make it a success. But it was Edelma's moving account of the MFI's cervical cancer screening clinic that detected her cancer early enough to initiate treatment, which truly captured the imagination of the audience that day. All were left in no doubt that MFIs have the potential to offer much more than just microcredit.

Life changing, or indeed lifesaving, stories of necessity entrepreneurs such as Edelma's are being played out daily across the globe as the microfinance industry increasingly leverages its position and influence within communities to integrate the provision of critical services using a common platform. Organizations that previously thought of integrated or complementary services as too expensive to provide are now developing sustainable business models wherein their hybrid offering allows them to attract a wider range of clients and differentiate themselves from the ever-growing competition. The ultimate beneficiaries remain the clients who, through their existing relationship with an MFI, now have access to services that they would otherwise be unable to pay for or unwilling to seek out.

This chapter will address the current movement within the microfinance sector toward MFIs offering a hybrid of integrated non-financial services and traditional loan products to necessity entrepreneurs who, without such assistance, would perhaps never break out of poverty. It will look at the fundamental role of MFIs before discussing why their impact will be limited with an approach that focuses on financial services alone. After detailing why MFIs are ideal platforms from which to provide a holistic approach to poverty alleviation for necessity entrepreneurs, specific approaches currently in operation will be analyzed including: microfinance plus microenterprise education and microfinance plus general education, microfinance plus technical assistance, and microfinance plus health education and services. Following a look at the risks and challenges faced by MFIs attempting to expand and diversify their services, the chapter will conclude with recommendations on the steps the industry must take to continue evolving as a genuine solution to the multidimensional issue of global poverty.

THE ROLE OF AN MFI

When the seeds of modern day microfinance were being sown in the 1970s, the early pioneers sought a solution to a problem they defined quite simply as a lack of access by impoverished people to mainstream financial services. Due to a combination of the necessities of economies of scale within financial institutions and the lack of available collateral from poor borrowers, those living in poverty were unable to take advantage of the loans, savings, insurance and money transfer products that were taken for granted by the financially enfranchised majority. Nobel Prize winner and one of the originators of microfinance, Muhammad Yunus, believed that it is this exclusion from the global economy that keeps people entrenched in a cycle of poverty. Yunus argued that all human beings are born with innate survival skills and that with access to credit these skills will be put into action and routes out of poverty will be found. To borrow from Darwin, 'it is a belief that the misery of the poor has been caused, not by the laws of nature, but by man-made institutions' and the remedy therefore lies within similar man-made institutions and systems.

It is a philosophy that focuses on promoting economic development and increased employment via small or micro business growth as the means to reduce the problems of the necessity entrepreneur.

There is a risk that such an approach is guilty of what Levitt described as marketing myopia in his seminal article of the same name (Levitt, 1960). For an industry to survive it must clearly understand both its business and its customer's needs. Is the main enterprise of microfinance really as basic as facilitating access to capital? Few of today's MFIs define their role so narrowly. Most acknowledge that they face a multidimensional problem that demands a multi-faceted solution. They speak of being double bottom line institutions, striving to effect measurable and sustainable social impact within the communities in which they work while at the same time helping their clients along the road to financial inclusion. Modern day mission statements are routinely dominated by bold declarations of institutions making critical and lasting social interventions, of empowering women, of adopting a holistic approach to poverty alleviation. These targets cannot be achieved through financial services alone and the limits of such a restrictive approach to providing solutions to poverty are axiomatic. In order to combat poverty effectively, and in order for necessity entrepreneurs to create lasting economic development from the bottom of the pyramid, all the basic needs of the poor must be met and this includes microenterprise education.

WHAT IS POVERTY?

So what is poverty? No longer is it defined in classic economic terms as a simple question of income and savings. The concept has evolved to include such deprivations as lack of food, housing, clothing, education, health care and civic participation (Ohri and Tulchin, 2004). A recent Freedom from Hunger report on health financing described illhealth and the inability to access health care as 'key factors both leading to and resulting from poverty' (Leatherman et al., 2012). It went on to emphasize the importance of facilitating access to health services for the poor by highlighting 'the disproportionate burden of disease among the poor; the burden of health costs with associated risk of further impoverishment; and the effect of poor health on productivity and progress towards economic empowerment' (Leatherman et al., 2012). A 2012 Microfinance and Health Alliance report describes the impact illness can have on a micro entrepreneur vis-à-vis the significant negative effects on a business. It goes on to state that 'poverty and poor health are so intimately connected that it is virtually impossible to distinguish between the causes of one and the effects of the other' (Metcalfe, Stack and Del Granado, 2012).

Insufficient education is another tell-tale sign of poverty. According to a 2012 World Literacy Foundation report, 796 million people worldwide cannot read and write, costing the global economy $1.19 trillion a year in lost earning potential. Unfortunately, many people who lack access to education remain 'trapped in a cycle of poverty with limited opportunities for employment or income generation and higher chances of poor health' (Cree, Kay and Steward, 2012). Additionally, other types of education such as business training and technical assistance are often necessary for a small enterprise to thrive. A large percentage[3] of the developing world earns a meagre living from agriculture but are unable to fully escape poverty without training on crop diversification and optimization or without guidance on how to access speciality markets and secure the best prices for their produce. The vast majority of necessity entrepreneurs are struggling to survive or reach their full potential due a lack of understanding of the fundamentals of budgeting, managing cash flows or asset investment.

WHY MFIS?

All of the above are pieces of the poverty puzzle and logically, any efforts to solve it must be multi-pronged in order to adequately address each issue simultaneously. Although some may argue that the role of microfinance is not to provide a panacea for every individual facet of poverty, there is perhaps no other industry better suited to taking on the challenge. According to Freedom from Hunger figures, there are over 3,500 MFIs worldwide providing financial services to more than 200 million households. This equates to ongoing and regular interaction with close to half a billion people living in poverty (Leatherman et al., 2012); an interaction that has helped MFIs build solidarity with communities and trust relationships with individuals. One of the great challenges service providers are confronted with is the geographical and cultural distance that often exists between urban centres and the rural areas in which the majority of microcredit borrowers reside. MFIs can help bridge this gap by opening up their distribution channels to health, education and technical assistance providers. Microfinance institutions have developed a robust and reliable global infrastructure and offer a platform from which to develop an integrated approach to improving the livelihoods for people living in poverty.

By simply making the most of their existing networks, MFIs are already in a position to: liaise with clients to determine what services are most needed and how to deliver them; lead community awareness campaigns; build local distribution points; link clients to third party service providers; strengthen local leadership; enhance coordination within local authorities to find solutions to poverty issues; and provide customized financing products. For example, the village banking model adopted by the majority of MFIs is currently proving an ideal forum for delivering health education, financial literacy training, and micro entrepreneurship education. These are just a few examples of the type of roles an MFI can play. Microfinance organizations must remain innovative in order to stay competitive. This drive to innovate produces the enabling conditions to create effective hybrids of integrated services. As adoption of these integrated service models expands, these models will become industry standard, and in certain regions, already have become the standard.

Furthermore, it is in the best interest of the microfinance sector to combine lending with non-financial services because this hybrid approach results in healthy, educated, skilled borrowers who represent a much lower credit risk. 'MFI clients and staff report that the cost of illness causes difficulties with loan repayment and savings deposits, often requiring clients to use their business loans and other household assets to pay for health-care expenses' (Metcalfe, Leatherman, Dunford, Gray, Gash, Reinsch and Chandler, 2010). A client with access to health care and health training is likely to miss fewer days due to personal sickness or caring for ill family members. In addition, savings and loan repayment rates are higher for healthy clients because they do not have to spend money on health care costs. There is also evidence placing poor health as a major reason for clients missing group meetings, which in turn undermines the group solidarity concept and threatens the integrity of the entire village banking lending model (Noble, 2001). Put simply, taking steps to minimize the risk of ill health amongst clients is a win–win situation for MFIs.

Additionally, a lack of business acumen or technical expertise may be a chief cause of under-performance amongst the microenterprises founded by necessity entrepreneurs. Providing technical training on crop diversification or teaching basic business skills such as budget management or stock maintenance increases the chances of MFI clients investing their credit sensibly, steadily improving the performance of their business, and comfortably servicing their loan. These are the type of borrowers that will remain with a microfinance organization for several years, successfully completing multiple loan cycles in the process. They are also ready-made potential customers for any new products or services the MFI develops.

Finally, MFIs operate in an extremely competitive market in which the competition grows and strengthens every year, making market saturation a real danger in some areas. They are in the business of selling a product and, as in every industry, product differentiation is often the key to success. Offering a combination of integrated services and financial products is one way to differentiate oneself in a crowded market, in addition to meeting broader client needs and therefore providing a greater social impact. Organizations such as the Microfinance and Health Alliance are already advocating with funders and governments in favour of integrated microfinance and health strategies.[4] Non-profit impact investor, Global Partnerships (GP), has invested over $85 million in more than 60 MFIs and cooperatives throughout Latin America and the Caribbean since its inception in 1994. As it evolved however, GP began to see and appreciate the impact benefits of using the microcredit platform to deliver additional critical services. As a result, for the past three years GP has invested exclusively in MFIs that demonstrate both a commitment to the hybrid approach and a successful track record of delivering an integrated model. Other institutional and private donors are increasingly supporting integrated models as well.

A HYBRID OF MICROFINANCE AND MICROENTERPRISE EDUCATION

> When people have low levels of financial literacy, they often make unproductive financial decisions: they spend their money in suboptimal ways, borrow too much, save too little, and miss opportunities for investing. (The MasterCard Foundation, 2011)

The title of this book demands a focus on microenterprise education born of necessity. It is therefore important to clarify some of the terms commonly used in discussions on this area of microfinance. This chapter treats microenterprise education as an amalgamation of three didactic approaches: financial literacy, business education, and technical assistance training. Financial literacy classes tend to entail guidance on budget management, debt management, and basic accounting principles. Business education traditionally focuses on such fundamentals as marketing, pricing, inventory control and client care. Technical assistance is tailored to specific enterprises or sectors but examples include agricultural training on crop rotation or training on using particular machinery or equipment or making particular products. However, with research suggesting that, in practice, financial literacy and business education topics frequently overlap in the programs developed and delivered by MFIs, this section will address those two fields together in considering how they impact on client knowledge and uptake and use of financial products. It will then

take a look at the effect technical assistance can have on the competitiveness and efficiency of a microenterprise. The terms financial education
and business education will be used interchangeably throughout the
chapter and should be read as referring to a combination of both subjects
which together are a key module in the holistic subject of microenterprise
education.

The Problem

Monitor Group's recent in-depth report investigating financial education
programs within MFIs opted to open Chapter 1 with the Scottish Financial
Services Authority definition of financial inclusion: 'Access to individuals to
appropriate financial products and services. This includes people having the
skills, knowledge and understanding to make the best of those products and
services' (Deb and Kubzansky, 2012). In other words, there are two over-
riding components to financial inclusion: access and capability.[5] Although
CGAP stated in 2009 that 2.7 billion persons worldwide remain unbanked
(CGAP, 2009), there is no doubt that in the past 40 years the microfinance
industry has made great strides to address access. Top estimates put the
number of low-income earners currently accessing financial services at 800
million. Of this number, 250 million hold deposit accounts, up to 190 million
have borrowed from MFIs, and between 30 and 45 million use mobile
banking (Deb and Kubzansky, 2012). These are already substantial figures,
which are likely to continue increasing. However, while the numbers of poor
with financial access increases, so too does the number using financial products with no formal financial education or training. Monitor Group (MG)
refers to this disconnect as the financial capability gap.

It is important that those working in microfinance appreciate the
dangers of this widening gap and take immediate action to reduce it.
An estimated 75 percent of MFI clients have had no exposure to financial capability building (Deb and Kubzansky, 2012). That equates to
a customer base of around 600 million unfamiliar with basic financial
principles such as budgeting, debt management and savings, yet freely
and independently using financial products. The inherent risks here are
obvious and perhaps most graphically illustrated by over-indebtedness
crises that have developed in recent years in various countries. Put simply,
microenterprises have a greater chance of survival and success when the
micro entrepreneur possesses the basic operational skills required to run
the business. There is a moral imperative for MFIs, particularly those
double bottom line institutions seeking to make a lasting social impact
on the livelihoods of the people they serve, to ensure their clients have
the financial capability to match the ever-increasing financial access

available. That means that MFIs must impart to clients the knowledge, skills and attitudes required for responsible use of financial products and services at the beginning of their relationship with the microfinance sector.

Some MFIs will also be spurred into action by a sense of self-interest. Customers should be trained on how to make best use of microfinance products and educated on the benefits of doing so. Providing such business training within a community will increase the size of the potential market that an MFI may wish to target. Financial education programs can also be utilized to maximize client retention or in the cross-selling of other services such as savings or insurance: not to mention the ever-important differentiation from competitors unable or unwilling to deliver an educational component to their services. And of course, a more financially literate market will almost certainly lead to less risk and healthier loan portfolios. All of the above will only strengthen the performance and viability of the average MFI.

The Opportunity

A recent CFI/Accion survey of over 300 MFIs confirmed that the industry is very much aware of the dangers of allowing the financial capability gap to grow. Sixty-six percent of respondents ranked 'financial education' as the top opportunity for financial inclusion. This was ranked above expanding product range, credit bureaus, mobile banking, and client protection regulations. In the same survey, 57 percent made 'limited financial literacy' the highest ranking barrier to financial inclusion which was ranked as more important than limited institutional capacity, MFIs' single product approach, limited understanding of clients, and political interference (Gardeva and Rhyne, 2011).

There is also global evidence that some MFIs have already begun leveraging their existing client relationships and distribution networks to take steps to develop and deliver business education programs in order to: broaden clients' understanding of financial options and principles, build the skills and knowledge necessary to maximize the potential of financial services, and encourage behaviors and actions that lead to more effective use of economic resources (Cohen and Nelson, 2011). One invaluable advantage that MFIs possess over other organizations is the 'ability to offer their clients an immediate opportunity to practise and apply newly-acquired financial management skills with actual financial products' (The MasterCard Foundation, 2011). MFI clients can walk out of an educational session and put their new training and knowledge to the test via the credit or savings products they currently use.

Generally speaking, three main types of delivery model are being utilized: the mass-market model of awareness raising campaigns via mass-media channels, the individual model of individual needs assessment and mobile messaging, and, by far the most common, the group-based model providing financial or technical training (Deb and Kubzansky, 2012). Regardless of the means used, the ends of each delivery model can be condensed into three objectives:

1. Improve knowledge and awareness;
2. Improve uptake and use of financial products; and
3. Improve competitiveness and efficiency.

This chapter intends to use these three goals as a framework within which it can analyze the work of a range of MFIs currently offering a hybrid of microfinance services and microenterprise education.

INTEGRATING MICROFINANCE AND MICROENTERPRISE EDUCATION TO:

Improve Knowledge and Awareness

In an effort to help the 600 million microfinance customers who are taking their first tentative steps towards financial inclusion while handicapped by an absence of fundamental financial skills or knowledge, many MFIs choose to integrate a general financial literacy education program into their services. The goal is simply to introduce their clients to basic financial concepts that will lead to better judgement and more informed financial decisions. Topics covered regularly include fundamentals such as: budgeting, debt management, investing, basic accounting principles, financial terms, financial negotiations, bank services, and the importance of saving.

In one of the largest initiatives of its kind, Microfinance Opportunities (MO) teamed up with Freedom from Hunger (FfH) in 2003 to launch the Global Financial Education Program (the GFEP). In consultation with five established MFIs,[6] the GFEP carried out extensive market research to gauge the needs of the target market before developing a series of modules that spanned all of the themes listed above. It then trained 239 organizations across six different countries to deliver the educational modules in-group sessions. The result was approximately 346,000 people receiving direct financial education and an additional 19 million were reached through print, radio, television or street theatre (Gray, Sebstad, Cohen and Stack, 2009). In addition, FfH created its own Credit with

Education curriculum consisting of learning sessions designed to address the most pressing needs of MFI borrowers living in poverty. Literacy is not a prerequisite as the dialogue-based sessions use story, role-play, demonstration, discussion and song to share experiences, explore new ideas and assist one another improve their livelihoods.[7]

Rather than simply following the syllabus of GFEP or FfH, other MFIs choose to adapt established content and materials and develop their own training modules to best suit the specific circumstances of their clients. FINCA in Peru collaborated with FfH and the alternative development services organization Atinchik to do just that. FINCA's clients received 22 entrepreneurship training sessions during monthly loan repayment meetings aimed at improving basic business practices such as: client treatment, use of profits, where to sell, and the use of discounts and credit sales.[8] Fundacion Espoir in Ecuador takes a similar approach by combining educational tools developed by FfH and the Gender Action Learning System (GALS) with content developed in-house following consultation with their clients to deliver dialogue-based business education modules during fortnightly village bank meetings.

Association ARARIWA in Peru uses the education methodology of FfH, but also employs agriculture, social, and food security promoters who work with clients on issues specific to the region, such as water, biodiversity, and forestation. Another entity of the Association offers training in the administration of rural enterprises, and another project targets the ultra-poor through education and technical assistance, and an initial donation such as a chicken or pig to kickstart a productive activity.

Improve Uptake and Use of Financial Products

Perhaps unsurprisingly given an MFI's need to do business, the most common approach to developing a hybrid of microfinance and financial education appears in the form of product-linked educational programs. Under this design, MFIs cover many of the themes previously mentioned but they tailor the content of modules for products and services they have on offer or already provide to clients. A good example is education on the benefits of having savings and training on savings strategies, combined with encouragement to clients to open and regularly use a savings account. It is often an ideal way to increase potential market size, boost product uptake and encourage client loyalty while simultaneously attempting to reduce the level of risk within the loan portfolio.

The Monitor Group outlines five distinct models within this approach: induction training, supplemental training, delinquency management, retention, and transaction intercept training (Deb and Kubzansky, 2012).

These models can be viewed as aids to help clients develop along a standard microfinance client continuum. The first two models are generally delivered to groups, the last to individuals, with models three and four delivered to a mixture of both groups and individuals. In practice, however, there is often much overlapping between the five. Below are some examples of MFIs who focus on product-linked education programs.

BRAC in Bangladesh, KASHF in Pakistan, and KWFT in Kenya all require prospective clients to attend induction programs in which loan officers deliver group training on topics such as: product features, repayment schedules, consumer rights and avoiding over-indebtedness. Vision Fund in Cambodia and SEWA Bank in India collaborate with specialist organizations such as the International Labour Organization (ILO) or GFEP to build upon the induction modules with content designed specifically for their target market. The Guatemalan based MFI Friendship Bridge (FB) is currently developing its own savings product and so, with one eye on marketing the new product, they have incorporated modules on savings techniques and the importance of having funds in reserve into their monthly education program.

As MFI clients move through loan cycles, attending the financial education classes along the way, their educational needs often become more individualized. Some will be performing well as borrowers and in order to retain and continue developing such individuals, KWFT in Kenya and the Mann Deshi Mahila Bank (MDMB) in India have designed microenterprise training programs specifically geared to assist business growth. For those clients struggling to service their debts, Banco Adopem in the Dominican Republic and SEWA Bank in India provide group or individual counselling and delinquency management advice in order to help clients sensibly manage their debts and meet repayment schedules. The final model, transaction intercept training, is when a customer is targeted at the point of making a financial transaction. The approach is more suited to institutions such as the commercial bank Banpro in Nicaragua and while it can be used as another entry point to provide financial education, it often appears more akin to direct product marketing (Deb and Kubzansky, 2012).

IMPROVE COMPETITIVENESS AND EFFICIENCY

In addition to the enhanced competitiveness and efficiency generated by a more financially literate and business-savvy client making the most of the available microfinancial products and services, MFIs are beginning to provide sector-specific technical assistance to improve microenterprise performance.

Currently, much of this technical assistance is designed to aid rural communities in which the vast majority of MFI clients earn at least a portion of their income from the agricultural sector. This can be as simple as Caja los Andes in Bolivia ensuring that most of their loan officers have degrees in agriculture, backgrounds in agronomy and experience with the local farming industry, and are therefore well placed to advise clients on issues such as crop diversification or rotation (Pearce et al., 2005). Confianza in Peru forms strategic partnerships with local public and private sector institutions to monitor weather patterns and agricultural commodity prices and keep their clients fully informed. These institutions have also been called upon by Confianza to provide technical training to their small farmer clients (Pearce and Reinsch, 2005).

Some of the best examples of technical education/skill development for improved livelihoods are seen in the agricultural cooperatives. Some of these cooperatives are organized as savings and credit cooperatives in agricultural regions, focusing on the needs of farmer-members, but organized to deliver credit much like an MFI. Others are agricultural cooperatives whose primary mission is to help farmers increase incomes and improve their livelihoods by providing training, technical assistance, processing facilities, and access to markets.

Also in Peru, APROCASSI, a Peruvian fair trade-certified coffee cooperative, provides technical assistance to all members on ways to improve coffee quality diversify farm-based productive activities. Additionally, the organization has begun an education program on farm expenses and investment planning. APROCASSI is a majority owner of a savings and credit cooperative, APROCREDI that allows them to combine these services with microcredit.

CESMACH, a Chiapas-based Mexican coffee cooperative, does both community-based training and individualized technical assistance on crop quality and productivity. The community-based training include both theoretical instruction and practice demonstrations; recent topics included wet mill management, pruning techniques, shade management, seed selection, and insect management, and were voluntarily attended by over 90 percent of member-producers. The cooperative also makes personal visits to farms that result in specific recommendations for the member-producer.

The microfinance industry could also learn from the approach of the Cooperative League of the USA (CLUSA) and its Rural Group Enterprise Development Program. This program sees hundreds of farmers in Mozambique linked together to form associations in order to establish stronger relationships and negotiate fairer contracts with commodity traders and other agribusinesses. CLUSA trained the farmers to combine their efforts to 'identify likely crop surpluses, control quality, collect and weigh harvests, arrange temporary storage, organize market days, coordinate the transportation of products to buyers and pay farmers' (Pearce et al., 2005). The program also encourages farmers to coordinate marketing campaigns, adhere to contracts and resist side sales,[9] and register as legal rural enterprises (Pearce et al., 2005).

Technical assistance is not of course restricted to agricultural clients. For the past decade IDEPRO in Bolivia has been striving to make its clients' microenterprises more competitive in agriculture but also in sectors as diverse as textiles, tourism and timber. In a holistic approach to microfinance, IDEPRO delivers technical assistance including training on: using specific machinery or equipment, drafting sales contracts, negotiating skills and techniques, and networking to expand their business through introductions to new buyers, suppliers and peers. IDEPRO believe its integrated value chain approach significantly increases the impact it has on clients and reports increasing microenterprise profits and job creation as well as improved client satisfaction and retention rates (Mahmood and Midberry, 2011). FB in Guatemala has formed alliances with a range of organizations in order to send its clients on courses to be trained in disciplines such as: candle-making, shampoo and soap production, piñata construction, food preservation, and jewellery design. The training is tailored for individual groups so that the women can return to their villages and immediately utilize their new skills and increase income within their existing businesses.

A more recent innovation within MFIs is the advent of environmentally-aware financial products. The EcoMicro program is training 12 MFIs in Latin America and the Caribbean to develop such green financial products and services. Fondo de Desarrollo Local (FDL) in Nicaragua is one organization set to benefit from the program. It has developed a service that combines technical assistance, a loan for investing in adaption initiatives, and crop microinsurance in order to reverse the adverse effects of climate change on its clients. Other MFIs, such as Te Creemos in Mexico and Caja de Arequipa in Peru, are piloting similar approaches that intend to reduce micro entrepreneurs energy costs, limit reliability on one energy source, and improve their stability and competitiveness. Technical assistance of this kind is likely to become more and more important as the effects of climate change continue to impact negatively on the livelihoods of an increasing number of MFI clients.

Impact

There is much debate in the microfinance industry as to the effectiveness of financial education and training and, while this debate rages, some

MFIs are unwilling to take the perceived risk of investing the time and money necessary to develop educational programs of their own. It is true that evaluations of financial education have often produced mixed results to fuel this lack of confidence. However, unlike other interventions such as health education, measuring the impact of microenterprise training has proved notoriously difficult due to a number of factors. Dunford highlights that 'outcomes are sensitive to the great variety of financial education objectives, content, delivery methods, delivery quality, delivery channels, audiences and contexts' (Dunford, 2013). Gray echoes this view in stating that the issue is not so much a lack of evidence of financial education having a positive effect as a lack of coherent goals, inconsistent or questionable research methods, and the timing of said assessments (Gray et al., 2009). It is also true that many organizational and external evaluations have come to the conclusion that business education modules do in fact have a positive impact on increasing financial capability and improving livelihoods amongst poor microfinance clients.

Innovations for Poverty Action's (IPA) evaluation of FINCA's business training concluded that the impact on business outcomes was 'significantly positive' and reported that amongst the 4,500 recipients of the education, sales were up 15 percent, returns increased by 26 percent and the women had 'better knowledge about business and how to use profits for business growth and innovation' (Karlan and Valdivia, 2005). Independent investigators have documented that MFI clients participating in FfH's Credit with Education program have 'more income and assets, a greater sense of personal empowerment to make decisions, and better nourished and healthier children'. The report goes on to say that these women also 'manage their businesses better and earn more money' than equivalent MFI clients not participating in the educational training (FfH website).[10] An evaluation of the GFEP found evidence of increased knowledge of: product characteristics, savings strategies, debt capacity and management calculations, and budgeting techniques. Overall, the report was able to conclude that 'the more financially literate the clients are, the better their financial decisions and overall financial well-being are compared to financially illiterate clients' (Gray et al., 2009). These reports all suggest that there is a place in the MFI market for microenterprise education.

The key to success lies in the preparation and subsequent quality and relevance of the education program that is developed. Market research in order to understand the level of client knowledge and capability is vital to inform the development of training modules. The GFEP evaluation concluded that business education works best when designed with input from the intended recipients and combined with the opportunity to immediately put new skills and knowledge into practice is available (Gray et al., 2009).

After ascertaining what is going to be taught and to whom, MFIs must then focus on guaranteeing both a high quality of content and an excellent standard of delivery. They need to be able to answer the question: how does our financial education add value to what these people already know and do (Dunford, 2013)? In other words, as far as is possible in what are typically group training sessions, the content and delivery should be tailored to maximize the positive effect it can have on the livelihoods of particular MFI clients. One aspect of such a bespoke approach is to accurately gauge the level of the educational modules. Fischer's review of the impact of two types of financial accounting training on ADOPEM customers in the Dominican Republic found that a delivery method based on simple 'rule of thumb' was much more effective than an approach which relied upon teaching the fundamentals of financial accounting (Drexler, Fischer and Schoar, 2010). Another may be to study how best to engage groups of adults with little or no experience of formal education in classroom-type settings. Perhaps the mantra of integrating microfinance with financial education should be: guarantee quality content and delivery while keeping it simple and relevant.

A HYBRID OF MICROFINANCE AND HEALTH SERVICES

> Single solutions continue to be inadequate in confronting the prevalent and persistent problems of poverty, social exclusion and ill health. (Sachs, 2005)

The Problem

The benefits of good health are self-evident to all and the links between health problems and poverty have long been established (Narayan, 2000; Dodd and Munck, 2002). Many people living in poverty lack access to adequate health care. Freedom from Hunger's report on alleviating poverty by leveraging the power of health service actors and microfinance providers in tandem defines three main barriers to health for those living in poverty (Metcalfe et al., 2010):

1. Insufficient knowledge and information about health risks, health-related behaviors, and appropriate use of health services.
2. Inadequate access to effective and appropriate health services and products.
3. Inability to afford necessary health services.

The above applies to sections of the population who often live in remote rural areas whose geographical distance from urban centres puts them beyond the reach of private and governmental health agencies. The challenges to delivering health services to people living in rural areas are extensive and as Leatherman states, 'worldwide, current public health programmes and health systems are proving to be inadequate to meet population needs' (Leatherman, S., Metcalfe, M., Geissler, K. and Dunford, C., 2011). This situation leaves those living in poverty incredibly vulnerable to a wide range of health risks. They also face the grim spectre of financial uncertainty if they decide to borrow or sell assets to pay for medical services. In fact, many choose to risk their own health rather than increase the financial burden on their family. Following a health loan pilot with Crecer in Bolivia, Freedom from Hunger reported that 12.2 percent of clients stated they 'would not have sought care at all' without the loan (Metcalfe et al., 2010).

The Opportunity

Due to their unique characteristics and capabilities, MFIs are well positioned to take on the challenge and facilitate the provision of health services to those hard-to-reach communities currently excluded from the existing health systems (Ohri and Tulchin, 2004). They can leverage the knowledge gained from long-standing trust relationships and regular meetings with clients to develop appropriate health products and services or forge partnerships with organizations and institutions that can. The group meetings also 'provide established distribution points for health-related information, products and services' (Metcalfe et al., 2010), and are ideal forums to unearth and nurture individuals to become local leaders and positively influence the community at large. In addition, the microfinance sector with its history of developing innovative financial products to meet client needs is the perfect environment for health financing solutions to emerge and eliminate a lack of wealth as a barrier to adequate health care. Table 5.1, taken directly from Leatherman's paper investigating integrating microfinance and health strategies, provides an overview of the principle barriers to obtaining adequate health care and examples of interventions MFIs can make to address the issues.

Driven by both the desire to make a lasting social impact and the financial benefits of having fit and healthy borrowers, many double bottom-line microfinance institutions have, throughout the last decade, begun developing hybrid products incorporating some of the above interventions. The following section will look at the efforts of a selection of those MFIs who are leading the way in searching for the most effective and efficient model

Table 5.1   Principle barriers to microfinance clients and examples of interventions

Barrier	Examples of Interventions
Knowledge, awareness and information	Health education
	Health promotion and screening
	Trained community health volunteers
Financial ability to pay	Loans for medical care
	Community and personal savings accounts
	Health microinsurance
Availability of effective products and services	Direct delivery of clinical patient care
	Contracts and linkages with providers
	Community pharmacies/drug dispensaries
	Referrals to providers
	Loans to providers for capital investment
	Microfranchising of health-related businesses

Source: Leatherman et al., 2011.

to deliver an integrated microfinance and health services package to their clients before assessing the impact their programs are having on medically disenfranchised communities.

INTEGRATING MICROFINANCE AND HEALTH SERVICES TO ADDRESS:

Insufficient Knowledge

For many MFIs, the first step towards integrated services is to provide basic health education to their clients. In comparison with interventions needed to tackle the issues of financing and facilitating access to health services, education is attractive to MFIs because it is relatively straight-forward to implement; flexible enough to suit a wide range of clients; and delivery and evaluation tools and materials already exist (Metcalfe et al., 2012). There are now countless examples of MFIs providing health education to their clients. Below are just a few.

After more than 20 years in Peru, FINCA began delivering 30-minute health education classes during regular loan meetings on topics chosen to target specific health needs. FINCA staff receive training in order to give the classes and key health messages are reinforced by radio broadcasts while additional information is disseminated via bulletin boards

(Metcalfe et al., 2012). Likewise in Ecuador, Cooperativa de Ahorro y Credito Mujeres Unidades (CACMU) have made individual health education a requirement of cooperative membership, and since 2008 they have covered topics such as nutrition, reproductive health, child health, first aid, oral health and healthy habits with 3,730 clients (Metcalfe et al., 2012). Popular health modules provided by other MFIs include: HIV/AIDS and malaria prevention knowledge (PADME in Benin), the financial costs of illness (CARD in the Philippines), and care of newborns and treating child diarrhoea (Bandhan in India). Bandhan chose to adapt the BRAC model of hiring staff to concentrate on teaching health modules in monthly forums open to entire communities, and then making home visits to reinforce the learning (Metcalfe et al., 2010). In Guatemala, Friendship Bridge report that the health topics delivered by loan officers as part of their general loan and non-formal education microcredit plus package frequently rank highest amongst clients completing customer satisfaction surveys.

Inadequate Access

While many of the health education classes delivered by MFIs focus on prevention and emphasize the importance of hygiene, nutrition and how to remain healthy, MFI clients are also educated on how to recognize and respond to health issues as they arise. It is at this point that the unmet demand for health services amongst the poor, especially in rural communities, becomes all too clear. The problem is both geographical and financial: remote areas suffer a huge shortage of health providers and those living in such areas often cannot afford to pay for what services are available. Again, microfinance institutions are ideally positioned to address the problem since MFIs are often located in remote or rural settings where many disenfranchised citizens reside.

To date, several successful models and mechanisms have been devised in an effort to increase access for clients to local health services and products. They range from simple linkage programs connecting clients to public or private health care institutions to MFIs taking it upon themselves to develop and provide health care services directly. Other models include MFIs that train and supervise local health promoters or health product distributors, offer discounted referral arrangements with private providers, and provide mobile health units delivering diagnostic and preventative services (Metcalfe et al., 2010).

In order to maintain as much control over the services as possible, Pro Mujer have installed doctor's surgeries in a large percentage of their offices in Bolivia and Peru. To reach the most isolated rural communities they also run mobile clinics staffed by medical specialists and equipped with the machinery needed for dental and gynaecological consultations. It continually evaluates and refines its services to guarantee it is focusing on the conditions most prevalent amongst its women clients. According to its website, Pro Mujer provides access to: pre- and post-natal monitoring, family-planning counselling, sexual and reproductive health services, screening for early detection of cervical and breast cancers, screening for early detection of asymptomatic chronic diseases as well as treatment and follow-up, mental health services and support groups, dental care and vaccinations.[11]

COOPROGESO, a savings and loan cooperative based in Ecuador, also use roving medical units to serve populations with limited or no access to primary medical services. These units are capable of carrying out diagnostic tests for bone density, mammograms, abdominal ultrasounds, electrocardiograms, eyesight examinations and de-worming (Metcalfe et al., 2012).

CRECER meanwhile has employed at least two distinct strategies for providing access to appropriate and affordable health care services for their clients. In the first, CRECER approached private health providers and negotiated discounted services before actively promoting these providers and referring their microfinance clients to these services. The second approach builds upon their strategic partnership with health providers to run 'Health Days' in which their branches are used by private health care providers to deliver their services for a fraction of the normal cost ($0.40 per client annually).

COMIXMUL, a Honduran women's cooperative, runs a Community Pharmacy Program, consisting of 190 rural community pharmacies established in the homes of member 'dispensers'. The volunteer dispensers are trained by an NGO in alliance with government or Red Cross personnel, and provide basic medicines at cost for the most common regional illnesses.

Finally, Friendship Bridge in Guatemala is currently investigating the synergies of partnering with Salud y Paz, an established health care NGO in the country. It is hoped that Friendship Bridge clients will soon be able to attend Salud y Paz's three week long Las Amigas health education courses designed and delivered by medical professionals. Themes covered include hygiene and nutrition, pregnancy and breast cancer, and practical first aid topics. A 'learner as teacher' approach is taken and upon completion of the course, graduates are equipped to return home and educate the rest of their towns and villages.

Inability to Pay

Economics is another obstacle for receiving adequate health care. One study calculated that the cost of malarial treatment in northern Ghana equates to 34 percent of a poor family's income (Barat, Palmer, Basu, Worrall, Hanson and Mills, 2004) whilst Freedom from Hunger's investigation of health financing found that direct health costs as a percentage of income ranged from 22 percent in Bolivia to 67 percent in Burkina Faso (Leatherman et al., 2012). These statistics give an indication of the financial burden borne when seeking medical treatment or consultation. When faced with health bills, many families are forced to turn to savings, selling assets, misusing microfinance loans or borrowing from family or less scrupulous lenders to survive – all of which can exacerbate financial instability within a household. We have already looked at some of the help being offered, however, such free services are often unsustainable and discounted services and products can only go so far. In order to provide a long-term solution to the problem, MFIs have used their expertise and market knowledge to develop a variety of financial products including: health loans, health savings, health microinsurance, and prepaid health programs. Such tools are vital in the drive to help clients face the impact of health costs and any loss of productivity due to ill health.

Reseau des Caisses Populaires du Burkina (RCPB) in Burkina Faso, Bandhan in India and CRECER in Bolivia all offer individual health loans to their clients. These credit products typically have a lower interest rate than standard microloans for business investment and enjoy more flexible repayment terms. RCPB also designed a health savings product that allows clients to deposit funds in an account that can only be accessed to pay for health related expenses. In the Philippines, CARD offers its clients the opportunity to opt into a government sponsored health insurance program and provides loans to pay the annual premium. The Adventist Development and Relief Agency (ADRA) in Peru has partnered with private clinics to offer health services which ADRA clients can pay for in instalments each month when they make a repayment on their microcredit. The entire amount is paid off during one full loan cycle, however clients and their family may begin accessing the health care after the first instalment is paid. One further example is the approach taken by Microcare Ltd in Uganda. Microcare acts as an independent intermediary organization, forming partnerships with MFIs in order to set up, offer and administer 'managed group health schemes that are pre-paid and risk pooled' to MFI clients and their families (Noble, 2001).

Finally, several MFIs have begun designing various models of microloans to boost the purchase of health-improving products such as water filters or eyeglasses. The Indian MFI Spandana for example has teamed up with global health innovators PATH and a local consumer goods company to expand the use of water filters and combat diarrhoeal disease. PATH reports that while post-pilot problems of correct and continued use of the filters is an issue that needs addressing, the scheme has at the very least created a demand for a health-improving product that previously did not exist in that particular market (PATH, 2012).

Impact

The Freedom from Hunger report on integrating health and microfinance services in the Andes concludes that a hybrid approach 'shows enormous potential for reducing the vulnerability of the poor' (Metcalfe et al., 2012). This view is reinforced by the multitude of studies that have found substantial increases in client health knowledge following health education delivered through MFI networks.[12] Further research has evidenced improved health practices and responses on issues such as diarrhoea, reproductive health, malaria and gender-based violence (Amin, St. Pierre, Ahmed and Hag, 2001; Smith, 2002; Pronyk, Hargreaves, Kim, Morison, Phetla, Watts, Busza and Porter, 2006; Pronyk, Kim, Abramsky, Phetla, Hargreaves, Morison, Watts, Busza and Porter, 2008). In terms of accessing health services, hybrids of microfinance and health services lead to increases in the percentage of clients seeking care for health issues such as sexually transmitted infections (Sherer, Bronson, Teter and Wykoff, 2004), vaccinations, and cancer screening (Smith, 2002; Dohn, Chavez, Dohn, Saturria and Pimentel, 2004).

Reports suggest that health loans 'enabled clients to reduce waiting times or gain access to treatment that they might not have otherwise' (Metcalfe et al., 2010) while microinsurance products greatly improve the likelihood of MFI clients utilizing hospital services (Jütting, 2003) and receiving care for the likes of malaria (Blanchard-Horan, 2007). Micro-loans have also proved successful in health capacity-building within local communities when disbursed to private health care providers. In addition, initial studies show that investing in improving facilities and services results in greater numbers of MFI clients receiving health care (Agha, Balal and Ogojo-Okello, 2004; Seiber and Robinson, 2007).

Overall the message is clear: MFIs leveraging their existing platforms and expertise can deliver health programs, products and services that make a real difference to the health of their clients. Leatherman's report, which reviews many of the studies referenced above, states that 'the evidence is instructive in clearly indicating that the addition of health-related programmes to microfinance services can change knowledge and behaviors associated with important and measurable health outcomes' (Leatherman, S., Metcalfe, M., Geissler, K. and Dunford, C., 2010).

THE FUTURE

Thus far a very positive picture has been painted of the potential impact MFIs can have on the economic development of their clients if they choose to integrate additional services with their financial products. It is however necessary to air a note of caution and draw attention to some of the challenges and risks involved when microfinance institutions choose to expand the scope of their work. As in most endeavours in global development, success lies firmly within the quantity and quality of research, preparation, implementation, feedback, and adaption undertaken.

In the first instance an MFI must ensure that it understands its own strengths and weaknesses. This requires an honest institutional assessment, with assistance from external agencies where possible, of whether an appropriate level of expertise and experience exists within an organization to begin diversifying products and services. It is important to remember that MFIs are set up first and foremost to facilitate access to financial services for those living in conditions of poverty. There is a danger that some institutions try to grow too fast, to provide too many products and services, and in the end only succeed in losing focus on what they originally did very well. Linked to this risk of doing too much too soon is the potential to put too much strain on the financial sustainability of an MFI that suddenly begins offering services without a model that can produce sustainable financial returns. A thorough cost analysis exercise is key and, once again, external agencies with expertise in risk management in a product development context can be of huge assistance in assessing the financial viability of expanding into integrated services.

Finally, when an MFI is confident that it is in a strong enough position to assimilate new educational or health services within their existing financial products, it must be prepared to put the necessary resources into researching, designing, testing and later, evaluating its new products and services. Microfinance organizations must know their customers and fully understand their needs. This can only be achieved by in-the-field research via one-on-one interviews, focus groups and informed observation of the challenges which clients face when running microenterprises. Literature reviews can play a part but it is important to appreciate that the business education needs of a rural community in Kenya may differ greatly from those of a rural community in Guatemala.

New products and services must therefore be tailored to address the specific needs of clients on an MFI by MFI basis. Even within individual microfinance institutions it is possible to segment the market further and develop genuinely bespoke products to meet the requirements of particular sectors, communities or clients. Ongoing monitoring and evaluation is then required to assess the impact and performance of the new hybrid approach and it may well take several iterations to iron out unforeseen issues in order to produce the most efficient and effective integrated services for that particular client base. An MFI not in a position to follow all of the above steps is an MFI that in all likelihood is not yet ready to convert to an integrated approach to poverty alleviation. However, for those that are ready and willing to evolve, their efforts may very well be rewarded by the seeing the progress their clients make in breaking out of the poverty cycle.

In many respects, the global microfinance industry is at an important juncture in its development. In recent years, those in the field have witnessed a huge shift in the approach of many MFIs who previously offered either a pure microfinance service or microfinance with a very basic financial literacy program attached. On the one hand there are MFIs up-scaling to become more and more like a small bank and less and less like the advocates for those at the bottom of the financial pyramid that they originally set out to represent. On the other hand, there is also a ground-swell movement towards integrated service models amongst MFIs, which maintain a focus on the best interests of their clients. This movement is perhaps most prominent in regions with relatively mature microfinance sectors, such as Bangladesh, India and Bolivia, but it is also beginning to take root in countries with less developed microfinance infrastructures. As success stories spread, other organizations are eager to become a part of this new wave of hybrid institutions, at times as much in an attempt to differentiate themselves from the competition as in response to client needs.

Nevertheless, the potential for social impact is clear and it is considerable. The pre-existing internal infrastructures of well-run MFIs, particularly with regard to village banking models, provide an excellent platform from which to deliver multiple services to the poor. Organizations that continue to focus solely on financial services are missing out on a huge opportunity to serve their clients through integrated models that are allowing clients to become healthier, better educated, better skilled, more successful financially and, subsequently, have better repayment records. It is true that banks and other single bottom line MFIs not serving the very bottom rung of the wealth ladder may find it more profitable to continue focusing on financial services alone. But for those microfinance institutions who stay true to their missions of alleviating the poverty of those at the bottom of the pyramid, their success will be more closely correlated with the progress of their clients and, for these MFIs, integrated models are undoubtedly a powerful source to accomplish their goals.

NOTES

1. The author would like to thank Paul Gibson, who was extremely helpful in preparing this chapter.
2. In this chapter the term MFIs refers to a broader set of institutions including microfinance institutions, savings and credit cooperatives, agricultural cooperatives that provide credit to farmers, and other associations which provide microcredit as part of their service offering.
3. Root Capital estimates that 500 million people around the world manage small-scale farms. http://www.rootcapital.org/.
4. Formed in 2011 by the Microcredit Summit Campaign and Freedom from Hunger, the Microfinance and Health Alliance seeks to leverage their technical expertise and communications platforms in order to expand the practice of integrating microfinance and health services. More information is available at www.microcreditsummit.org.
5. The Monitor Group has developed the concept of there being seven components to financial inclusion that they describe as levers. As well as financial education they include: Public Awareness Campaigns, Voluntary Conduct Codes, Regulatory Actions, Incentives, and Appropriate, Affordable and Available Products.
6. SEWA Bank (India); Al Amana (Morocco); Teba Bank (South Africa); Equity Building Society (Kenya); and Pro Mujer (Bolivia).
7. Further information on Freedom from Hunger's credit with education program can be found on their website: www.freedomfromhunger.org/credit-education.
8. http://www.poverty-action.org/project/0020.
9. Side-selling is when a farmer ignores the terms of an agreement and takes part or all of a harvested crop and sells it to another buyer for a higher price.
10. http://www.freedomfromhunger.org/programs/cwe.php.
11. http://promujer.org/what-we-do/.
12. Examples include: Hadi's 2001 and 2002 studies in Bangladesh, De la Cruz, Crookston, Gray, Alder, and Dearden's 2009 study in Ghana, and Smith's 2002 study in Honduras and Ecuador.

REFERENCES

Agha, S., Balal, A. and Ogojo-Okello, F. (2004). The impact of a microfinance program on client perceptions of the quality of care provided by private sector midwives in Uganda. *Health Services Research*, *39*(6.2), 2081–2100.

Amin, R., St. Pierre, M., Ahmed, A. and Haq, R. (2001). Integration of an essential services package in child and reproductive health and family planning with a micro-credit program for poor women. *World Development*, *29*(9), 1611–1621.

Barat, L., Palmer, N., Basu, S., Worrall, E., Hanson, K. and Mills, A. (2004). Do malaria control interventions reach the poor? A view through the equity lens. *American Journal of Tropical Medicine and Hygiene*, *71*(2), 174–178.

Blanchard-Horan, C. (2007). Health microinsurance in Uganda: Affecting malaria treatment seeking behaviour. *International Journal of Public Administration, 30*(8–9), 765–789.

Capsuto, T. (2010). Microfinance and education. Skoll World Forum. Retrieved from http://skollworldforum.org/2010/09/13/microfinance-and-education/.

CGAP (2006). *Emerging lessons in agricultural microfinance: Selected case studies.* Washington, DC: International Fund for Agricultural Development.

CGAP (2009). *Financial Access 2009* [Data file]. Retrieved from http://www.cgap.org/publications/financial-access-2009.

Cohen, M. and Nelson, C. (2011). *Financial literacy: A step for clients towards financial inclusion.* Washington, DC: Microfinance Opportunities.

Cree, A., Kay, A. and Steward, J. (2012). *The economic and social cost of illiteracy: A snapshot of illiteracy in a global context.* Grandville, MI: World Literacy Foundation.

De la Cruz, N., Crookston, B., Gray, B., Alder, S. and Dearden, K. (2009). Microfinance against malaria: Impact of freedom from hungers malaria education when delivered by rural banks in Ghana. *Transactions of the Royal Society of Tropical Medicine and Hygiene, 103*(12), 1229–1236.

Deb, A. and Kubzansky, M. (2012). *Bridging the gap: The business case for financial capability.* New York, NY: Monitor Group and Citi Foundation.

Deutsch Bank Community Development Finance Group (2013). *Microfinance customer service highlights.* Retrieved from http://www.mixmarket.org/sites/default/files/microfinance_customer_service_highlights_-_deutsche_bank.pdf (last accessed 7 March 2013).

Dodd, R. and Munck, L. (2002). *Dying for change: Poor people's experience of health and ill health.* Geneva, Switzerland: World Health Organization.

Dohn, A., Chavez, A., Dohn, M., Saturria, L. and Pimentel, C. (2004). Changes in health indicators related to health promotion and microcredit programs in the Dominican Republic. *Revista Panamericana de Salud Publica, 15*(3), 185–193.

Drexler, A., Fischer, G. and Schoar, A. (2010). *Keeping it simple: Financial literacy and rules of thumb.* Barcelona, Spain: CEPR Development Economics Worskshop.

Dunford, C. (2013). *The power of suggestion (i.e. financial education) to further build household resilience* [Web log post, 5 February]. Retrieved from http://microfinanceandworldhunger.org/wordpress/2013/02/the-power-of-suggestion-i-e-financial-education-to-further-build-household-resilience/.

Freedom from Hunger. (2013). *Credit with education.* Retrieved from https://www.freedomfromhunger.org/credit-education.

Gardeva, A. and Rhyne, E. (2011). *Opportunities and obstacles to financial inclusion.* Washington, DC: Centre for Financial Inclusion.

Gray, B., Sebstad, J., Cohen, M. and Stack, K. (2009). *Can financial education change behavior? Lessons from Bolivia and Sri Lanka.* Washington, DC: Global Financial Education Program.

Hadi, A. (2001). Promoting health knowledge through micro-credit programmes: Experience of BRAC in Bangladesh. *Health Promotion International, 16*(3), 219–227.

Hadi, A. (2002). Integrating prevention of acute respiratory infection with micro-credit programme: Experience of BRAC, Bangladesh. *Public Health, 116*(4), 238–244.

Innovations for Poverty Action (2005). *Innovations for poverty action evaluation summary: Business education for microcredit clients in Peru.* Retrieved from http://www.poverty-action.org/project/0020 (last accessed 7 March 2013).

Jütting, J. (2003). *Health insurance for the poor? Determinants of participation in community-based health insurance schemes in rural Senegal.* OECD Development Centre Working Papers 204, OECD Publishing.

Karlan and Valdivia (2005). In Innovations for Poverty Action (2005). *Innovations for poverty action evaluation summary: Business education for microcredit clients in Peru.* Retrieved from http://www.poverty-action.org/project/0020 (last accessed 7 March 2013).

Leatherman, S., Metcalfe, M., Geissler, K. and Dunford, C. (2010). *Integrating microfinance and health strategies: Examining the evidence to inform policy and practice.* Oxford: Oxford University Press.

Leatherman, S., Metcalfe, M., Geissler, K. and Dunford, C. (2011). Integrating microfinance and health strategies: Examining the evidence to inform policy and practice. *Health Policy and Planning, 26*(1), 1–17.

Leatherman, S., Geissler, K., Gray, B. and Gash, M. (2012). Health financing: A new role for microfinance institutions? *Journal of International Development,* doi: 10.1002/jid.2829.

Levitt, T. (1960). Marketing myopia. *Harvard Business Review,* 45–56. Retrieved from http://s3.amazonaws.com/files.posterous.com/cjlambert/kIMWyE KRGR mvFoUZJ1Vi4nL8Sv0vd8Voy7LopsnDzEsOejFLD37UoH3dOY30/MARKE TING_MYOPIA.pdf?AWSAccessKeyId=AKIAJFZAE65UYRT34AOQ&Ex pires=1362671297&Signature=zWx9aD8l8d%2FY75Ih6RmjagnSFuo%3D.

Mahmood and Midberry (2011). In Deutsch Bank Community Development Finance Group (2013). *Microfinance customer service highlights.* Retrieved from http://www.mixmarket.org/sites/default/files/microfinance_customer_ser vice_highlights_-_deutsche_bank.pdf (last accessed 7 March 2013).

The MasterCard Foundation (2011). *Taking stock: Financial education initiatives for the poor.* Toronto, Canada: Microfinance Opportunities and Genesis Analytics.

Metcalfe, M., Leatherman, S., Dunford, C., Gray, B., Gash, M., Reinsch, M. and Chandler, C. (2010). *Health and microfinance: Leveraging the strengths of two sectors to alleviate poverty.* Davis, CA: Freedom from Hunger.

Metcalfe, M., Stack, K. and Del Granado, A. (2012). *Integrated health and microfinance: Harnessing the strengths of two sectors to improve health and alleviate poverty in the Andes.* Davis, CA: Freedom from Hunger.

Murphy, K. (2009). Lending talent, and money, on a micro scale. *New York Times,* 24 June. Retrieved from ttp://www.nytimes.com/2009/06/25/business/ smallbusiness/25sbiz.html?_r=0.

Narayan, D. (2000). Voices of the poor. Retrieved from http://web.worldbank.org/ WBSITE/EXTERNAL/TOPICS/EXTPOVERTY/0,,contentMDK:20622514~ menuPK:336998~pagePK:148956~piPK:216618~theSitePK:336992,00.html.

Noble, G. (2001). *Healthy wealthy and wise: An introduction to microfinance based group health schemes.* Retrieved from http://www.microinsurancecentre.org/ resources/documents/doc_details/36-healthy-wealthy-and-wise-an-introduction-to-microfinance-based-group-health-schemes.html.

Ohri, C.G. and Tulchin, D. (2004). *Working Paper on microfinance and health: A case for integrated service delivery.* Washington, DC: Social Enterprise Associates.

OMIN (2012). Four Latin American microfinance institutions to develop green

financial products. (4 October.) Retrieved from http://www5.iadb.org/mif/
  portada/noticias/comunicadosdeprensa/tabid/511/artmid/3819/articleid/22/four-
  latin-american-microfinance-institutions-to-develop-green-financial-products.
  aspx.
PATH (2012). Microfinancing boosts uptake of water filters. (January.) Retrieved
  from http://www.path.org/publications/files/TS_swp_micro_hul_india_fs.pdf.
Pearce et al. (2005). In CGAP (2006). *Emerging lessons in agricultural microfinance:
  Selected case studies.* Washington, DC: International Fund for Agricultural
  Development.
Pearce and Reinsch (2005). In CGAP (2006). *Emerging lessons in agricultural
  microfinance: Selected case studies.* Washington, DC: International Fund for
  Agricultural Development.
Pronyk, P., Hargreaves, J.R., Kim, J.C., Morison, L.A., Phetla, G., Watts, C.,
  Busza, J. and Porter, J.D. (2006). Effect of a structural intervention for the pre-
  vention of intimate partner violence in rural South Africa: A cluster randomised
  trial. *The Lancet, 368*(9551), 1973–1983.
Pronyk, P., Kim, J.C., Abramsky, T., Phetla, G., Hargreaves, J.R., Morison, L.A.,
  Watts, C., Busza, J. and Porter, J.D. (2008). A combined microfinance and
  training intervention can reduce HIV risk behaviour in young female partici-
  pants. *AIDS, 22*(13), 1659–1665.
Sachs, J. (2005). *The end of poverty: Economic possibilities for our time.* New York,
  NY: The Penguin Press.
Seiber, E. and Robinson, A. (2007). Microfinance investments in quality in private
  clinics in Uganda: A case-control study. *BMC Health Services Research, 7*, 168.
Sherer, R.D., Bronson, J.D., Teter, C.J. and Wykoff, R.F. (2004). Microeconomic
  loans and health education to families in impoverished communities:
  Implications for the HIV pandemic. *Journal for the International Association of
  Physicians in AIDS Care, 3*(4), 110–114.
Smith, S. (2002). Village banking and maternal and child health: Evidence from
  Ecuador and Honduras. *World Development, 30*(4), 707–723.

6. Entrepreneurship in developing economies: transformation, barriers and infrastructure

Claudine Kearney and Robert D. Hisrich

INTRODUCTION

Over a century ago Joseph Schumpeter (1883–1950) recognized the importance of entrepreneurship for economic development. Schumpeter (1911/1963) conceptually identified the 'entrepreneur as innovator' as a major influence in driving economic growth and development. Schumpeter predicted that an increase in the number of entrepreneurs would result in an increase in economic growth. Writings on economic history pre-twentieth century provide detailed statements that entrepreneurship is critical to long-term economic growth and prosperity. His theory is highly influential, and it is recognized today that entrepreneurship plays a central role in the economy by establishing and developing businesses, which in turn create markets and organizations. Entrepreneurs are major contributors to economic growth, development, and prosperity (Baumol, Litan and Schramm, 2007). They significantly contribute to product and process technological innovation, which drive economic transformation and international trade. They develop new forms of organizations and innovative approaches to business.

Organizations today are facing challenges due to the increasing number of businesses, the opening of new markets, intense competition, and the global economic downturn. From the first stage of the global economic downturn, the world has experienced major transformation. In today's economy entrepreneurship is an economic necessity for organizations and economies rather than the natural emergence of major opportunities as occurred during more prosperous economic times. Now more than ever economies need to take corrective action to overcome the difficulties occurring by developing and stimulating entrepreneurship as a key contribution to economic growth and development. Understanding the factors that contribute to and influence entrepreneurship as well as the entrepreneurial skills needed is important for the economic system of the world, particularly in the current economic climate of developed and, most significantly, developing economies where 'necessity entrepreneurs' abound.

The process of entrepreneurship can be dramatically different depending on the context and level of economic development of an economy. Governments and policy makers are a major determinant of economic transactions and have a strong influence in supporting or deterring entrepreneurial activity. Entrepreneurship is the focus of many policy questions related to sustainability, poverty, human capital, employment, resources, competitiveness and so forth. Over the last six decades major diversity has occurred across the globe, from positive economic structural transformations (East Asia), a combination of positive and negative transformations (countries of the former Soviet Union), significant innovation leading to high growth (Finland, India, Ireland, and the US), and stagnated growth and conflict (African countries). In the last decade the global economic downturn has had major direct or indirect negative implications on many developed and developing economies around the world.

Entrepreneurship is not only relevant for developing countries, it is of major importance for developed countries to gain and regain competitiveness and overcome the challenges they face in a global economic downturn. The focus on entrepreneurship in developing countries is on generating and developing economic growth and prosperity, and creating change to the infrastructure of economies. In developed economies the focus is mainly on generating new and innovative sources of productivity and growth leading to greater competitiveness. Therefore understanding the diverse contexts of entrepreneurship is fundamental to the knowledge of how important entrepreneurship is for economic growth and prosperity and how entrepreneurship can be utilized to further enhance economic development.

The purpose of this chapter is to provide an understanding of the key factors that promote entrepreneurship and the required skills necessity entrepreneurs need in developing economies in the current economic climate. The chapter is structured in the following manner. Firstly, the importance of entrepreneurship in developing economies, including entrepreneurial drivers in economic transformation and development, country barriers to entrepreneurship and business creation and ways in which countries can manage and effectively overcome these barriers towards an entrepreneurial climate that generates economic growth and development, will be discussed. Next, the importance of training and education to encourage and engender entrepreneurship within a society and the required infrastructure for support in developing economies in the current economic climate will be explored. This chapter concludes with a discussion on the future of entrepreneurship endorsed by government, society, educational institutions, and corporations.

IMPORTANCE OF ENTREPRENEURSHIP IN DEVELOPING ECONOMIES

Entrepreneurship is a key driver for innovation and economic growth and development. Fueled by entrepreneurship, developing economies go through stages of growth, improving the financial viability of nations. The role of the entrepreneur as a significant contributor of economic growth and employment creation in society has gained considerable attention both in literature and policy of developed and developing economies (Lauder, Bookcock and Presley, 1994).

Roles and functions of entrepreneurship vary over time and across developed and developing economies. These variations are partly explained by the interdependencies between economic development and institutions (Acs, Bardasi, Estrin and Svejnar, 2011). A major determinant of economic behavior and transactions, institutions can directly and indirectly affect both the supply and the demand of entrepreneurs (Acs et al., 2011). Policies set by institutions can affect entrepreneurship activity, which in turn shape economic development.

Current research makes the following three observations. (1) While in general, entrepreneurship enhances economic growth (for example, Carree and Thurik, 2003; Audretsch and Keilbach, 2004; Van Praag and Versloot, 2007), however, Van Stel, Carree and Thurik (2005) find that entrepreneurial activity by budding entrepreneurs and owner/managers of new businesses only enhances economic growth for countries with a high level of per capita income. (2) High-growth businesses, usually started by opportunity entrepreneurs, typically make a more significant contribution to economic growth than newer and smaller scaled firms (for example, Friar and Meyer, 2003; Wong, Ho and Autio, 2005). (3) With an abundance of policy measures focusing on entrepreneurship or small businesses (for example, Landstrom and Stevenson, 2005; Acs and Stough, 2008) and high-growth firms being the main focus of policy makers (for example, Fischer and Reuber, 2003; Smallbone, Baldock and Burgess, 2002), researchers have given limited attention to policies affecting the contributions entrepreneurs add through the diverse aspirations and created opportunities that help growth in developed and developing economies. Policies directed at particular industries and sectors can affect entrepreneurs differently in their contribution to economic growth. In particular, institutions develop policies that encourage the development of some sectors and create environments that stimulate certain business activities over others. Ultimately, entrepreneurs respond to environmental factors. Therefore, businesses in certain sectors or in a particular growth phase will be incentivized to act over others.

Through individual aspirations and interests, entrepreneurs can affect economic growth differently. For instance, entrepreneurs focused on producing novel products, growing and developing their company, or engaging in export activities are likely to make a greater impact on economic growth than those who produce more ordinary products or do not aspire to gain substantial market share from its competition. Regardless of the aspiration and motivation, entrepreneurs need to be supported by the environment in which they are positioned if economic growth is to be achieved.

Despite the economic contributions, entrepreneurs do not create a business for the sole purpose of generating employment or economic growth at the national level. Individuals are motivated by personal profitability or autonomy; or sometimes, entrepreneurship is forced upon them as a result of redundancy or unemployment, as is the case with necessity entrepreneurs. In fact, the degree of individual entrepreneurial drive and motivation may influence the goals and aspirations for their business, which may then determine macroeconomic outcomes (Hessels, van Gelderen and Thurik, 2008). While in developing countries, many local economies are reliant upon necessity entrepreneurs, or individuals who have little to no access to employment, and therefore, employ themselves; in developed nations, opportunity entrepreneurs, or individuals who seek and identify opportunities, help local and national economies grow. The significance of entrepreneurship for economies is manifested not only by new businesses entering the market but also by innovative and imitative entries by existing businesses into new markets. Referred to as corporate entrepreneurship, this type of activity is critical for economic and social progress. The creation of small and medium enterprises (SMEs) and the entry of existing businesses into new markets, and their subsequent expansion through successful growth and development, contributes to the productive capacity of a society. Regardless of the drive and motivation, it is critical that policy makers recognize the key factors that influence entrepreneurship and ensure that they are supported by the institutions and policies of the nation if entrepreneurship is to contribute to economic growth.

Entrepreneurship can be characterized as productive, unproductive or even destructive (Desai, Acs and Utz Weitzel, 2011). Productive entrepreneurship contributes to economic growth and the output of a society, which generally derive from opportunity entrepreneurs. Unproductive entrepreneurship reduces social income and wealth, generating no net positive value for society, which is predominately the case with the firms created by necessity entrepreneurs. Destructive entrepreneurship is undesirable entrepreneurial activities. One extreme example is the selling of illicit and illegal substances. Frequently, an entrepreneur makes no productive contribution to the real output of an economy and in some situations plays a destructive role (Baumol, 1990). Government plays a major role in creating the conditions for productive entrepreneurship to grow and develop in an advanced transition setting. Therefore, it is important for policy makers to take the necessary action to reduce the barriers for new business creation and development. This requires, for example, proper laws and legislation, a fair and transparent tax system, financial stability, and the promotion of opportunities for new as well as existing entrepreneurs. By ensuring that entrepreneurs can generate profits and benefit from their activities, government and policy makers can facilitate positive entrepreneurship.

Historically, developing economies have underestimated the economic importance of entrepreneurship. Research has illustrated that small businesses play a major role in the economic growth and development of countries. A major driver of innovation, competitiveness and growth, entrepreneurship is a fundamental component of a nation's development and prosperity. Promoting entrepreneurship is one of the principal measures to accelerate economic growth and development. Many developed and developing countries recognize the importance of new business creation as a way of reducing poverty, unemployment, and creating economic growth and prosperity. Therefore, countries should focus on promoting economic policies that will encourage new business creation and the development of existing businesses.

ENTREPRENEURIAL DRIVER OF ECONOMIC TRANSFORMATION AND DEVELOPMENT

Since the late 1970s, the world has witnessed fundamental economic transformation in former centrally planned economies. One of the core objectives of the transformation is to improve the economic performance of a nation. The degree of transformational success is determined, to a large extent, by whether the institutional environment has become more conducive to drive entrepreneurial activities and whether firms respond to such change by adopting strategies aimed at enhancing performance.

Economic development has emerged as a result of the structural transformation of countries from traditional societies to modern economies influenced by manufacturing and services. Although a key driver of economic transformation and development within society, the role of entrepreneurship in economic development is more than increasing per capita income and output; it involves change in the structure of business and society. This change is linked to growth and increased output, which allows for the greater distribution of wealth among participants. Entrepreneurship and innovation are crucial to economic growth and development, not only in new product or service development but also in promoting investment opportunities in the creation of new business ventures. Entrepreneurship has assisted in revitalizing economies. Developing economies can be stimulated through creating structural changes that support entrepreneurship. Entrepreneurship injects energy, innovation and opportunity into an economy. The more entrepreneurs there are starting and developing businesses, the more significant the transformations will be seen in a country's economy. In developing economies, public and private sectors need to work together to strengthen the entrepreneurial infrastructure – from better support agencies to finance start-ups to more competitive supply chains. The key for developing economies is to ensure that more necessity entrepreneurs across a various industries and regions of the country have the capital, skills training and expert networks that can help them create and develop businesses that can take advantage of these growing market opportunities. Thriving entrepreneurship is essential for long-term economic transformation, growth and competitiveness of an economy.

Knowledge is recognized as an essential entrepreneurial driver of economic transformation and growth. Not only can knowledge lead to technological advancement and increase productivity, it can also lead to innovation, resulting in entrepreneurial activities, including new business creation and development of new products, processes and services. For the sake of encouraging innovation and its benefits, policies should support knowledge-creation and entrepreneurial activities. In order to identify, assimilate, and exploit externally created knowledge, research and development activities are also necessary (Cohen and Levinthal, 1990; Zucker, Darby and Brewer, 1998). In fact, the creation of new businesses can be viewed as a mechanism for knowledge diffusion and as the application of knowledge (Mueller, 2007). New businesses may emerge from entrepreneurial opportunities based on new knowledge and its application. If commercialized, the creation and exploitation of knowledge and entrepreneurial activity in developing economies can drive economic transformation and growth.

By supporting and encouraging entrepreneurship, developing economies can attract competent, educated, and innovative entrepreneurs who will generate employment, develop and grow businesses, add economic diversity through recognizing opportunities and production possibilities, and support and facilitate the implementation of new technology. This can transform an emerging economy. Sustained growth and competitiveness will depend on whether the nation can continue to attract productive entrepreneurs and whether existing competent and educated entrepreneurs can utilize their knowledge to capitalize on emerging opportunities. A nation's investment in driving entrepreneurship will transform their economy, assist in economic recovery, generate motivation and energy through innovation, and leverage innovation and job creation through the entrepreneur.

BARRIERS TO ENTREPRENEURSHIP

In order to promote entrepreneurial activity, it is important to know the barriers that affect new business creation and ways to overcome these impediments and implement new policies and measures to promote entrepreneurship. There are a number of barriers to entrepreneurship and business creation, depending on the country, industry sector, and type of enterprise. Major types of barriers in developing economies include regulatory, cultural and social, and financial and economic.

Typical Barriers to Entrepreneurship and Business Creation Among Developing Economies

Typical barriers include:

- Regulatory:
  - Creating an environment conducive to entrepreneurship and business creation requires supportive policies, including fiscal and monetary policies that are necessary for a stable macroeconomic environment, and structural policies that determine the economic framework in which the business operates. Strict regulations can become a major barrier of entrepreneurship and business creation. Legal barriers to entry should be avoided unless their importance can be justified. An example of a barrier to entry includes the numerous legal forms of business, each with different policies, procedures and registration requirements. Exit barriers may also inhibit entry because exit and entry rates are usually interconnected. When a business enters a new market, it is exposed to risk associated with investing in non-transferable and often illiquid assets without

any guarantee of success. Therefore, institutions that have costly exit rates create a major barrier to entry.

- Cultural and Social:
  - o Entrepreneurship and business creation requires knowledge and understanding of a country's legislation, cultural environment, market conditions, institutions, and language. A country that promotes an entrepreneurial culture will attract locals and foreigners to create businesses. On the other hand, without having a clear understanding of the cultural and social environment, the associated costs of business creation, including risk and consequences of failure, greatly increases, creating an international barrier for business creation. Communication, information and resources are critical tools that can be provided by institutions to assist in lowering the risks. However, limited availability and access to these resources can be a significant entry barrier.
- Financial and Economic:
  - o Proper financial access is crucial for all businesses in all sectors to achieve their objectives, particularly for new and expanding businesses. Capital markets are more favorable towards larger firms. On the other hand, newer and smaller growth firms can face barriers to entrepreneurship by finding difficulty in raising a relatively small amount of capital, especially during the current economic global downturn.

Ways Developing Economies can Overcome Barriers to Entrepreneurship and Business Creation

Actions necessary to support and encourage new business creation and development:

- Improve legislation and regulation to support business creation;
- Promote the creation of an entrepreneurial environment and increased opportunities for employment;
- Develop stronger, more effective representation of the interests of small enterprises nationally and internationally;
- Provide education and training for entrepreneurship and business creation that creates an entrepreneurial mindset;
- Create accessible communication and information support systems;
- Utilize successful e-business models and develop high quality small business support;
- Highlight the importance of networking and knowledge transfer for

business competitiveness through the development of networks of key stakeholders;
- Eliminate unreasonable barriers to entry or exit;
- Create a strong country culture for entrepreneurship and business creation;
- Develop sources of finance and support for business creation and development;
- Provide knowledge of financial support that is available to help small businesses through the various stages of business creation and development.

Entrepreneurship thrives by operating in a well-functioning business and regulatory environment. By understanding the regulatory, cultural and social, financial and economic barriers to entrepreneurship, new business creation and entrepreneurial activities in a country can be promoted. Government, institutions, policy makers, and other stakeholders need to work together to maximize the opportunities and attractiveness of new business creation and reduce the barriers within the country.

TRAINING AND EDUCATION NEEDED

With today's increasingly changing globalized economy, entrepreneurship and new business creation is very important to the economic development of the future. Training and education have a key role in creating the next generation of entrepreneur and corporate entrepreneurs with the skills and tools necessary to succeed – for both necessity and opportunity entrepreneurs. It is the application of those skills and competencies learned and developed over the career of an individual which generates benefits to the economy and society at large. This is of great significance for developing economies that need more opportunity entrepreneurs, innovation and employment opportunities. It is important to educate entrepreneurs at an early stage to provide the young generation with new creative, independent and successful entrepreneurial knowledge.

Entrepreneurship education has been identified as being able to promote entrepreneurial behavior that is critical for economic success (for example, Harrison and Leitch, 2010; Crayford, Fearon, McLaughlin and van Vuuren, 2012). By offering training and education, especially to necessity entrepreneurs, an entrepreneurial and innovative culture in developing economies can be created, as well as stronger and more sustainable companies. Its importance is evident not only in skills and level of education obtained, but it helps entrepreneurs to make decisions and manage internal and external problems they may face at an operational or strategic level. The ability to interact and communicate clearly and concisely is fundamental in all entrepreneurial activities. General education as well as specific entrepreneurial education facilitates the development of new knowledge, generating more opportunities for success and development.

Entrepreneurial knowledge and insight as well as practical training in new business creation and development are important across all disciplines. In developing economies, training and education are needed to transform economies and drive entrepreneurship. Objectives should be clearly defined and outcomes should be measured to ensure that the intended results are being achieved. Developing economies' entrepreneurialism, competitiveness, innovation and economic growth depend on their ability to generate leaders with entrepreneurial skills and mindsets, whether by creating their own businesses or innovating in larger corporations. Entrepreneurship skills and education is the first and most important, sustainable step for embedding an innovative culture among all entrepreneurs in developing economies.

As unemployment continues to increase globally, it becomes necessary for developing economies to move towards developing entrepreneurship skills and education in order to produce future opportunity entrepreneurs who will create employment opportunities and contribute to economic growth seen already in developed economies. For entrepreneurship skills and education to be fully integrated into the curricula in developing economies, schools must have the infrastructure and support similar to those of university systems in developed countries. Universities must have the support of academics, students, governments, private sector and donor agencies in order to be successful. Entrepreneurs who developed skills and knowledge through education are more likely to develop growth-orientated, organized and well-connected businesses. Effective entrepreneurship education at school and university provides a strong foundation for future entrepreneurs in diverse economies.

INFRASTRUCTURE SUPPORT

In recent decades globalization has created major opportunities for well-developed economies, while also creating difficulties for developing economies with limited infrastructure support for entrepreneurship. Regional support at national government level is critical for economic competitiveness and support for survival and growth of entrepreneurship. The terms 'entrepreneurship' and 'innovation' are fundamental and frequently used in most economies, but its implementation is not an easy task, particularly in developing economies that do not have the infrastructure to support such entrepreneurial activities. Inadequate infrastructure may impede entrepreneurship and investment in developing economies.

New business ventures are ingrained in the economic and social environment in which they were founded. The relationship between the economy and infrastructure is critical to promote entrepreneurship and create new businesses in developing economies. A major deterrent of entrepreneurship in many developing economies is the high cost of transport, energy and limited Internet access. This is compelling governments to advance infrastructure in order for these economies to become more competitive in the global marketplace. Investments in roads reduce transport costs while ports and other logistics infrastructure reduce the cost associated with trade. Ultimately, infrastructure developments improve the competitiveness of firms and generate opportunities for developing economies.

An entrepreneur setting up a business in a developing economy is concerned about a significant lack of infrastructure and resources such as roads, electricity, communication systems, banking facilities systems, educational systems, well-developed legal systems, business ethics and norms, and cultural diversity – leaving the necessity entrepreneurs to exist and operate in the informal economies. Technological advancement and development variances among countries may pose a challenge. For instance, uniform products that meet industry standards in one country may not meet standards imposed in a different country. This variation in standards creates difficulty in achieving consistent quality standards. The new products that are created based on the conditions and infrastructure operating in one country but must meet the standards of another country, pose a key challenge for developing economies, which may lack the support and infrastructure of the country of its target market. Such factors vary greatly in countries and can be the most influential inhibitor of entrepreneurship and innovation in developing countries, both at local and international levels.

THE FUTURE OF ENTREPRENEURSHIP

The term 'entrepreneurship' means different things to different people and can be considered from different perspectives. However, there are some common components such as innovation, creativity, risk taking, independence, and rewards. These components will continue to accelerate entrepreneurship in the future. Entrepreneurship is now recognized as being important for economic development, and this is endorsed by government, society, educational institutions, and corporations. Most specifically since the global economic downturn, governments all over the world are taking an increased interest in entrepreneurship to stimulate economic growth and development. Individuals are encouraged to create new businesses and are supported with tax incentives, buildings, infrastructure, and a communication system to facilitate this creation process. Government and institutional encouragement should continue in the future in both developed and developing economies as policy makers recognize that new business creation generates employment and increases economic growth and development.

Society's support for entrepreneurship and business creation will develop into the future. The media is a key factor in the development of societal support for entrepreneurship. The media plays and will continue to play a major role by reporting on the general entrepreneurial spirit in a country and highlighting the successes of new business ventures. Media coverage through television, radio, newspapers, business magazines, and so on supports a positive image of entrepreneurs in growing businesses and focuses on their contributions to society.

Entrepreneurship education is growing worldwide. Many universities and colleges throughout the world have well-developed undergraduate and postgraduate programs in entrepreneurship, with faculty actively engaged in entrepreneurial research. The study of entrepreneurship and the education of future entrepreneurs are essential to a country's economic prosperity. Considering the recognized importance of entrepreneurship to society, further investment in education is necessary in both developed and, more importantly, developing economies.

Large corporations have an interest and need to engage in corporate entrepreneurship. These organizations utilize their research and development through entrepreneurship and innovation in today's highly competitive, dynamic environment in order to remain competitive. They will need to create more new businesses in the future through corporate entrepreneurial activity, particularly in light of the global economic downturn and the demands of globalization.

Beyond simply increasing national income through the generation of employment, entrepreneurship is a positive force in economic growth and development by serving as the bridge between innovation and the marketplace (Hisrich, Peters and Shepherd, 2013). The challenge for entrepreneurship in developing economies is for entrepreneurs to continue to work within the existing system but also to work towards developing financial systems, legal structures, and labor markets that are necessary to promote entrepreneurial activities. Successful entrepreneurs from developing economies are embedded in continuous institutional structures that influence their activities.

CONCLUSION

In many countries entrepreneurship policies are already shifting their focus from seeking to increase the quantity of entrepreneurs to improving the quality of entrepreneurship, which is reflected in policies that focus on high-growth entrepreneurship (Fischer and Reuber, 2003; Smallbone et al., 2002). The main challenge for policy makers is to facilitate market entry (and exit) as well as to improve the general environment in order to stimulate growth and development of new and existing businesses without introducing too much bureaucracy (Sauka and Welter, 2007). Research has illustrated that policy makers should discourage entrepreneurship that is necessity-motivated, since this type of entrepreneurship is not likely to contribute to innovation, job creation, and export (Hessels et al., 2008).

Successful entrepreneurs link the knowledge gained from their previous ventures into future innovation strategies. Entrepreneurship is not just about new business creation; it is also about developing existing and mature organizations in all sectors, industries and economies. It includes innovations such as new business creation, new and novel combinations of existing products, new forms of production, and new markets. Today more than ever, due to globalization, technological advancement and development, intensified competitiveness, and the global economic downturn, there is a greater need for entrepreneurship in developing economies. Entrepreneurship impacts all members of society and is important to individuals, organizations, and governments and will continually impact consumers and economic growth of economies in the future.

Entrepreneurship skills and education are important not only because it helps entrepreneurs better fulfill their personal needs but because of the economic contributions of new business creation and development. Beyond improving national income by job creation, entrepreneurship acts as a positive driving force in economic growth by bridging the gap between innovation and the marketplace. The study of entrepreneurship and the skills and education of potential entrepreneurs are essential components of any objective to strengthen this link to a nation's economic well-being.

The intersection of the individuals, opportunities, organizations, combined with government, societal, academic and institutional support, can promote entrepreneurship within developing economies. This is not an easy task and resources must be utilized and effectively managed. The differences between countries and between developed and developing economies will be of less significance as globalization, technological advancement and development, improved educational systems, and infrastructure support become more widely available to developing economies.

REFERENCES

Acs, Z.J. and Stough, R. (2008). *Public Policy in an Entrepreneurial Economy*. New York, NY: Springer.

Acs, Z.J., Desai, S. and Hessels, J. (2008). Special issue on entrepreneurship, economic development and institutions. *Small Business Economics*, *31*(3), 219–234.

Acs, Z.J., Bardasi, E., Estrin, S. and Svejnar, J. (2011). Introduction to special issue of small business economics on female entrepreneurship in developed and developing economies. *Small Business Economics*, *37*, 393–396.

Audretsch, D.B. and Keilbach, M. (2004). Entrepreneurship capital and economic performance. *Regional Studies*, *38*(8), 949–959.

Baumol, W. (1990). Entrepreneurship: Productive, unproductive and destructive. *Journal of Political Economy*, *98*, 893–921.

Baumol, W.J., Litan, R.E. and Schramm, C.J. (2007). *Good Capitalism, Bad Capitalism, and the Economics of Growth and Prosperity*. New Haven: Yale University Press.

Carree, M.A. and Thurik, A.R. (2003). The impact of entrepreneurship on economic growth. In D.B. Audretsch and Z.J. Acs (eds), *Handbook of Entrepreneurship Research* (pp. 437–471). Boston, MA: Kluwer Academic.

Cohen, W.M. and Levinthal, D.A. (1990). Absorptive capacity: A new perspective on learning and innovation. *Administrative Science Quarterly*, *35*(1), 128–152.

Crayford, J., Fearon, C., McLaughlin, H. and van Vuuren, W. (2012). Affirming entrepreneurial education: Learning, employability and personal development. *Industrial and Commercial Training*, *44*(4), 187–193.

Desai, S., Acs, Z.J. and Utz Weitzel, U. (2011). A theory of destructive entrepreneurship. *Small Business Economics* (forthcoming).

Fischer, E. and Reuber, A.R. (2003). Support for rapid-growth firms: A comparison of the views of founders, government policymakers, and private sector resource providers. *Journal of Small Business Management*, *41*, 346–365.

Friar, J. and Meyer, M. (2003). Entrepreneurship and start-ups in the Boston region: Factors differentiating high-growth ventures from micro-ventures. *Small Business Economics*, *21*, 145–152.

Harrison, R. and Leitch, C. (2010). Voodoo institution or entrepreneurial university? Spin-off companies, the entrepreneurial system and regional development in the UK. *Regional Studies*, *44*(9), 1241–1262.

Hessels, J., van Gelderen, M. and Thurik, R. (2008). Entrepreneurial aspirations, motivations, and their drivers. *Small Business Economics*, *31*, 323–339.

Hisrich, R.D., Peters, M.P. and Shepherd, D.A. (2013). *Entrepreneurship*, 9th Edition, New York, NY: McGraw-Hill.

Landstrom, A. and Stevenson, L.A. (2005). *Entrepreneurship Policy*. New York, NY: Springer.

Lauder, D., Bookcock, G. and Presley, J. (1994). The system of support for SMEs in the UK and Germany. *European Business Review*, *94*(1), 9–16.

Mueller, P. (2007). Exploiting entrepreneurial opportunities: The impact of entrepreneurship on growth. *Small Business Economics*, *28*, 355–362.

Sauka, A. and Welter, F. (2007). Productive, unproductive and destructive entrepreneurship in an advanced transition setting: The example of Latvian small enterprises. In M. Dowling and J. Schmude (eds), *Empirical Entrepreneurship in*

Europe (pp. 87–111). Cheltenham, UK and Northampton, MA, USA: Edward Elgar.

Schumpeter, J.A. (1963). *The Theory of Economic Development: An Inquiry into Profits, Capital, Credit, Interest and the Business Cycle* (R. Opie, Trans.). Oxford, UK: Oxford University Press. (Original work published 1911).

Smallbone, D., Baldock, R. and Burgess, S. (2002). Targeted support for high-growth start-ups: Some policy issues. *Environment and Planning C, 20*(2), 195–209.

Van Praag, C.M. and Versloot, P.H. (2007). What is the value of entrepreneurship? A review of recent research. *Small Business Economics, 29*(4), 351–382.

Van Stel, A.J., Carree, M. and Thurik, A.R. (2005). The effect of entrepreneurial activity on national economic growth. *Small Business Economics, 24*(3), 311–321.

Wong, B., Ho, Y. and Autio, E. (2005). Entrepreneurship, innovation and economic growth: Evidence from GEM data. *Small Business Economics, 24*(3), 335–350.

Zucker, L.G., Darby, M.R. and Brewer, M.B. (1998). Intellectual human capital and the birth of US biotechnology enterprises. *American Economic Review, 88*(1), 290–306.

7. Entrepreneurial intentions of nascent entrepreneurs motivated out of necessity

Wendy A. Lindsay

INTRODUCTION

Developing countries represent the majority of countries in the world; 160 of the 192 listed United Nations member countries are classified by the International Monetary Fund (2011) as 'developing countries'. Developing countries are often characterized by extremes in wealth with significant proportions of the populations living in abject poverty – many in urban areas – while small concentrated proportions enjoy affluence (Massey, 1996; Luiz, 2006). Wealth extremes can contribute to economic and political instability and ultimately, if left unchecked, can lead to civil unrest and the destabilizing of regions as the effects of the unrest spread (Massey, 1996; Luiz, 2006; Arat, 2003). Thus, it is in the best interests of developed countries to assist in reducing poverty and to assist in the economic development of developing countries (Massey, 1996; Luiz, 2006; Arat, 2003).

Although there are considerable variations in the levels of entrepreneurial activities that exist in developing countries, entrepreneurs who establish businesses 'out of necessity' represent the majority of businesses established in these countries (Acs, 2006; Reynolds, Bygrave, Autio, Cox, and Hay, 2002). Since developing countries represent the majority of countries in the world (International Monetary Fund, 2011), when this is extrapolated on a global basis, it is not inconceivable that the majority of businesses globally are established 'out of necessity' – notwithstanding that two-thirds of entrepreneurs classified themselves as 'opportunity-motivated' while only one-third classified themselves as 'necessity-motivated' (Reynolds et al., 2002). For this reason, improving our understanding of necessity established businesses is important particularly since there is growing evidence of the link between entrepreneurship and economic development in developing countries (Acs and Virgill, 2010) where entrepreneurial activity helps to plug gaps in imperfect markets (Leff, 1979).

Improving our understanding of would-be (nascent) entrepreneurs is an imperative in developing countries since these countries are often characterized by high levels of unemployment (Massey, 1996; Luiz, 2006; Arat, 2003). Many who do not have a job seek an alternative income stream and consider starting a business as a result (Acs, 2006; Reynolds et al., 2002). Thus, developing a better understanding of nascent necessity entrepreneurs in developing countries is important. In line with this goal, this research aims to understand to what extent entrepreneurship training helps to improve/strengthen the entrepreneurial intentions of nascent necessity entrepreneurs. While much research has been undertaken into entrepreneurship education and training of entrepreneurs in high income countries (see, for example, Levie and Autio, 2008; Acs, Desai, and Hessels, 2008), little research has been undertaken into the effects of entrepreneurship training of entrepreneurs motivated to start businesses out of necessity in lower income countries. This research aims to contribute toward bridging this gap in the literature.

RESEARCH CONTEXT

South Africa provided the context for this research. South Africa was chosen because there are only limited employment opportunities in the black socially and economically disadvantaged communities where most of the population live. Because employment prospects are limited, there is a need to encourage entrepreneurial activity in these communities. Thus, research that leads to improving our understanding of entrepreneurship in South Africa has value; yet, most behavioral science research that is published in many top tier journals occurs within a context of *Western, Educated, Industrialized, Rich, and Democratic (WEIRD) societies* (Henrich, Heine, and Norenzayan, 2010). In a recent survey of the top tier psychology journals, 96 percent of the participants in those studies were from the USA and Europe (which represented countries with only 12 percent of the world's population) with most of the participants being students (Henrich et al., 2010). Yet, WEIRD participants in such research are atypical compared to the rest of the global population and are least representative for generalizing to the human species (Henrich et al., 2010). This research, by design, focuses on a developing, rather than developed, country where the population of interest is necessity-motivated rather than opportunity-motivated nascent entrepreneurs.

HOW ENTREPRENEURSHIP IS DEFINED IN THIS RESEARCH

Various psychological, sociological, and economic entrepreneurship studies have examined how and why entrepreneurs create ventures and how entrepreneurship facilitates economic growth (Thornton, Ribeiro-Soriano, and Urbano, 2011; Shane and Venkataraman, 2000). Although entrepreneurship does not necessarily involve new venture creation (Shane and Venkataraman, 2000), new venture creation is crucial for developing countries. In this research, entrepreneurial intention precedes new venture creation and is central to the research question: *To what extent does an entrepreneurship training program affect the entrepreneurial intentions of nascent entrepreneurs who establish businesses out of necessity?* Although true cause and effect is difficult to determine, the longitudinal nature of the research allows for insights to be made and tentative conclusions to be drawn. Of interest is the individual nascent entrepreneur who, while motivated out of necessity, intends starting a for-profit business based upon an identified business opportunity (Casson and Wadeson, 2007; McMullen and Shepherd, 2006) and who will put in place the necessary activities to start that business (Kirzner, 1997; Schumpeter, 2004).

Implicit in the entrepreneurial process leading up to the commencement of the business is the entrepreneur's ability to discover, evaluate, and exploit an opportunity to create future goods and services (Shane and Venkataraman, 2000). Thus, while motivated out of necessity to start businesses due to social and economic disadvantage, it is indeed possible that necessity entrepreneurs can search for quality opportunities upon which to found their businesses that reflect attributes that will improve the sustainability of their businesses. Being a nascent entrepreneur motivated by necessity does not necessarily exclude an entrepreneur from seeking an opportunity that will enhance the sustainability of the business (though, it is acknowledged that the focus of most necessity entrepreneur businesses is self-employment only (Acs, 2006)).

Entrepreneurship in Developing Countries

There is no common definition of entrepreneurship and, as Davidsson (2005) states, 'no one can claim to have the right answer to the question of what entrepreneurship really is' (p. 6) though there are certain agreed upon characteristics that should be present:

> entrepreneurship consists of the competitive behaviors that drive the market process (Kirzner, 1973, pp. 19–20) . . . it is based jointly on behavior and

outcomes . . . (it) makes a difference, or else it isnt entrepreneurship . . . (and) it puts entrepreneurship squarely in a market context and makes clear that it is the suppliers who exercise entrepreneurship – not customers, legislators, or natural forces that also affect outcomes in the market. (Davidsson, 2005, p. 6)

This statement has universal relevance; however, entrepreneurship in a developed country can take a different form to that which occurs in developing countries (Acs and Virgill, 2010). In developing countries, words such as entrepreneurship, small and medium enterprise (SME), petty capitalism, and the informal sector are sometimes used interchangeably (Acs and Virgill, 2010, Smart and Smart, 2005). For example, throughout Africa, most enterprises are small traders that operate with a handful of employees and family helpers (Fafchamps, 2001; Acs and Virgill, 2010). These businesses tend to be frail but they do make a contribution toward GDP – particularly the SMEs (Ayyagari, Beck, and Demirguc-Kunt, 2003). Entrepreneurship is crucial for economic development in developing countries because entrepreneurs plug key gaps in incomplete and underdeveloped markets that often exist in these countries (Leff, 1979). Market imperfections are tackled by entrepreneurs implementing 'various gap-filling and, perhaps, second-best solutions. In extreme cases, where market and non-market failures are pervasive, entrepreneurs are pushed out of the formal sector into the informal sector. In less severe cases, large diversified indigenous business groups (form). Importantly, these groups engage in entrepreneurial behavior' (Leff, 1978, p. 669; cited in Acs and Virgill, 2010, p. 23). Thus, an important strategy for solving the economic ills of a country involves stimulating greater business activity and business start-ups since 'in the absence of the wealth-creating and job-creating activities of entrepreneurial businesses, the depth and extent of world poverty would be far greater' (Singer, 2006, p. 225). However, although facilitating business start-ups is important and should be supported, achieving the sustainability and continuity of these start-ups is paramount if economic development is to be perpetuated.

Bearing in mind Davidsson's (2005) insights into entrepreneurship, while embracing a Schumpeterian entrepreneurship perspective where entrepreneurial businesses engage in innovation in the form of developing new products, entering new markets, and/or developing new processes, the distinction between entrepreneurship, SMEs, petty capitalism, and the informal sector can be blurred. Of importance for entrepreneurship research in developing countries, 'as Schumpeter (1947, p. 151) (points) out, . . . the 'new thing' (whether it is a product, market, or process) need not be spectacular or of historical importance' (cited in Acs and Virgill, 2010, p. 27). Thus, consistent with Acs and Virgill's (2010) reasoning, this research embraces a broad interpretation of entrepreneurship where the innovations underpinning the entrepreneurial activity have some novelty and perceived consumer value relative to the environment of interest at its stage of development.

Entrepreneurship in a Developing Country: South Africa

As a developing country, South African SMEs play a significant role in job creation and poverty alleviation (Booyens, 2011). SMEs generate 50 percent of South African GDP and employ 60 percent of the labor force (Munshi, 2009). South Africa, however, is not necessarily regarded as having a robust entrepreneurial economy. For example, in terms of early-stage entrepreneurship activity, South Africa was ranked 23rd out of 43 countries in the 2008 Global Entrepreneurship Monitor (GEM) (Herrington, Kew, and Kew, 2008). The 2010 GEM reported an improvement over previous years (Herrington, Kew, and Kew, 2010); however, the 2011 GEM showed no real improvements over 2010 (Simrie, Herrington, Kew, and Turton, 2011). There appeared to be little improvement for 2012 with the *Global Entrepreneurship and Development Index* (Acs and Szerb, 2012) ranking South Africa toward the bottom of this Index. The South African government has attempted to improve the levels of entrepreneurship through supporting the delivery of a range of entrepreneurship training programs across the country; however, these efforts have not necessarily been successful in producing sustainable businesses. Although South Africa's nascent entrepreneurial activity in terms of business start-ups is elevated when compared to some European countries, there is a real issue in the sustainability and continuity of these businesses (Booyen, 2011). For those businesses that do survive, however, innovation is present and, thus, entrepreneurs and enterprises that are innovative or that are capable of becoming innovative are of interest to South African government entrepreneurship and innovation policy makers (Booyen, 2011). Gauteng Province, where Johannesburg is located (and where this research was conducted), is regarded as a South African innovation hub. Ironically, it also has the largest concentration of *informal* community settlements and poverty (OECD, 2011).

NECESSITY ENTREPRENEURS

Individuals engage in entrepreneurial activities for one of two reasons (Reynolds et al., 2002): (1) because they perceive a business opportunity and, as a result, they start a venture to develop that opportunity; or (2) because 'other employment options are either absent or unsatisfactory' (Hechavarria and Reynolds, 2009, p. 418) and so they start a business out of necessity (Van Stel, Wennekers, Thurik, and Reynolds, 2004; Kelley, Singer, and Herrington, 2011). Using this taxonomy, Reynolds et al. (2002) state that 97 percent of those who are entrepreneurially engaged can be defined as either 'opportunity entrepreneurs' or 'necessity entrepreneurs'.

Necessity entrepreneurship is at its highest in developing countries such as South Africa, Argentina, Brazil and Chile where there is a decreasing function of per capita income and where more generous social security systems may be less prevalent (Van Stel et al., 2004; Reynolds et al., 2002; Acs, Gorman, Szerb, and Terjesen, 2007) and/or in countries where there are uneven income distributions. As economic wealth levels increase, 'necessity' decreases as a motivator for becoming an entrepreneur (Kelley et al., 2011).

Necessity entrepreneurs may not be driven by the same factors as those that stimulate opportunity entrepreneurs into action (Reynolds et al., 2002; Acs et al., 2007). From a policy perspective, it is therefore important to understand the underlying entrepreneurial motivations for individuals if effective entrepreneurship encouragement and support programs are to be developed and implemented.

Although entrepreneurial activity of any form will benefit a country (Leff, 1979), there is evidence to suggest that some forms of entrepreneurship may fail to be a mechanism for economic development (Naude, 2010): Necessity entrepreneurs contribute least to economic development and opportunity entrepreneurs most (Acs, 2006; Reynolds et al., 2002; Acs et al., 2007). If necessity entrepreneurship is equated with self-employment (and it often is – Acs, 2006) then,

> entrepreneurship will not lead to economic development because there is no mechanism to link the activity to development. In fact, we know that self-employment declines as economies become more developed. It is only when economies are able to remove people from self-employment that we start to see an increase in development. . . . As more and more of the population becomes involved in opportunity entrepreneurship and as more and more people leave necessity entrepreneurship (self-employment), the more we see rising levels of economic development. (Acs, 2006, p. 102)

Thus, there is an imperative to transition necessity entrepreneurs whose businesses are characterized by self-employment to businesses that are aligned with, and founded upon, robust sustainable opportunities and where those businesses are capable of employing others. In this way, real contributions toward economic development can be achieved.

NASCENT ENTREPRENEURS

Nascent entrepreneurship involves the commencement of activities that are intended to result in a viable new business (Hechavarria and Reynolds, 2009). Nascent entrepreneurs are individuals who intend to start new businesses (McGee, Peterson, Mueller, and Sequeira, 2009) and who engage in gestation activities associated with the business creation process (Davidsson and Honig, 2003). To accomplish their entrepreneurial goals, nascent entrepreneurs embrace a series of activities that they anticipate will culminate in their entrepreneurial intentions becoming reality (Carter, Gartner, and Reynolds, 1996). Aldrich and Martinez (2001, p. 43) state that to be regarded as nascent entrepreneurs, individuals must 'not only say they are currently giving serious thought to the new business, but (they) also are engaged in at least two entrepreneurial activities, such as looking for facilities and equipment, writing a business plan, investing money, or organizing a start-up team'. Various factors influence individuals to become entrepreneurs including a range of traits, personal attributes, experiences, backgrounds, and dispositions (Krueger, Reilly, and Carsrud, 2000; Shane, Locke, and Collins, 2003; Baron, 2004; Arenius and Minniti, 2005) with social, network, and mentoring capabilities being important predictors of nascent entrepreneurship (Davidsson and Honig, 2003).

TEACHING ENTREPRENEURSHIP

The teaching of entrepreneurship entails covering a range of topics across many disciplinary areas. Aside from discovery and/or idea generation, topics taught on entrepreneurship programs tend to be derivatives from other disciplines; for example, the topic of the funding of entrepreneurial ventures stems from the finance discipline and the management of growth stems from the organizational area (Fiet, 2000a). Because entrepreneurship does not have a 'distinctive domain' (p. 3), Fiet (2000a) argues that many entrepreneurship programs do not have a strong enough theoretical base and that they 'focus excessively on describing the entrepreneurial phenomenon rather than on developing theory to enable aspiring entrepreneurs to make predictions' (p. 2) and that some entrepreneurship textbooks add to these shortcomings because they are deficient in theoretical underpinnings. He therefore encourages entrepreneurship educators to strengthen the theoretical content of their programs – as it relates to entrepreneurship – by avoiding only describing what entrepreneurs do and by emphasizing deductive teaching (rather than inductive) so that students understand how to apply the theory to their specific entrepreneurial business situations when they graduate. He argues that this is central to producing students with the relevant cognitive skill-sets that will facilitate their becoming effective entrepreneurial decision-makers. Pedagogically, Fiet (2000b) recognizes that students may become disinterested if content are not presented in a stimulating manner. Thus, Fiet (2000b) argues that entrepreneurship educators need to change from being only teachers to facilitators of *knowledge transfer* so that students develop an interest in the topic and leave the classroom wanting to develop additional competencies so that they can become successful practicing entrepreneurs.

Neck and Greene (2011) argue that it is time to explore new frontiers of entrepreneurship teaching where entrepreneurship is taught as a method. They categorize the existing 'known worlds of entrepreneurship education' (p. 57) into three; the entrepreneur world ('influenced by a lecture teaching methodology, basically a stand-and-deliver approach' (p. 58)), the process world ('one of planning and prediction' (p. 59) . . . '(that) focuses on a linear process' (p. 60)), and the cognition world ('which recognizes the potential for learning how to think entrepreneurially' (p. 60)). Because the entrepreneurship environment is dynamic and changing and is reflective of increasing uncertainty and 'unknowability' (p. 68), they argue that the mainstream entrepreneurship educational practice approaches are not in sync with the environment, with the mainstream approaches being dated and needing to incorporate action and practice in the learning experience (and even venture failure and all that goes with this).

ENTREPRENEURIAL INTENTIONS

Intentions are derived from a mixture of personal and contextual factors (Ajzen, 1991). They flow from the attitudes that individuals develop and become the immediate determinant of behavior (Fishbein and Ajzen, 1975; Ajzen, 1991). Social learning theory (Bandura, 1977) formed the basis for early intentions studies; however, there were problems with the explanatory power and predictive validity of these studies (Krueger et al., 2000) and, thus, Ajzen and Fishbein's (1977) and Ajzen's (1985, 1991) theory of planned behavior provided a more promising research direction.

Whereas Shapero's (1982) theory of an entrepreneurial event posits entrepreneurial intentions as a function of individual perceptions concerning the feasibility, desirability, and propensity to act, Ajzen's (1985, 1991) theory of planned behavior identifies intentions as a function of an individual's attitude, subjective norms, and perceived feasibility (control) (Hindle, Klyver, and Jennings, 2009). The entrepreneurship literature has supported both Ajzen's (1985, 1991) model (Krueger et al., 2000; Shook,

Priem, and McGee, 2003) and Shapero's (1982) model (Krueger, 1993; Krueger et al., 2000; Shook et al., 2003).

Although Bird (1988) was an early pioneer of entrepreneurial intentions, Krueger (1993, 2000, 2003), in association with various colleagues (Krueger and Dickson, 1993, 1994; Krueger and Brazeal, 1994; Krueger and Carsrud, 1993; Krueger et al., 2000; Shepherd and Krueger, 2002), developed 'the most prominent and sustained body of (entrepreneurial intentions) work in the field' (Hindle et al., 2009, p. 36). Krueger's (1993) model (as well as Ajzen's (1985, 1991) theory of planned behavior) has been widely used for predicting entrepreneurial intentions and behavior (Elfving, Brannback, and Carsrud, 2009). Krueger's (1993) model is based upon both Ajzen and Fishbein's (1977) and Ajzen's (1985, 1991) theory of planned behavior and Shapero's (1982) theory of an entrepreneurial event with entrepreneurial intentions defined as a commitment to commencing a business. This definition of entrepreneurial intentions is used in this research. Since nascent entrepreneurs are intending entrepreneurs, it is expected that they will have intentions of starting businesses. These intentions may be influenced via an entrepreneurship training process but, by definition, nascent entrepreneurs will demonstrate entrepreneurial intentions prior to any entrepreneurship training process they may engage in. Thus, it is expected that, in this research,

H1:   Nascent entrepreneurs motivated out of necessity will demonstrate entrepreneurial intentions prior to commencement of the entrepreneurship training and mentoring intervention program (T1).

Krueger (1993) identifies the perceived feasibility and perceived desirability of an entrepreneurial opportunity to be the primary components underpinning the development of entrepreneurial intentions. McMullen and Shepherd (2006) use knowledge as a substitute for perceived feasibility and an appetite for bearing risk as a substitute for perceived desirability (Douglas, 2009). Other researchers support this notion that the nascent entrepreneur's possession of prior proprietary knowledge and his/her resulting alertness underpin the development of the intention to become an entrepreneur (Kirzner, 1973, 1997; Gaglio and Katz, 2001; Gifford, 2003).

Although intentions per se are important, some argue that research into new venture creation does not engage enough with knowledge about social and human capital (Hindle et al., 2009). The acquisition of relevant knowledge and experience, as sources of human capital, inform new venture creation decisions together with social capital non-redundant information (derived from entrepreneurs' social networks and surroundings) and this allows them to enhance their entrepreneurial performance (Hindle et al., 2009). Hindle et al. (2009) argue for an enhanced model of entrepreneurial intentions that builds upon Krueger's (1993) model but which incorporates both human and social capital as endogenous variables in the model. They argue that by including human and social capital, the model is no longer about intentions to start a business; it is about *'informed intent'* to start a business – where entrepreneurial intentions are informed by human and social capital (p. 45). They also argue that women may require more human and social capital than men to form the same level of entrepreneurial intentions and that gender distinctions need to be made in entrepreneurial intentions research. This research adopts this recommendation and it is therefore expected that there will be differing levels of entrepreneurial intentions between women and men. Thus,

H2:   The entrepreneurial intentions of women and men nascent entrepreneurs motivated out of necessity will differ.

Since entrepreneurial decision making is non-linear, entrepreneurial intentions will be dynamic and therefore may change over time (Krueger, 2009). Effectuation theory supports this (Sarasvathy, 2001). As entrepreneur goals evolve, different corridors toward achieving those goals evolve; thus, entrepreneurial intentions may advance in a non-linearly manner. Krueger (2009) states that, 'We certainly may wish to think about intentions as a stepwise process and consider modeling intentions toward each step' (p. 58) and that 'it might be quite rewarding to monitor entrepreneurial intentions at both the overall level and for each step of their trajectory' (p. 70). Thus, it is expected that entrepreneurial intentions will change over time.

H3:   The entrepreneurial intentions of nascent entrepreneurs motivated out of necessity will be changeable and will be non-linear.

Krueger (2009) raises the issue of bricolage (Baker and Nelson, 2005) and intent. These are important issues since most entrepreneurs experience significant resource constraints in the venture creation and venture growth stages (Shepherd et al., 2000). Bricolage is associated with resourcefulness using what is currently available (making do with what is at hand) and recombining resources for novel uses (Baker and Nelson 2005).

Krueger (2009) asks the question, 'If entrepreneurs move forward with limited resources and must improvise with what they perceive as available, then what does that mean for how we model intent?' (p. 58). Thus, consider the intentions model applied to nascent entrepreneurs who have access to a plentiful supply of scarce resources versus the situation where there are little or no scarce resources. Resources are more than financial and include intellectual. Krueger (2009) argues that although the model should hold overall, the variance explained may be 'masking some deeper issues' (p. 58). Thus, where perceived resources increase, it is expected that there will be corresponding increases in entrepreneurial intentions and so, where intellectual resources increase as a result of participation in an entrepreneurship training, it is expected that there will be a corresponding increase in entrepreneurial intentions. Since it is possible to teach entrepreneurship (Neck and Greene, 2011), learning how to establish and grow a business will foster an enhanced intention to start a business as the learning process will reduce the uncertainty associated in business start-up. Thus, this leads to the following hypothesis:

H4:   The entrepreneurial intentions of nascent entrepreneurs motivated out of necessity will increase after the entrepreneurship training intervention program.

RESEARCH METHOD

The research occurred in Johannesburg, South Africa. Due to the research question addressed, the research design was longitudinal with repeated measures taken at three points in time. Baseline (T1) measures were taken prior to commencement of the study. An entrepreneurship training intervention was introduced immediately after T1 and finished at T2. T2 occurred 12 months after T1. Repeated measures were taken at T2. Repeated measures were also taken at T3 – 3.5 years after T2. Paired samples t-tests were undertaken in comparing T1–T2, T2–T3, and T1–T3 overall and gender specific entrepreneurial intention mean results. Gender related independent samples t-tests were also taken at T1, T2, and T3.

Participants

There were 287 participants in the study. All participants were previously socially and economically disadvantaged[1] (as classified by the South African government) – they were black South Africans and were unemployed and were from a group that had been discriminated against under the previous apartheid government. Participant ages ranged from 18 to 39 years with 84 percent in the 21–30 year age bracket; 51 percent were women and 49 percent were men; 22 percent had a university degree. Participants were recruited by promoting the study in various communities and asking for individuals who had intentions of establishing businesses to participate.

Since social security benefits payable to the longer term unemployed are somewhat absent in South Africa, the participants were motivated out of necessity to establish businesses because there was an imperative to generate an income to support themselves and/or their families. Continuous employment for the socially and economically disadvantaged is difficult to achieve in South Africa. Establishing a business is an alternative income-generating strategy to employment (if sustainability can be achieved), with begging, stealing, and starvation also being alternative possibilities/outcomes.

Because a significant part of the training process focused on opportunity identification which also involved helping participants identify viable opportunities upon which to found their businesses, participants developed an appreciation of the importance of the quality of the underlying opportunity in the entrepreneurship process. Thus, while 'necessity' was a motivating context for participants, the opportunity was paramount in their entrepreneurial decision making. From this perspective, the training that participants engaged in was designed to increase the sustainability of their ventures since many necessity entrepreneurs (when left to their own devices) found unsustainable businesses as a result of low quality opportunities (see, for example, Reynolds et al., 2002). While the literature divides entrepreneurs into those who are 'necessity-motivated' and those who are 'opportunity-motivated', there is room for a third category of entrepreneur; those who are necessity motivated but who are opportunity driven.

All participants stated that they had intentions of establishing businesses in the foreseeable future. In addition, in accordance with Aldrich and Martinez (2001) and McGee et al. (2009), the participants were classified as nascent entrepreneurs because they had engaged in at least two of the following:

1. Had attended a 'start your own business' planning seminar or conference (all participants in this research were engaged in a one-year entrepreneurship training program and were paid a small stipend while they attended the program).
2. Had written or were writing a business plan or had participated in seminars that focus on writing a business plan (participants were developing business plans for their businesses based upon opportunities that they had identified).
3. Had or were putting together start-up teams (some participants

worked in teams – either with other participants on the program or with others outside the program).

4. Were looking for a building or equipment for their businesses (around six months into the one-year program, participants were provided with a business incubator environment and were mentored by experienced consultants who encouraged participants to begin taking actions that would lead to venture start-up; however, raising the necessary funds for premises and equipment was problematic for many participants).

5. Had been saving money to invest in the business (in this research, few individuals had sufficient funds to save and invest in their businesses), and

6. Had been developing a product or service appropriate for their business (in this research, participants generally had no idea about the types of products or services they could offer and so needed mentoring and training support in this regard. To spark ideas, workshops were conducted that focused on possible business opportunities that participants could exploit to develop their businesses upon).

Thus, the participants satisfied the recommended nascent entrepreneur criteria identified by Aldrich and Martinez (2001) and McGee et al. (2009) in that they engaged in a number of the identified prerequisite criteria.

Training Intervention

The duration of the training intervention was 12 months. It involved the development of a program with theoretical foundations but with practical applications that focused on entrepreneurship and the skills and knowledge necessary to establish and develop businesses. The program involved participants attending classes that were delivered by practical instructors who had an in-depth knowledge of entrepreneurship. The first part of the program involved mainly classroom tuition that involved the delivery of a range of topics including opportunity identification, marketing, team building, and legal aspects of establishing a business. A business-oriented competitive game was introduced during this phase to help participants understand the relevance of some of the topics. The second half of the program primarily involved the mentoring of participants as they developed their business concepts in line with the business opportunities that they had identified. Mentors were experienced with practical backgrounds. All had university qualifications and were 'business savvy'. Thus, the mentors complemented the in-class training sessions and helped participants understand how to apply what they learned in the classroom situations.

Measures

Participants were asked two sets of questions to ascertain their degree of nascency. One set of questions asked: 'Do you intend to actually start a business in the foreseeable future?'. The response options were 'Yes' or 'No'. All 287 respondents answered 'Yes' to this question at each time measures were taken. This question was used to classify the participants as nascent entrepreneurs. A second question involving a 7-point likert scale was used to identify the '*degree* of participant nascency' at each point measures were taken. The question asked was: 'How *likely* is it that you will start a business in the foreseeable future?'. A '1' = 'Extremely Unlikely' and a '7' = 'Extremely Likely'. This question was used in the analysis and provided the data for the paired samples t-tests (that compared the means of two variables – for example, the entrepreneurial intention of nascent entrepreneurs at T1 and T2 – to determine if the average difference at these two points was significantly different from zero) and the independent samples t-tests (that compared the mean scores of the two groups – men and women nascent entrepreneurs – on entrepreneurial intention at each point in time).

RESULTS

Figure 7.1 provides details of the overall entrepreneurial intention means over the 4.5 years duration of the study. As can be seen, entrepreneurial intentions peaked at T2 but then decreased at T3. However, the T3 results were higher than those that existed at T1. Table 7.1 provides details of the

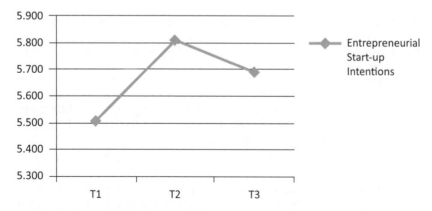

Figure 7.1   Entrepreneurial intention means – overall

Table 7.1   Paired samples t-test results – overall

Paired Samples Statistics

		Mean	N	Std. Deviation	Std. Error Mean
Pair 1	intenta1	5.51	287	.844	.050
	intenta2	5.81	287	.852	.050
Pair 2	intenta2	5.81	287	.852	.050
	intenta3	5.69	287	.863	.051
Pair 3	intenta1	5.51	287	.844	.050
	intenta3	5.69	287	.863	.051

Paired Samples Statistics

		N	Correlation	Sig.
Pair 1	intenta1 and intenta2	287	.756	.000
Pair 2	intenta2 and intenta3	287	.753	.000
Pair 3	intenta1 and intenta3	287	.701	.000

Paired Samples Test

		Paired Differences							
		Mean	Std.Deviation	Std.Error Mean	95% Confidence Interval of the Difference Lower	Upper	t	df	Sig. (2-tailed)
Pair 1	intenta1 – intenta2	−.300	.592	.035	−.368	−.231	−8.575	286	.000
Pair 2	intenta2 – intenta3	.118	.603	.036	.048	.189	3.329	286	.001
Pair 3	intenta1 – intenta3	−.181	.660	.039	−.258	−.105	−4.651	286	.000

paired samples t-tests. This indicates that there were significant differences between the T1 and T2 (p = 0.000), T2 and T3 (p = 0.001), and T1 and T3 (p = 0.000) entrepreneurial intention mean results.

Figure 7.2 provides details of the gender-specific entrepreneurial intention means over time for the women and men participants. As can be seen, for both women and men nascent entrepreneurs, entrepreneurial intentions peaked at T2. The T3 entrepreneurial intention results were higher than that which existed at T1. Table 7.2 provides details of the paired

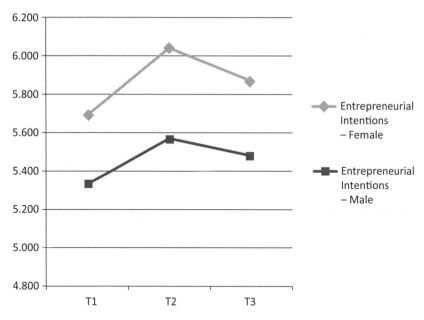

Figure 7.2   Entrepreneurial intention means – gender

Table 7.2   Paired samples t-test results – gender

Paired Samples Statistics

		sexenton	Mean	N	Std. Deviation	Std. Error Mean
71	Pair 1	intenta1	5.69	146	.784	.065
		intenta2	6.04	146	.813	.067
	Pair 2	intenta2	6.04	146	.813	.067
		intenta3	5.87	146	.849	.070
	Pair 3	intenta1	5.69	146	.784	.065
		intenta3	5.87	146	.849	.070
81	Pair 1	intenta1	5.33	141	.866	.073
		intenta2	5.57	141	.830	.070
	Pair 2	intenta2	5.57	141	.830	.070
		intenta3	5.51	141	.842	.071
	Pair 3	intenta1	5.33	141	.866	.073
		intenta3	5.51	141	.842	.071

Table 7.2 (continued)

Paired Samples Correlations

	sexenton		N	Correlation	Sig.
71	Pair 1	intenta1 and intenta2	146	.680	.000
	Pair 2	intenta2 and intenta3	146	.658	.000
	Pair 3	intenta1 and intenta3	146	.633	.000
81	Pair 1	intenta1 and intenta2	141	.801	.000
	Pair 2	intenta2 and intenta3	141	.824	.000
	Pair 3	intenta1 and intenta3	141	.740	.000

Paired Samples Test

			Paired Differences							
		sexenton	Mean	Std. Deviation	Std.Error Mean	95% Confidence Interval of the Difference Lower	Upper	t	df	Sig. (2-tailed)
71	Pair 1	intenta1 – intenta2	−.349	.639	.053	−.454	−.245	− 6.607	145	.000
	Pair 2	intenta2 – intenta3	.171	.688	.057	.059	.284	3.005	145	.003
	Pair 3	intenta1 – intenta3	−.178	.702	.058	−.293	−.063	− 3.067	145	.003
81	Pair 1	intenta1 – intenta2	−.248	.537	.045	−.338	−.159	−.5.493	140	.000
	Pair 2	intenta2 – intenta3	.064	.496	.042	−.019	.146	1.528	140	.129
	Pair 3	intenta1 – intenta3	−.184	.616	.052	−.287	−.082	−3.552	140	.001

samples t-tests. As can be seen, there were significant differences between the T1 and T2, T1 and T3, and T2 and T3 entrepreneurial intention mean results for women participants. For the men, there were significant differences between the T1 and T2 and T1 and T3 entrepreneurial intention results; however, there were no significant differences for the T2 and T3 entrepreneurial intention results.

Table 7.3 provides the details of the independent samples t-tests for the gender-specific entrepreneurial intention means at T1, T2, and T3. As can

Table 7.3 Independent samples t-test results – gender

Group Statistics

	sexenton	N	Mean	Std. Deviation	Std. Error Mean
intenta1	71	146	5.69	.784	.065
	81	141	5.33	.866	.073
intenta2	71	146	6.04	.813	.067
	81	141	5.57	.830	.070
intenta3	71	146	5.87	.849	.070
	81	141	5.51	.842	.071

Independent Samples Test

		Levene's Test for Equality of Variances		t-test for Equality of Means					95% Confidence Interval of the Difference	
		F	Sig.	T	df	Sig. (2-tailed)	Mean Difference	Std. Error Difference	Lower	Upper
intenta1	Equal variances assumed	1.811	.179	3.751	285	.000	.366	.097	.174	.557
	Equal variances not assumed			3.745	279.980	.000	.366	.098	.173	.558
intenta2	Equal variances assumed	2.529	.113	4.812	285	.000	.467	.097	.276	.657
	Equal variances not assumed			4.810	284.102	.000	.467	.097	.276	.658
intenta3	Equal variances assumed	1.265	.262	3.598	285	.000	.359	.100	.163	.556
	Equal variances not assumed			3.599	284.800	.000	.359	.100	.163	.556

be seen there were significant differences between women and men nascent entrepreneurs at each point with women demonstrating a significantly higher entrepreneurial intention at each of the three points where measures were taken.

Details of the results in terms of whether they support the hypotheses generated appear below.

H1 stated that nascent entrepreneurs motivated out of necessity will demonstrate entrepreneurial intentions prior to commencement of the entrepreneurship training and mentoring intervention program (T1). This hypothesis was confirmed. The entrepreneurial intentions mean for the group was 5.51.

H2 stated that the entrepreneurial intentions of women and men nascent entrepreneurs motivated out of necessity will differ. This hypothesis was confirmed. The entrepreneurial intentions means for women was consistently higher than men at each of the three measurement points (5.69 versus 5.33 at T1; 6.04 versus 5.57 at T2; and 5.87 versus 5.51 at T3).

H3 stated that the entrepreneurial intentions of nascent entrepreneurs motivated out of necessity will be changeable and will be non-linear. This hypothesis was supported. The overall entrepreneurial intentions mean at T2 was 5.81 compared with 5.51 at T1 and 5.69 at T3. There were similar trends for both women and men participants.

H4 stated that the entrepreneurial intentions of nascent entrepreneurs motivated out of necessity will increase after the entrepreneurship training intervention program. This hypothesis was supported overall for the group as well as for women and men.

DISCUSSION

As was expected, participants demonstrated an entrepreneurial intention prior to the commencement of the study – both in terms of the categorical 'Yes/No' entrepreneurial intentions question and the continuous likelihood of establishing a business question. Of interest though is that although all said they intended starting businesses, there were apparent reservations otherwise they would all have said that it would have been extremely likely that they would start a business (with a mean of 7.0 on this question). This 'reduced' scale response, no doubt, partly reflects the apprehension, intrepidation, and uncertainty experienced by any nascent entrepreneur (whatever his/her social and financial circumstances) due to the risks that they will face when starting a new business. In addition, it probably also reflects the disadvantaged economic environment and circumstances that the participants faced. Being economically disadvantaged, they may have been unsure of whether they could actually start a business due to the lack of resources they had at their disposal.

Participants' entrepreneurial intentions peaked immediately after the entrepreneurship training and mentoring intervention. Although the cause of this spike in entrepreneurial intention cannot be explained definitively, it is likely that the training contributed toward at least some of the increased entrepreneurial intentions at T2. Thus, it would seem that a comprehensive entrepreneurial training program can enhance the entrepreneurial intentions of nascent entrepreneurs motivated by necessity. However, the effects were not necessarily permanent. The overall entrepreneurial intention means decreased after the end of the intervention. There was a significant overall difference between the T2 and T3 entrepreneurial intention means. However, the intervention did have a sustainable effect in that the results were significantly different and enhanced over the commencing results at T1. Thus, while the total effects of the intervention did not demonstrate a continuing overall presence at T3, there were apparent effects that endured after the training. To this extent, the intervention was beneficial to the participants. A program of entrepreneurial training and associated mentoring that is targeted at nascent entrepreneurs who are motivated to establish businesses out of necessity can make a difference.

However, while there was a significant overall difference in the entrepreneurial means between T2 and T3 when gender was considered, additional insights were provided. Consistent with the overall results, the women participants demonstrated a significant reduction in their entrepreneurial intentions between T2 and T3 (though their T3 intentions were significantly higher than those they demonstrated at T1). The men participants, however, demonstrated no significant differences between their T2 and T3 entrepreneurial intentions (with their T3 intentions being significantly higher than their T1 intentions). Thus, to the extent that the training affected participants' entrepreneurial intentions, the training had a greater lasting effect on the men versus the women nascent entrepreneurs. There are various possible explanations for this including: the men were more attentive and diligent in class than the women; the women had other family-related duties to attend to and so were unable to devote the time and attention as much as the men; and/or the women were less sure of themselves – even after acquiring intellectual resources about starting a business – than the men. Given the disadvantaged situations and the environment that the participants came from, men assume a more prominent role in society and this may be reflective of the results achieved.

However, women demonstrated consistently higher entrepreneurial intentions than men at each of the three points (T1, T2, and T3) that measures were taken. One explanation for this could be that women felt more helpless at being unemployed and had a greater desire or need to start a business to generate an income; for themselves, for their immediate family, and for their extended family. Another explanation could be that women were not as risk averse as the men or did not perceive the risks associated with starting a business as being as high as the men. Alternatively, they may have been more risk ignorant than the men and/or may have had less to lose than the men in terms of reputation if they failed. A third possible explanation could be that the women were more motivated to move from the social position they occupy in the community and starting a business provided a means for them achieving this. Leveraging off the social capital foundations they develop may help them achieve this.

As a final comment, in line with theory (Krueger, 2009), entrepreneurial intentions were not stable – they were indeed volatile over the duration of the study. To this end, depending on the research questions being asked, cross-sectional studies that examine entrepreneurial intentions need to be interpreted with some caution as intentions may be affected by introduced stimuli and environmental contexts. Longitudinal empirical studies of entrepreneurial intentions may provide more insightful results.

RESEARCH LIMITATIONS AND FUTURE DIRECTIONS

This research was exploratory and made contributions to existing theory as well as practice. Theoretically, it contributed toward our understanding of the nature of entrepreneurial intentions. Building upon prior studies, the research provides insights into how entrepreneurial intentions are changeable over time. It also demonstrates that the entrepreneurial intentions of women nascent entrepreneurs who are motivated by necessity may differ from those of men. Thus, gender should be taken into consideration in intention models – at least in so far as they focus on nascent entrepreneurs who are driven to start businesses because of their adverse social and/or economic circumstances. From a practical perspective, policy makers can take heart that it would appear that a comprehensive entrepreneurial training program can make a difference with nascent entrepreneurs motivated by necessity. Both the women and men nascent entrepreneur participants in this research had a significantly enhanced entrepreneurial intention of starting a business three and a half years after they completed the entrepreneurship training and mentoring program.

One limitation of this research is that the research does not address how comprehensive should an entrepreneurship training program be for nascent entrepreneurs who are necessity-motivated, what duration should it be, what balance of classroom-imparting of knowledge versus mentoring should there be, and what disciplinary components of the teaching component are more essential than others for it to make a difference. These are questions that need to be addressed in future studies.

A second limitation is that the research involved nascent entrepreneurs who were motivated to establish businesses out of necessity from Johannesburg, South Africa – an urbanized city. Thus, the results may not be generalizable to rural areas, other developing countries, and entrepreneurs who are opportunity-motivated to start a business. To this extent, future studies need to be undertaken to address these questions. However, although the participants were motivated by necessity, they were driven by opportunity – to identify businesses that were founded on viable opportunities. To this extent, the research makes a contribution in that it demonstrates that necessity motivated entrepreneurs can have an opportunity focus.

A third limitation is that the sample was not randomly sampled from the population. However, random sampling of the target population was impossible and the approach adopted was assessed to be the best that could be undertaken given the circumstances. As Davidsson (2005, p. 74) states,

> The simple fact is that there is no fully satisfactory solution to the challenge of obtaining a representative sample of on-going, independent start-up processes. There is no way we will ever be able to sample strictly randomly (or probabilistically) from the universe of venture ideas . . . (however) . . . The fact that obtaining the ideal sample is impossible does not mean that trying to approach that ideal is a futile effort.

SUMMARY

This research examined a group of socially and economically disadvantaged individuals who intended establishing businesses. All participants were unemployed. To this extent, they could be regarded as nascent entrepreneurs who were motivated to start businesses out of necessity. A one-year entrepreneurship training and mentoring program was introduced at the beginning of the study and this helped participants to identify opportunities upon which to develop their businesses. Thus, though the participants were necessity-motivated, they were encouraged to develop businesses that were underpinned by real opportunities. Repeated measures were taken of participants' intentions of starting businesses immediately prior to the commencement of the study, immediately at the end of the training program, and three and a half years after the training finished (end-of-study). Although entrepreneurial intentions increased significantly at the end of the training program, overall they decreased by the end-of-study. In investigating this further, the women's decrease in intentions was responsible for the overall decrease since the men's intentions did not decrease significantly at the end-of-study. Women, however, demonstrated consistently higher entrepreneurial intentions than the men at each of the three points that measures were taken.

NOTE

1. For insights into the term, the US government defines 'socially and economically disadvantaged' individuals under its Small Business Act (15 USC 637) . . . (5) *Socially disadvantaged individuals* are those who have been subjected to racial or ethnic prejudice or cultural bias because of their identity as a member of a group without regard to their individual qualities. (6)(A) *Economically disadvantaged individuals* are those socially disadvantaged individuals whose ability to compete in the free enterprise system has been impaired due to diminished capital and credit opportunities as compared to others in the same business area who are not socially disadvantaged. In determining the degree of diminished credit and capital opportunities the Administration shall consider, but not be limited to, the assets and net worth of such socially disadvantaged individuals.

REFERENCES

Acs, Z. (2006). How is entrepreneurship good for economic growth? *Innovations*, 1(1), 97–107.
Acs, Z., Desai, S. and Hessels, J. (2008). Entrepreneurship, economic development and institutions. *Small Business Economics*, 31, 219–234.
Acs, Z.J., Gorman, C., Szerb, L. and Terjesen, S. (2007). Could the Irish miracle be repeated in Hungary? *Small Business Economics*, 28(2–3), 123–142.
Acs, Z. and Szerb, L. (2012). *Global Entrepreneurship and Development Index*. Cheltenham, UK and Northampton, MA, USA: Edward Elgar Publishing.
Acs, Z. and Virgill, N. (2010). *Entrepreneurship in Developing Countries*. Hanover, MA: Now Publishing.
Ajzen, I. (1985). From intentions to actions: A theory of planned behavior. In J. Kuhn and J. Beckman (eds), *Action-Control: From Cognition to Behavior*. Heidelberg: Springer.
Ajzen, I. (1991). The theory of planned behavior. *Organizational Behavior and Human Decision Processes*, 50, 179–211.
Ajzen, I. and Fishbein, M. (1977). Attitude-behavior relations: A theoretical analysis and review of empirical research. *Psychological Bulletin*, 84, 888–918.
Aldrich, H.E. and Martinez, M.A. (2001). Many are called, but few are chosen: An evolutionary perspective for the study of entrepreneurship. *Entrepreneurship Theory and Practice*, 25(4), 41–56.

Arat, Z.F. (2003). *Democracy and Human Rights in Developing Countries.* Authors Guild Backinprint.com, iUniverse, USA.

Arenius, P. and Minniti, M. (2005). Perceptual variables and nascent entrepreneurship. *Small Business Economics*, 24(3), 233–247.

Ayyagari, M., Beck, T. and Demirguc-Kunt, A. (2003). Small and medium enterprises across the globe. *World Bank Policy Research Working Paper, 3127.*

Baker, T. and Nelson, R. (2005). Creating something from nothing: Resource construction through entrepreneurial bricolage. *Administrative Science Quarterly*, 50(3), 329–366.

Bandura, A. (1997). *Self-Efficacy: The Exercise of Control.* New York, NY: Freeman.

Baron, R.A. (2004). The cognitive perspective: a valuable tool for answering entrepreneurship's basic 'why' questions. *Journal of Business Venturing*, 19, 221–239.

Bird, B. (1988). Implementing entrepreneurial ideas: The case for intention. *Academy of Management Review*, 13, 442–453.

Booyens, I. (2011). Are small, medium- and micro-sized enterprises engines of innovation? The reality in South Africa. *Science and Public Policy*, 38(1), February, 67–78.

Carter, N.M., Gartner, W.B. and Reynolds, P.D. (1996). Exploring start-up event sequences. *Journal of Business Venturing*, *11*, 151–166.

Casson, M. and Wadeson, N. (2007). The discovery of opportunities: Extending the economic theory of the entrepreneur. *Small Business Economics*, 28(4), 285–300.

Davidsson, P. (2005). *Researching Entrepreneurship.* New York, NY: Springer.

Davidsson, P. and Honig, B. (2003). The role of social and human capital among nascent entrepreneurs. *Journal of Business Venturing*, 18, 301–331.

Douglas, E. (2009). Perceptions – Looking at the world through entrepreneurial lenses. In Carsrud, A.L. and Brännback, M. (eds), *Understanding the Entrepreneurial Mind: Opening the Black Box.* New York, NY: Springer.

Elfving, J., Brannback, M. and Carsrud, A.L. (2009). Toward a contextual model of entrepreneurial intentions. In Carsrud, A.L. and Brännback, M. (eds), *Understanding the Entrepreneurial Mind: Opening the Black Box.* New York, NY: Springer.

Fafchamps, M. (2001). Networks, communities and markets in Sub-Saharan Africa: Implications for firm growth and investment. *Journal of African Economics*, 10(2), 109–142.

Fiet, J.O. (2000a). The theoretical side of teaching entrepreneurship. *Journal of Business Venturing*, 16, 1–24.

Fiet, J.O. (2000b). The pedagogical side of entrepreneurship theory. *Journal of Business Venturing*, 16, 101–117.

Fishbein, M. and Ajzen, I. (1975). *Beliefs, Attitudes, Intentions, and Behavior: An Introduction to Theory and Research.* Reading, MA: Addison-Wesley.

Gaglio, C.M. and Katz, J.A. (2001). The psychological basis of opportunity identification: Entrepreneurial alertness. *Small Business Economics*, 16(2), 95–111.

Gifford, S. (2003). Risk and uncertainty. In Acs, Z.J. and Audretsch, D.B. (eds), *Handbook of Entrepreneurial Research.* New York, NY: Springer, 37–54.

Hechavarria, D.M. and Reynolds, P.D. (2009). Cultural norms and business start-ups: the impact of national values on opportunity and necessity entrepreneurs. *International Entrepreneurship Management Journal*, 5, 417–437.

Henrich, J., Heine, S.J. and Norenzayan, A. (2010). The weirdest people in the world? *Behavioral and Brain Sciences*, 33, 61–135.

Herrington, M., Kew, J. and Kew, P. (2008). *Global Entrepreneurship Monitor 2008*. Cape Town, South Africa: Centre for Innovation and Entrepreneurship, UCT Graduate School of Business.

Herrington, M., Kew, J. and Kew, P. (2010). *Global Entrepreneurship Monitor 2010*. Cape Town, South Africa: Centre for Innovation and Entrepreneurship, UCT Graduate School of Business.

Hindle, K., Klyver, K. and Jennings, D.F. (2009). An 'informed' intent model: Incorporating human capital, social capital, and gender variables into the theoretical model of entrepreneurial intentions. In Carsrud, A.L. and Brännback, M. (eds), *Understanding the Entrepreneurial Mind: Opening the Black Box*. New York, NY: Springer.

International Monetary Fund (2011). World Economic Outlook: Tensions from the Two-Speed Recovery – Unemployment, Commodities, and Capital Flows, April, retrieved from http://www.imf.org/external/pubs/ft/weo/2011/01/pdf/text.pdf, last viewed 11 January 2012.

Kelley, D.J., Singer, S. and Herrington, M. (2011). *Global Entrepreneurship Monitor: 2011 Global Report*, Babson College, Universidad del Desarrollo, Universiti Tun Abdul Razak.

Kirzner, I. M. (1973). *Competition and Entrepreneurship*. London: University of Chicago Press.

Kirzner, I.M. (1997). Entrepreneurial discovery and the competitive market process: An Austrian approach. *Journal of Economic Literature*, 35(1), 60–85.

Krueger, N.F. (1993). The impact of prior entrepreneurial exposure on perceptions of new venture feasibility. *Entrepreneurship Theory and Practice*, 18, 5–21.

Krueger, N.F. (2000). The cognitive infrastructure of opportunity emergence. *Entrepreneurship Theory and Practice*, 24, 5–23.

Krueger, N.F. (2003). The cognitive psychology of entrepreneurship. In Acs, Z.J. and Audretsch, D.B. (eds), *Handbook of Entrepreneurship Research: An Interdisciplinary Survey and Introduction*. Boston: Kluwer Academic, 105–140.

Krueger, N.F. (2009). Entrepreneurial intentions are dead: Long live entrepreneurial intentions. In Carsrud, A.L. and Brännback, M. (eds), *Understanding the Entrepreneurial Mind: Opening the Black Box*. New York, NY: Springer.

Krueger, N.F. and Brazeal, D.V. (1994). Entrepreneurial potential and potential entrepreneurs. *Entrepreneurship Theory and Practice*, 18, 91–104.

Krueger, N.F. and Carsrud, A.L. (1993). Entrepreneurial intentions: Applying the theory of planned behavior. *Entrepreneurship and Regional Development*, 5, 315–330.

Krueger, N.F. and Dickson, P.R. (1993). Self-efficacy and perceptions of opportunities and threats. *Psychological Reports*, 722 (3, pt.2.), 1235–1240.

Krueger, N.F. and Dickson, P.R. (1994). How believing in ourselves increases risk taking: Perceived self-efficacy and opportunity. *Decision Sciences*, 25, 385–400.

Krueger, N.F., Reilly, M.D. and Carsrud, A.L. (2000). Competing models of entrepreneurial intentions. *Journal of Business Venturing*, 15, 411–432.

Leff, N.H. (1978). Industrial organization and entrepreneurship in the developing countries: The economic groups. *Economic Development and Cultural Change*, 26(4), 661–675.

Leff, N.H. (1979). Entrepreneurship and economic development: The problem revisited. *Journal of Economic Literature*, 17(1), 46–64.

Levie, J., and Autio, E. (2008). A theoretical grounding and test of the GEM model. *Small Business Economics*, 31(3), 235–263.

Luiz, J.M. (2006). The wealth of some and the poverty of Sub Saharan Africa. *International Journal of Social Economics*, 33(9), 625–648.

Massey, D.S. (1996). The age of extremes: Concentrated affluence and poverty in the twenty-first century. *Demography*, 33(4), 395–412.

McGee, J.E., Peterson, M., Mueller, S.L. and Sequeira, J.M. (2009). Entrepreneurial self-efficacy: Refining the measure. *Entrepreneurship Theory and Practice*, 965–988, July.

McMullen, J.S. and Shepherd, D.A. (2006). Entrepreneurial action and the role of uncertainty in the theory of the entrepreneur. *Academy of Management Review*, 31(1), 132–152.

Munshi, R. (2009). Small and medium enterprises in numbers. *Financial Mail*, 31 July, 28.

Naude, W. (2010). Entrepreneurship, developing countries, and development economics: New approaches and insights. *Small Business Economics*, 34 (1), 1–12.

Neck, H.M. and Greene, P.G. (2011). Entrepreneurship education: Known worlds and new frontiers. *Journal of Small Business Management*, 49(1), 55–70.

OECD (2011). OECD Territorial Reviews: South Africa 2011. OECD Publishing, http://dx.doi.org/10.1787/9789264122840-en Accessed 1 July 2012.

Reynolds, P.D., Bygrave, W.D., Autio, E., Cox, L.W. and Hay, M. (2002). *Global Entrepreneurship Monitor, 2002 Executive Report*, Wellesley, MA: Babson College.

Sarasvathy, S.D. (2001). Causation and effectuation: Toward a theoretical shift from economic inevitability to entrepreneurial contingency. *Academy of Management Review*, 26(2), 243–288.

Schumpeter, J.A. (1947). The creative response in economic theory. *The Journal of Economic History*, 7(2), 149–159.

Schumpeter, J.A. (2004). *The Theory of Economic Development*. New Brunswick, NJ: Transaction Publishers.

Shane, S., Locke, E.A. and Collins, C. (2003). Entrepreneurial motivation. *Human Resource Management Review*, 13, 257–279.

Shane, S. and Venkataraman, S. (2000). The promise of entrepreneurship as a field of research. *Academy of Management Review*, 16(2), 23–45.

Shapero, A. (1982). Social dimensions of entrepreneurship. In Kent C., Sexton D. and Vesper K. (eds), *The Encyclopedia of Entrepreneurship*. Englewood Cliffs, NJ: Prentice Hall.

Shepherd, D.A., Douglas, E.J. and Shanley, M. (2000). New venture survival: Ignorance, external shocks, and risk reduction strategies. *Journal of Business Venturing*, 15(5–6), 393–410.

Shepherd, D.A. and Krueger, N.F. (2002). An intentions-based model of entrepreneurial teams' social cognition. *Entrepreneurship: Theory and Practice*, 27, 167–185.

Shook, C.L., Priem, R.L. and McGee, J.E. (2003). Venture creation and the enterprising individual: A review and synthesis. *Journal of Management*, 29, 379–399.

Simrie, M., Herrington, M., Kew, J. and Turton, N. (2011). *GEM South Africa 2011 Report*. Cape Town, South Africa: Centre for Innovation and Entrepreneurship, UCT Graduate School of Business.

Singer, A.E. (2006). Business strategy and poverty alleviation. *Journal of Business Ethics*, 66, 225–231.

Smart, A. and Smart, J. (2005). *Petty Capitalists and Globalization: Flexibility, Entrepreneurship, and Economic Development*. New York, NY: State University of New York Press.

Thornton, P.H., Ribeiro-Soriano, D. and Urbano, D. (2011). Socio-cultural factors and entrepreneurial activity. *Small Business Journal*, 29, 105–118.

Van Stel, A., Wennekers, S., Thurik, R. and Reynolds, P. (2004). Explaining variation in nascent entrepreneurship, *Research Report H200401*. SCALES-initiative (SCientific AnaLysis of Entrepreneurship and SMEs), June.

8. The role of family capital in necessity entrepreneurship

W. Gibb Dyer

Entrepreneurship is the economic engine fueling the economies of many countries throughout the world. Some entrepreneurs start their ventures with significant experience and expertise along with the ability to identify business opportunities. Others have access to labor and capital through formal networks and thus are able to acquire the resources needed to start a business. On the other hand, other individuals start businesses out of necessity – they lose a job, a family member who was providing income becomes sick, or their nation's economy cannot provide enough employment opportunities for all its citizens. In these cases, out of necessity, these individuals launch a new business – often with just themselves as the only employee. These 'necessity entrepreneurs' often have greater difficultly gaining access to the resources they need as compared with those more experienced entrepreneurs who have established resource networks. However, most necessity entrepreneurs can access one form of capital that can help them succeed – family capital. 'Family capital' is the human, social, and financial resources that are available to individuals or groups as a result of family affiliation (Danes, Stafford, Haynes and Amarapurkar, 2009).

In this chapter I will describe what family capital is and why it is important for necessity entrepreneurs. Second, I will discuss how family capital may influence successful start-up activity among various racial and ethnic groups in the United States and across nations, and finally I will discuss how necessity entrepreneurs might gain access to family capital and the public policy implications for those who would like to assist necessity entrepreneurs.

THREE TYPES OF FAMILY CAPITAL

Francis Fukuyama notes that 'virtually all economic endeavors start out as family businesses' (Fukuyama, 1995, p. 63). Why does there appear

to be such an important connection between families and the founding
of new enterprises? Families supply entrepreneurs with certain types
of capital that allow them to start and grow successful enterprises. For
necessity entrepreneurs who do not often have formal resource networks
readily available, they may need to turn to these family resource networks
to help them succeed. While not all necessity entrepreneurs have supportive family members who can supply them with the kinds of capital that
they need, families may provide three types of family capital which have
been described by various scholars (Dyer, 2006; Rodriguez, Tuggle and
Hackett, 2009; Danes et al., 2009). These are: (1) family human capital, (2)
family social capital, and (3) family financial capital (and other tangible
assets).

FAMILY HUMAN CAPITAL

Families can help necessity entrepreneurs by providing ideas and man-
power needed to start a new business. Research has shown that children
of self-employed parents are more likely to start a new business (Fairlie
and Robb, 2008). This is due to the fact that parents and other family
members discuss business matters regularly – not only at work, but at
home as well. Thus, parents or other family members are able to impart
both the mechanics and the art associated with running a business. This
explains why certain industries, such as agriculture, distilled spirits, and
funeral homes are dominated by family businesses. By teaching family
members how to run a business family elders pass on the 'secrets' of the
business and how to gain competitive advantage in their industry. Fairlie
and Robb (2008) report that 'business outcomes are 15 to 27 percent better
if the owner worked in a family business prior to starting his or her own
business' (p. 179). Thus, necessity entrepreneurs might be more successful
if they: (1) worked for a family member before launching a new business,
or (2) gained knowledge from family members about how to start a successful enterprise.

Moreover, if necessity entrepreneurs employ family members, the family
members may be more motivated and committed to the business since the
owner is their relative (Rosenblatt, de Mik, Anderson and Johnson, 1985).
Family members may also be willing to be flexible about when they are
paid – and may even work for free under certain circumstances – to help a
family member succeed in his or her new enterprise (Light and Gold, 2008;
Rosenblatt et al., 1985).

FAMILY SOCIAL CAPITAL

Necessity entrepreneurs may also be able to draw upon the social capital of family members to help them succeed. Social capital involves the relationships between the family and others – customers, suppliers, bankers, and so on – whose help may be needed to start a new enterprise. Families may have some unique advantages in developing social capital between the family and firm stakeholders since they have the ability to develop long-standing relationships across generations (Ermisch, Jantti and Smeeding, 2012; Sirmon and Hitt, 2003; Steier, 2001). Moreover, firm stakeholders may develop personal attachments to a family that owns and operates a business creating important social ties (Meek, Woodworth and Dyer, 1988).

Some writers indicate that family connections bring certain advantages by attracting customers because of the goodwill generated by the family name (Micelotta and Raynard, 2011). A recent SC Johnson advertisement by Fisk Johnson, a 5th generation Johnson makes the connection between the family name and the family's business:

> For years, we've said that SC Johnson is a family company . . . To us, family is more than a relation. It's our inspiration. Inspiration to care. To try to do what's right. To always be better. Times may have changed since my great-great-grandfather started SC Johnson, but the inspiration behind what we do remains exactly the same. (*Parade* Magazine, 2 May 2010)

While necessity entrepreneurs may not have a familial reputation to draw upon, to the extent that they can tap into their family's social network may determine their ultimate success.

FAMILY FINANCIAL CAPITAL AND OTHER ASSETS

The last form of family capital is financial capital and other tangible assets such as the family home as the place to do business, or tools, or other implements owned by the family that can be used to start a new business. Sirmon and Hitt (2003) note that family 'survivability capital' – capital available through family connections – can provide the necessity entrepreneur the capital needed to withstand downturns in the marketplace. They write, 'survivability capital can help sustain the business during poor economic times or, for example, after an unsuccessful extension or new market venture. This safety net is less likely to occur in non-family firms due to the lack of loyalty, strong ties, or long-term commitments on the part of employees' (Sirmon and Hitt, 2003, p. 343). This pooling of capital by families has helped Chinese entrepreneurs start and grow their businesses (Fukuyama, 1995; Light and Gold, 2008). Bates (1997) reports that Asian Americans borrow three times more frequently from family and friends than do white Americans. Along with many other researchers, Fairlie and Robb (2008) concluded that 'an important limiting factor' for business start-ups was access to financial capital (p. 107). Thus tapping into the family's financial resources is likely to be critical for a necessity entrepreneur, given that banks and other formal lending institutions – even microcredit organizations – may be reluctant to lend money to them.

DISTINCT ADVANTAGES OF FAMILY CAPITAL

Family capital is important because it has significant advantages for a necessity entrepreneur. These advantages are: (1) It is difficult to imitate; (2) It can be mobilized quickly; (3) It has low transaction costs; and (4) It can be transferred efficiently across generations. Family members can easily transfer important knowledge about how to run a business. For example, Barley (1983) describes how two brothers who took over their father's funeral home had learned distinctive routines and semiotic 'codes' regarding 'taking the call, removing the body, making arrangements with the family, embalming and preparing the body, holding a wake, holding a funeral, and, finally, internment' all with the goal of 'creating a set of signs to mitigate those perceptions of death they believe might disturb participants' (Barley, 1983, p. 402). The passing of such knowledge by the father to his sons helped the sons succeed. Family relationships also promote the mobilization of family capital. Family members will often supply knowledge, labor, contacts, or financial resources to help a family member in need without contractual legal protection, thus reducing transaction costs.

To illustrate the advantages of family capital let's take the hypothetical case of a necessity entrepreneur who happens to have a fairly well-off uncle who is a small business owner. The necessity entrepreneur may be able to get the uncle to give him some tips about what types of businesses would be successful. Even better, the uncle would let his nephew work for him for a short period of time or at least let him watch how he runs his business. The necessity entrepreneur might ask the uncle who to contact to help him get his business started, who might help him run the business, and where he might get some start-up capital. The uncle may even be willing to loan his nephew some money to get started. While not all necessity entrepreneurs have a 'well-off uncle' the principle of looking first to family resources and networks still applies, since it may be the most efficient and effective way to gain resources to get started. The bonds of reciprocity that exist in a family enable family members to gain access to resources more easily than attempting to go outside the family network to more formal channels.

FACTORS INFLUENCING ACCESS TO FAMILY CAPITAL

We will now turn our attention briefly to examine those factors that tend to undermine family capital and make it more difficult for necessity entrepreneurs to access it. Prior research has suggested that family human capital is strengthened by: (1) opportunities for family members to gain skills and experience, (2) opportunities within the family to share knowledge and learn from one another, and (3) opportunities to work with family members, particularly in a family-owned enterprise. Family social capital would likely be strengthened by: (1) the size of the entrepreneur's nuclear and extended family, and (2) opportunities to engage in behaviors that would strengthen norms of reciprocity and social obligation within the family. And family financial capital would be affected by (1) the family's ability to generate wealth, and (2) the family's willingness and ability to share that wealth among family members and across generations. Factors that would affect family capital are likely to be: (1) marriage rates, (2) cohabitation rates, (3) divorce rates, (4) birth rates, and (5) out-of-wedlock birth rates. These factors affect familial trust, interaction, cooperation, the development and dispersion of family capital, and the extent of the family resource network. We will now describe how these factors can influence family capital.

Marriage Rates

Marriage provides a potential entrepreneur several forms of human, social, and financial capital. Spouses can supply labor, provide contacts, and provide money needed to start a new enterprise. The findings from various studies indicate that firms founded by married entrepreneurs are likely to have more staying power than those businesses founded by entrepreneurs who are not married (Fairlie and Robb, 2008). If the necessity entrepreneur's spouse is employed, he or she can provide both a financial safety net and a psychological safety net to help his or her spouse during difficult times that will inevitably occur when starting a new business. Sanders and Nee (1996) in their study of Asian and Latino immigrants to the US found that 'being married and living with the spouse increases the odds of self-employment for each ethnic group' (pp. 240–241). For both men and women being married increases one's chance for self-employment by 20 percent (Fairlie and Robb, 2008). And marriage seems to influence not only start-up rates but success as well. Fairlie and Robb (2008) report that married business owners have the best business outcomes while never-married owners have the worst. Thus, the institution of marriage seems to provide a wide range of familial capital to start-up entrepreneurs.

But recent demographic trends in the United States point to decline in marriage rates. The age at first marriage in the United States has increased for men (and women) from 22.5 (20.5) in 1970, to 25.5 (23.7) in 1988, to 28.4 (26.5) in 2009. In addition, marriage rates in the US have decreased from 76.5 marriages per 1,000 unmarried women in 1970 to 61.4 in 1980 to the latest figure of 36.0 in 2009 (Wilcox, Marquardt, Popenoe and Whitehead, 2010).

Cohabitation Rates

Cohabitation, where an unmarried couple lives together in an emotionally and/or sexually intimate relationship, is another factor that influences family capital. Current research notes that cohabitation fails to provide couples with many of the benefits of marriage. When compared to married couples, cohabiting couples report poorer physical and mental health (Waite, 1995), lower happiness (Stanley, Whitton and Markman, 2004), decreased productivity at work (Korenman and Neumark, 1992), and shorter longevity (Lillard and Waite, 1995). Cohabiting couples also tend to be less connected than married couples to the larger community (Waite, 1996). Cohabiters are also less likely to pool their resources (Larson, 2001). They tend to act more as individuals than as a husband and wife team.

Cohabitation rates have increased significantly in the US in recent years. It increased more than 450 percent between 1977 and 1997 (Casper, Cohen and Simmons, 1999). Cohabiters marry only 60 percent of the time, but when they do they are 46 percent more likely to divorce than those who did not live together before they were married. It appears that cohabitation may also be contributing to the increasing age of first marriage and to less stability in marriage.

Divorce Rates

Divorce can also have a significant impact on family capital. Working and associating with one's parents can have a positive impact on family capital. For example, research has shown that working in a family business has a positive impact on future entrepreneurial success, and the disruptions of family ties via divorce may make it more difficult for children to find employment in the family firm when divorced parents live significant distances from one another. Fairlie and Robb (2008) state: 'having only one parent at home limits potential exposure to family business, particularly if the absent parent is the father' (p. 187). Amato (2005) also notes that 'children in divorced families tend to have weaker emotional bonds with mothers and fathers than do their peers in two-parent families' (p. 77). Under such circumstances family ties will be undermined and family capital will be affected negatively.

The United States is experiencing historically high divorce rates. The number of divorces per 1,000 married women in 1960 was 9.2. The divorce rate rose to 14.9 in 1970, and peaked at 22.6 in 1980; it showed a slight decline in 1990 to 20.9 and has leveled out at 16.4 in 2009 (Wilcox et al., 2010). In a divorce, family financial capital is usually undermined since family assets are divided up between spouses and are not pooled as they once were.

Birth Rates

Because of smaller families in today's society, Aldrich and Cliff (2003) write: 'Individuals from smaller-sized families may perceive that they have inadequate potential resources available from kin members, and thus decide against starting their own firm. Shrinking family size clearly has negative implications for the resource mobilization process, particularly for securing human resources. When it comes to attracting employees, many entrepreneurs rely on family members, whether paid or unpaid' (p. 581). Aldrich and Langton (1998) reported that 25 percent of the firms in their sample employed family members at the time of start-up. The larger the family the more opportunities to acquire resources. One example of this is the Amish community, where it is not uncommon for couples to have ten children. Thus, the average Amish person has 90 first cousins 'each of whom is available as a potential lender' (Light and Gold, 2008, p. 87). But finding family members to work with may prove more difficult in the future. Total fertility rates have plummeted in the United States in recent years from 3.65 in 1960, to 2.48 in 1970 to 1.84 in 1980 and since have risen slightly to 2.09 in 2008 (Wilcox et al., 2010).

Out-of-wedlock Births

The final factor we will consider as to its impact on family capital is out-of-wedlock births. The Fragile Families Study based at Princeton University summarized the findings about children born to unwed parents: (1) they often grow up in poverty; (2) they have more anxiety and depression; (3)

they have more behavioral problems; and (4) they do poorly in school compared to their peers with two married parents (Carlson, McLanahan and England, 2003). While there are exceptions, in general, children in a household with only one parent tend to have a more disruptive home life and are less able to draw on familial resources that would enable them to become competent adults and able to meet the demands of an entrepreneurial career. Unfortunately, out-of-wedlock births have increased in the United States from 5 percent of live births to unmarried women in the 1960s to 18 percent in the 1980s to 41 percent in 2009 (Wilcox et al., 2010).

FAMILY CAPITAL AND ENTREPRENEURSHIP

The previous discussion has argued that there is evidence that access to family capital helps entrepreneurs launch new businesses, and would be very helpful to necessity entrepreneurs who may only have family to turn to for help in starting an enterprise. There is some data from various racial and ethnic groups in the United States that those groups with higher marriage and birth rates, and lower rates of cohabitation, divorce, and out-of-wedlock births tend to be more likely to start and own their own businesses. Table 8.1 shows the differences along these five dimensions for the four prominent racial and ethnic groups in the United States.

Overall, Asian-Americans appear to have the 'strongest' families, and therefore it's not surprising that 12 percent of Asian-Americans are self-employed and own their own businesses. Eleven percent of whites are self-employed, while 7 percent of Hispanics and 5 percent of African-Americans own their own business (Fairlie and Robb, 2008). Moreover, Asian-Americans businesses are larger and are more successful than those from other racial/ethnic groups in the US. Fairlie and Robb (2008) note that: Asian-American-owned firms 'clearly have the strongest performances among all major racial and ethnic groups' (p. 10). Asian-American-owned firms are 16 percent less likely to close, 21 percent more likely to have profits of at least $10,000, are 27 percent more likely to hire employees, and have mean sales 60 percent higher than white-owned firms. In contrast, African-American-owned companies have lower sales, profits, hire fewer people, and have higher closure rates than white-owned firms. Hispanic firms also have lower sales and hire fewer employees than white-owned firms. While family capital does not account for all the differences in self-employment rates and business success rates among these groups, I believe it accounts for a significant part of the variance that we see between these groups.

Table 8.1   Racial/ethnic groups in the United States in regards to marriage, cohabitation, divorce, birth rate and out-of-wedlock births

	% Ever Married[1]	% Cohabit[2]	% Divorced[3]	Birth Rate Per 1000[4]	Out-of-wedlock Births Per 1000[5]
Asians	71.6	5.0	4.9	17.2	26
Whites	72.5	8.2	10.8	13.7	32
Hispanics	64.0	12.2	7.8	23.4	106
Blacks	53.9	17.0	11.5	16.9	72

Notes:
1. US Census, 2009 (Average of Data on Men and Women).
2. Simmons and O'Connell, 2003.
3. US Census 5-Year community study, 1 January 2005 to 31 December 2009.
4. National Vital Statistics Reports for 2007, Vol. 58, No. 4.
5. Ventura, 2009.

WORLDWIDE TRENDS REGARDING THE FAMILY

The trends we see in the United States regarding marriage, cohabitation, fertility rates, divorce, and out-of-wedlock births are similar in many parts of the world. Despite recent declines, the United States generally leads the world in marriage rates – 9.8 per 1,000 people per year. Other selected countries' marriage rates per 1000 are as follows: Russia, 8.9; Portugal, 7.3; Israel, 7; New Zealand, 7; Australia, 6.9; Denmark, 6.1; Greece, 5.8; Japan, 5.8; Italy, 5.4; France, 5.1; Finland, 4.8, and Sweden, 4.7 (United Nations Monthly Bulletin of Statistics, April 2001).

Another trend is declining birth rates. Given current birth rates various studies project that Europe will have approximately 40 to 100 million fewer people by 2050 (www.xist.org/earth/pop_continent.aspx). A sample of the fertility rates of developed countries are (2.10 is replacement rate): France, 2.08; United States, 2.06; United Kingdom, 1.91; Chile, 1.87; Australia, 1.77; Russia, 1.61; Canada, 1.59; China, 1.55; Italy, 1.40; Ukraine, 1.29; Czech Republic, 1.27; Taiwan, 1.10; and Singapore, 0.78 (Central Intelligence Agency, 2012). Eleven countries with the highest birth rates are in Africa; however poor nutrition and disease (particularly AIDS) has led to a significant number of families in Africa headed by single parents as well as a significant number of orphans. In South Africa alone there are 5.6 million people infected by AIDS with 310,000 dying of the disease each year (CIA, 2012). Hvistendahl (2011) and Hudson and den Boer (2005) report that due to selective abortions in Asia there are well over 100 million fewer women than men in Asia. Thus, many young men in Asia will not be able to find a mate who can provide them with family capital. And smaller families may mean fewer familial resources to draw on to start a business.

Divorce rates vary dramatically across the world. The highest divorce rates are in Europe (for example, Sweden, 54.9 percent), Australia (46 percent), the United States (45.8 percent) and Russia (43.3 percent), while divorce rates in the Middle East (for example, Turkey, 6 percent) and Asia (for example, India, 1.1 percent) are much lower (www.divorcemag. com/statistics/statsWorld.shtml). One of the more significant changes in families worldwide in recent years has been the increase in the number of children born to unwed parents. However, this varies greatly by country. In Japan, for example, only 2 percent of all births are out-of-wedlock. However in Europe the rates are significantly higher: Italy, 21 percent; Spain, 28 percent; Ireland, 33 percent; Netherlands, 40 percent; Sweden, 55 percent; Iceland 66 percent (www.usatoday.com/news/health/2009-05-13-unmarriedbirths_N.htm). Worldwide trends suggest that families in Asia are generally more stable than those in the West – there are more marriages, fewer divorces, and fewer out-of-wedlock births. But family size and the fewer women available for marriage could have a negative impact on Asian family capital. In North America, Europe, and Australia family size, along with divorce, marriage, and out-of-wedlock birth rates are likely to undermine the familial capital. In Africa and South America birth rates are relatively high compared to other continents, but out-of-wedlock births, divorce, and marriage rates are still problematic in many countries on these continents.

So do these trends regarding the family affect entrepreneurial activity? Data from the Global Entrepreneurship Monitor (GEM) suggests a connection between the family patterns we have just described and entrepreneurial activity (Kelley, Singer and Herrington, 2012). In 2011 GEM researchers interviewed over 140,000 adults regarding their feelings and intentions toward entrepreneurship. Unfortunately, the respondents' access to family capital was not assessed in the survey. Countries with the highest entrepreneurial intentions were Columbia (55 percent), Chile (46 percent), China (42 percent), and Algeria (41 percent). Overall, South American countries had respondents most likely to start new businesses. European countries however had the lowest percentage of those who intended to start new businesses (for example, Russia, 3.6 percent; Germany, 5.5 percent; Ireland, 5.8 percent; Denmark, 6.7 percent. The GEM survey also determined the percentage of the population in what they called 'early-stage start-up activity.' In the survey, China ranked number one (24 percent), with Chile (23.7 percent), and Peru (22.9 percent) close behind. European countries exhibited significantly lower rates of entrepreneurial activity (for example, Slovenia, 3.7 percent; Russia and Denmark, 4.6 percent; Germany, 5.6 percent; and Belgium and France at 5.7 percent). Although access to family capital by potential entrepreneurs will not explain all the difference in start-up rates, it is likely to be a significant factor.

IMPLICATIONS OF FAMILY CAPITAL FOR NECESSITY ENTREPRENEURS

There are a number of implications regarding the development and use of family capital for necessity entrepreneurs as well as countries, regions, cities, and states that might want to encourage entrepreneurship and help necessity entrepreneurs succeed. Those who feel a need to start a business out of necessity must first look to their family network for ideas, labor, contacts, and capital that may help them succeed. Of course it may be the case that the reason they must start a new business is because they do not have a 'family safety net' to help them during difficult times. But clearly, family relationships, if available, are very important for a fledgling entre-preneur. Necessity entrepreneurs should be encouraged to develop and maintain relations with family members – even distant ones. Working with and learning from family members can also prove helpful, as can eventu-ally getting married and having a partner to help with the challenges of starting a new business. From a public policy standpoint the key is to develop policies that: (1) encourage marriage and births in the context of marriage; and (2) discourage divorce and cohabitation. Such efforts would encourage the formation of and sustenance of family capital. Economist and Nobel laureate Gary Becker supports the notion that strong families are important to economic development when he writes, 'the family is still crucial to a well-functioning economy and society, and I believe – in the long run – that those economies that will advance most rapidly will tend to have strong family structures' (http://www.um.edu.uy/docs/revistafcee/2002/humancapitalBecker.pdf, p. 2). Governments through tax policy and other incentives should encourage their citizens to marry and to provide for their children in the context of marriage. Encouraging larger families, when the parents can provide sufficiently for the children, is another step that is important. China, for example, is already reviewing its 'one child' policy due to potential problems in the future. Governments can also provide more support for individuals contemplating divorce or mitigating the impact of divorce through required training programs and mediation. Given current trends it's not likely that we will see a return to the traditional family patterns of the past, but it is important for governments to recognize the importance of family capital to economic activity and take steps to ensure that family capital will be strengthened and supported in the future.

POTENTIAL 'DARK SIDE' OF FAMILY CAPITAL

While family capital can be an important factor in helping entrepreneurs – particularly necessity entrepreneurs – succeed, I should note that some family patterns can undermine one's ability to start a new business. For example, Stack (1974) in her study of one African-American community describes how social obligations among family members and friends actually stifle entrepreneurship. Stack demonstrates that some families may have a difficult time accumulating capital since they must use such funds to help others in their social network. She gives an example: 'When Magnolia and Calvin inherited a sum of money, the information quickly spread to every member of their domestic network. Within a month and a half all of the money was absorbed by participants in their network whose demands and needs could not be refused' (Stack, 1974, pp. 36, 37). Stack notes that those in the black community known as 'The Flats' are 'trapped in a web of obligations' and that family and friends 'exploit one another . . . and expect to be exploited in return' (p. 39). In contrast, Asian-Americans tend to accumulate capital, rather than disperse it among all their relatives, thus providing the necessary funds to form new enterprises. In another study, Banfield (1958) described how the families in southern Italy were so distrusting of those outside the family that little collaboration in the broader community occurred to improve the local economy. Family networks can be particularly useful when they are leveraged with resources from outside the family. Therefore, families that lack resource networks outside the family might have difficulty in starting new businesses. Thus we must recognize that strong families are not necessarily a panacea to all the problems facing necessity entrepreneurs. However, it is important to recognize that family capital is an important resource to be drawn upon by entrepreneurs who have little hope of finding resources through more formal channels, and by strengthening their families and family networks, necessity entrepreneurs might be more likely to succeed.

CONCLUSION

In this chapter I have argued that family capital is likely to be an important resource for necessity entrepreneurs to draw upon if they are to succeed in starting and growing a new business. Human, social, and financial capital are often crucial to the success of an entrepreneurial venture, and necessity entrepreneurs may find that family is their only source for these important assets. In addition to strengthening family relationships as I suggested previously, the necessity entrepreneur could enhance his or her own human capital by developing those skills and gaining the experience needed to be a successful entrepreneur. Gaining basic skills in accounting, marketing and sales, as well as inventory management may prove critical to the success of a necessity entrepreneur, particularly if he or she does not have role models in their social network to observe and rely upon. It may be that finding microenterprise educational opportunities might prove important *before* the necessity entrepreneur decides to launch a business. It also may prove important to use other vehicles to start a business such as microfranchising, where the necessity entrepreneur can get help and support from the micro franchisor who develops the franchise and supports the franchisees (Fairbourne, Gibson and Dyer, 2007). In some sense, the micro franchisor provides an alternative resource network to family capital that the necessity entrepreneur can draw upon. Thus, necessity entrepreneurs who may not have family capital to draw upon may have to develop their own human capital via personal development and education and then rely on other resource networks such as microfranchising to provide them with the resources they will need to succeed. While finding substitutes for family resources may not be easy – and I have argued, family capital often proves easier to access due to family relationships – the necessity entrepreneurs should be proactive in seeking out other non-family resources as well to hopefully create a successful enterprise that will support themselves and their loved ones.

REFERENCES

Aldrich, H.E. and Cliff, J.E. (2003). The pervasive effects of family on entrepreneurship: Toward a family embeddedness perspective. *Journal of Business Venturing, 18*, 573–596.

Aldrich, H.E. and Langton, N. (1998). Human resource management and organizational life cycles. In Reynolds, P.D., Bygrave, W., Carter, N.M., Davidsson, P., Gartner, W.B., Mason, C.M. and McDougall, P.P. (eds), *Frontiers of entrepreneurship research 1997. Babson College, Center for Entrepreneurial Studies* (349–357). Wellesley, MA: Babson College.

Amato, P.R. (2005). The impact of family formation change on the cognitive, social and emotional well-being of the next generation. *Future of Children, 15*(2), 75–96.

Banfield, E. (1958). *The moral basis of a backward society*. Glencoe, IL: The Free Press.

Barley, S.R. (1983). Semiotics and the study of occupational and organizational culture. *Administrative Science Quarterly, 28*(3), 393–413.

Bates, T. (1997). *Race, self-employment and upward mobility: An elusive American dream.* Washington, DC: Woodrow Wilson Center Press.

Carlson, M., McLanahan, S. and England, P. (2003). Union formation and dissolution in fragile families. *Fragile Families Research Brief*, no. 4. Bendheim-Thoman Center for Research on Child Wellbeing, Princeton, NJ: Princeton University.

Casper, L.M., Cohen, P.N. and Simmons, T. (1999). *How does POSSLQ measure up? Historical estimates of cohabitation.* Paper presented at the Annual meeting of the Population Association of America, Spring, MD.

Central Intelligence Agency. (2012). In *The World Factbook, Country comparison: Total fertility.* Retrieved from https://www.cia.gov/library/publications/the-worldfactbook/rankorder/2127rank.html.

Danes, S.M., Stafford, K., Haynes, G. and Amarapurkar, S.S. (2009). Family capital of family firms: Bridging human, social, and financial capital. *Family Business Review, 22*(3), 199–215.

Dyer, W.G., Jr. (2006). Examining the 'family effect' on firm performance. *Family Business Review, 19*(4), 253–273.

Ermisch, J., Jantti, M. and Smeeding, T. (eds) (2012). *From parents to children: The intergenerational transmission of advantage.* New York, NY: Sage.

Fairbourne, J., Gibson, S.W. and Dyer, W.G. (2007). *Microfranchising: Creating wealth at the bottom of the pyramid.* Cheltenham, UK and Northampton, MA, USA: Edward Elgar Publishing.

Fairlie, R.W. and Robb, A.M. (2008). *Race and entrepreneurial success.* Cambridge, MA: MIT Press.

Fukuyama, F. (1995). *Trust: The social virtues and the creation of prosperity.* New York, NY: Free Press.

Hudson, V.M. and den Boer, A.M. (2005). *Bare branches: The security implications of Asia's surplus male population.* Cambridge, MA: MIT Press.

Hvistendahl, M. (2011). *Unnatural selection: Choosing boys over girls and the consequences of a world full of men.* New York, NY: Public Affairs.

Kelley, D.J., Singer, S. and Herrington, M. (2012). *The global entrepreneurship monitor: 2011 global report.* Babson Park, MA: Babson College.

Korenman, S. and Neumark, D. (1992). Marriage, motherhood, and wages. *Journal of Human Resources, 27*, 233–255.

Larson, J. (2001). The verdict on cohabitation vs. marriage. *Marriage and families.* Retrieved from http://marriageandfamilies.byu.edu/issues/2001/January/cohabitation.htm.

Light, I. and Gold, S.J. (2008). *Ethnic economies.* Bingley, UK: Emerald.

Lillard, L.A. and Waite, L.J. (1995). Till death do us part: Marital disruption and mortality. *American Journal of Sociology, 100*, 1131–1156.

Meek, C., Woodworth, W. and Dyer, W.G., Jr. (1988). *Managing by the numbers: Absentee owners and the decline of American industry.* Reading, MA: Addison-Wesley.

Micelotta, E.R. and Raynard, M. (2011). Concealing or revealing the family? Corporate brand identity strategies in family firms. *Family Business Review, 24*(3), 197–216.

Rodriguez, P., Tuggle, C.S. and Hackett, S.M. (2009). An exploratory study of how potential family and household capital impacts new venture start-up rates. *Family Business Review*, *22*(3), 259–272.

Rosenblatt, P.C., de Mik, L., Anderson, R.M. and Johnson, P.A. (1985). *The family in business*. San Francisco, CA: Jossey-Bass.

Sanders, J. and Nee, V. (1996). Social capital, human capital, and immigrant self-employment: The family as social capital and the value of human capital. *American Sociological Review*, *61*(2), 231–249.

Simmons, T. and O'Connell, M. (2003). Married-couple and unmarried-partner households: 2000. Available online. Washington, DC: US Department of Commerce, Economics and Statistics Administration, US Census Bureau.

Sirmon, D.G. and Hitt, M.A. (2003). Managing resources: Linking unique resources, management, and wealth creation in family firms. *Entrepreneurship: Theory and Practice*, *27*(4), 339–358.

Stack, C. (1974). *All our kin*. New York, NY: Basic Books.

Stanley, S.M., Whitton, S.W. and Markman, H.J. (2004). Maybe I do: Interpersonal commitment and premarital or nonmarital cohabitation. *Journal of Family Issues*, *25*, 496–519.

Steier, L. (2001). Next-generation entrepreneurs and succession: An exploratory study of modes and means of managing social capital. *Family Business Review*, *14*(3), 259–276.

Ventura, S.J. (2009). *Changing patterns of nonmarital childbearing in the United States*. NCHS Data Brief, No. 18.

Waite, L.J. (1995). Does marriage matter? *Demography*, *32*, 483–507.

Waite, L.J. (1996). Social science finds: Marriage matters. *Responsive Community*, *6*, 26–35.

Wilcox, W.B., Marquardt, E., Popenoe, D. and Whitehead, B.D. (2010). *When marriage disappears: The state of our unions, marriage in America*. University of Virginia: National Marriage Project. Retrieved from http://stateofourunions.org/2010/SOOU2010.pdf.

9. Policy analysis for entrepreneurship education in necessity-based contexts: a Sri Lankan case study

Eva Balan-Vnuk, Manjula Dissanyake and Allan O'Connor

INTRODUCTION

The development of entrepreneurs in order to stimulate economic growth is a key component of government policies (Hannon, 2006), and policy makers appear to consider entrepreneurship education and training as 'an efficient mechanism for increasing entrepreneurial activity' (Martinez, Levie, Kelley, Sæmundsson and Schøtt, 2010, p. 43). Government policies encouraging the education and development of entrepreneurs are evident in countries around the globe (Xavier, Kelley, Kew, Herrington and Vorderwülbecke, 2012), however evaluating the contribution of entrepreneurship education to a country and its economy has proved challenging (O'Connor, 2013).

In this chapter we analyze policies for entrepreneurship education in a country that exhibits a high level of necessity-based entrepreneurship. Necessity-driven entrepreneurs are defined as 'those who are pushed into starting businesses because they have no other work options and need a source of income'. This is contrasted with opportunity-driven entrepreneurs who undertake entrepreneurial activities in order to pursue a perceived opportunity (Xavier et al., 2012, p. 8). There is very little academic research regarding necessity-driven entrepreneurs, and even less so in countries that are in relatively early stages of development.

Sri Lanka is considered a transitional early stage economy moving from being factor-driven to efficiency-driven (Schwab, 2012). Although entrepreneurship activity data specific to Sri Lanka is unavailable, based on the authors' familiarity with Sri Lanka and Sri Lanka's transitional state, a significant number of necessity-driven entrepreneurs can be observed, and this is also reflected in the language used and the policies of the Sri Lankan government. Having recently emerged from a decade-long civil war, Sri Lanka is in the process of rebuilding its economy.

This chapter is structured as follows. We first examine necessity entrepreneurship within the context of economic purposes. We then review the literature on entrepreneurship education to explicate the diverse array of arguments and purposes that are purported to underpin its delivery. In particular we locate entrepreneurship education in the practice of policy making. We next provide an overview of the research method applied in this case study, and discuss the findings. Finally, we conclude with implications and limitations of our research, and future research opportunities.

THEORETICAL BACKGROUND

Necessity Entrepreneurship and Economic Purpose

This chapter interprets entrepreneurship from an economic perspective as 'a social process involving the efforts of individuals in enterprise activity', where enterprise is viewed, in the Schumpeterian sense, as 'the *introduction* of new products, services, processes and materials, and so on, that result in market disruption' (O'Connor, 2013, p. 547). In turn, the terms 'introduction', 'new' and 'market disruption' deliberately imply that enterprise activity is about innovation.

This raises the question: when one considers necessity entrepreneurship, is it based upon innovation in terms of the introduction of new products, services, processes and materials and so on that result in market disruption? In this framing of necessity entrepreneurship it highlights a disparity in definition. Necessity entrepreneurship is defined by the push motivation (Verheul, Wennekers, Audretsch and Thurik, 2002) or the circumstances that conspire to force or prompt an individual into entrepreneurship but it does not define the type of opportunity the necessity entrepreneur might pursue.

Therefore, in thinking about policy for entrepreneurship in necessity-based contexts it is important to distinguish the motivations of the entrepreneur from the type of opportunity discovered or created by the entrepreneur. That is, a necessity entrepreneur may act upon different types of opportunities and in neither case does the motivation define the type of opportunity nor does the type of opportunity define the motivation.

Following O'Connor's (2013) argument further, innovation is linked at the macro-level to the economic development function which is specifically positioned by the introduction of new products, services, processes and materials and so on that result in market disruption. The activity of innovating is assumed to be outside of the existing market dynamics or, more specifically, with the knowledge sector of the economy rather than the trading market economy. Upon the introduction of an innovation into a market, it accordingly disrupts the functioning market and displaces incumbent firms' products, services, and processes with new products, services, and processes. However, innovations *within* market dynamics also occur, apparent by shifts and maneuvers around competitive positioning. This less radical and 'within market' form of innovation (that some may call incremental innovation) brings about changes in an economy's productivity by lowering costs and/or broadening the reach of existing products, services, and processes through pricing, cost arbitrage, and quality differentiations among firms in the formalized and trading 'corporate' sector of the economy.

Given that the motivation of the entrepreneur and the opportunity that they pursue are distinct concepts, policy for necessity entrepreneurship cannot be exclusively positioned within either the knowledge or the market sectors. O'Connor (2013) further draws attention to the social sector of the economy and argues that entrepreneurship within this sector draws upon the utility of market economics to address social issues. In short this means that issues of social inequity or disadvantage are addressed by using market-led entrepreneurship. An example from within the Australian economy highlights how the social disadvantage of the Indigenous communities is attracting policy designed to stimulate business activity and trading to create economic activity by the Aboriginal peoples and restore economic independence for the Indigenous communities. Policy for necessity entrepreneurship perhaps more closely resembles this model whereby stimulating entrepreneurship acts as a means to empower the unemployed, create jobs and address labor-market inefficiencies (Cécora, 2000).

Acs (2006) argues that less developed economies, as a priority, need to strengthen the small and medium enterprise sector by creating 'policies that are focused at firms, not at individuals' (p. 104). Acs (2006) emphatically argues that if entrepreneurship is taken to mean 'self-employment either in agriculture or very small-scale industry, then in most cases entrepreneurship will not lead to economic development because there is no mechanism to link the activity to development' (p. 102). Acs continues to say that 'In fact, we know that self-employment declines as economies become more developed. It is only when economies are able to remove people from self-employment that we start to see an increase in development' (p. 102). From this position it is apparent that for a transitioning economy, entrepreneurship policy may be best placed within the market sector and improving productivity to grow established small and medium firms and exploit scale economies (Wennekers, Van Stel, Thurik and Reynolds, 2005). Similarly, by distinguishing the necessity motivation for entrepreneurship from the type of opportunity, it also suggests that new firms with high potential that exploit market gaps and productivity improvement and/or knowledge based innovation opportunities would provide better foundations for the economy than an entrepreneurship policy that creates self-employment and sole-proprietor businesses.

The background of this theoretical economic discussion about necessity entrepreneurship leads to our overall research question, which is: How is entrepreneurship education policy used in practice to support the development of necessity-driven entrepreneurs in Sri Lanka? Will the empirical evidence from Sri Lanka shed light on whether government policy for entrepreneurship is socially skewed in necessity-based contexts? Can we expect that the alleviation of poverty and reduction of unemployment will dominate the entrepreneurship policy agenda or will a more enlightened approach recognize the importance of entrepreneurship in the knowledge and market sectors of the economy?

Entrepreneurship Education and the Necessity-based Context

Stevenson and Lundström (2002) outline the general thrust of the definitions of entrepreneurship and enterprise education as:

> Imparting of a set of personal attributes, attitudes and behaviors and a set of knowledge and skills (know-how), which in the broadest sense can be applied to any walk of life, and in the narrowest sense can be applied to the starting and managing of one's own business. (Stevenson and Lundström, 2002, p. 273)

This summary of the definitional stance highlights the two broadly accepted schools of thought about the purpose of entrepreneurship and the closely related concept of enterprise education. The first stance aims to fulfill the broad purpose of instilling enterprising and entrepreneurial behaviors and attitudes across a general population and the second is more specifically aimed at inspiring business start-up and developing skills and competencies that support the success of new businesses. However, others argue that the purpose behind entrepreneurship (which hereafter includes enterprise) education can vary across a third spectral divide. Apart from preparing an individual to start, own and manage a business or providing more generic life and work skills, entrepreneurship education can also introduce students to the world of commerce and industry. This trio of purposes is neatly referred to as being either 'for', 'through' or 'about' entrepreneurship (Caird, 1990; Scott, Rosa and Klandt, 1998).

Putting the multiple purposes argument to one side for the moment, understanding the impact or influence of entrepreneurship within an economy is also further complicated when entrepreneurship education is found to be inconsistent in its content, pedagogy and general approach (Peterman and Kennedy, 2003). In addition, the relationship between entrepreneurship and education is regularly associated with higher levels of general education rather than specifically entrepreneurship education with respect to having more people successfully start and grow a business within an economy (Leffler and Svedberg, 2005; Van der Sluis, Van Praag and Vijverberg, 2003; Minniti, Bygrave and Autio, 2006). The inconsistencies within the field of entrepreneurship education, and the overlap with general education arguments, add to the difficulties of evaluating the contribution of entrepreneurship education to the development of an economy.

Despite these observations, some are drawing attention to the significance of entrepreneurship for community growth and development, which implies a broader relevance to developing and growing economies (Taylor and Plummer, 2003). For instance Jaafar and Aziz (2008) argue that entrepreneurship education embedded in higher education will assist industry development in developing countries with more potential graduate entrepreneurs entering an industry. Similarly Block and Koellinger (2008) suggest that training and teaching of entrepreneurial skills will raise awareness of business opportunities. Yet, there has also been significant criticism of entrepreneurship education with respect to its ability to deliver economic value (Van Praag and Versloot, 2007) or more specifically at the individual level whether it does much at all to enhance entrepreneurship skills and motivation (Oosterbeek, Van Praag and Ijsselstein, 2010).

Given the multiple purposes that motivate entrepreneurship education and the uncertainty around the impact of entrepreneurship education, O'Connor (2013) argues that there is a need for explicit distinctions in purpose at higher units of analysis above and beyond successful entrepreneurs and entrepreneurial businesses. This position is also supported by Henry, Hill, and Leitch (2005) and Gordon, Hamilton, and Jack (2010) who also claim that entrepreneurship programs need to clearly define the purpose in order to achieve specific regional economic development outcomes. Perhaps even more relevant to this study is the finding by Bhola, Verheul, Grilo and Thurik (2006) that suggests policies designed to stimulate opportunity entrepreneurship may not be valid for encouraging necessity entrepreneurs.

The distinction between necessity- and opportunity-driven entrepreneurs is important when a government seeks to understand the impact and positioning of entrepreneurial programs. If the focus of entrepreneurship education is just naively adding more entrepreneurs (as business owners) to an economy it ignores the fact that the financial reward for most entrepreneurs (those who start a business) is generally poorer than for those who seek employment (Shane, 2008). Similarly others argue that when entrepreneurship education becomes a response to labor-market deficiencies, in effect it appears to offer little to entrepreneurship and the long-term economic well-being of a region (Cécora, 2000). Thus, the type and ambition of the entrepreneur along with the type and potential of the opportunity need to be taken into account with respect to the objectives of an entrepreneurial education or program intervention.

From this vantage point it justifies Acs' (2006) argument that policies in developing countries should focus on bringing in foreign direct investment to employ people to attract them away from agriculture and self-employ-ment. He adds that a strong commitment to education and training, both at the elementary and secondary levels, are important as those with less education will end up in necessity entrepreneurship.

Returning to our earlier economic perspective then, entrepreneurship education, if it is to influence the development of a transitioning economy, will need to focus on established firms to stimulate high growth activity. Further, for new or nascent entrepreneurs, regardless of their motivation, the focus should be on developing skills of opportunity recognition and exploitation to establish firms that have higher growth potential that can provide stable jobs. A general thrust for higher levels of education would also underpin a progressive shift of the types of businesses that will be established from self-employment to knowledge-based ventures with high growth potential.

This leads us to frame our second research question which asks: How does the Sri Lankan government understand entrepreneurship education in the context of policy documents, and what are the focus areas for micro-enterprise development? This question will seek to establish the purpose of entrepreneurship education, 'for', 'through' or 'about' with respect to policy in a transitioning economy. Is entrepreneurship education specifi-cally a focus or are educational levels more generally being raised? What positioning is targeted for entrepreneurship education within the scope of market, knowledge or social sectors of the economy?

RESEARCH METHODOLOGY AND METHOD

Research Context: Sri Lanka

In this study we acknowledge the points raised by Acs, Desai, and Hessels (2008) that a 'one size fits all' policy approach for entrepreneurship within

developing economies is not appropriate and we seek to add to our understanding and make explicit the different approaches to entrepreneurship
education, and how these may be influenced by the dynamics of economic development. We adopt a single country case study of a transition
economy, namely Sri Lanka.

The World Economic Forum's (WEF) Global Competitiveness Report
categorizes three phases of economic development; factor-driven, efficiency-driven and innovation-driven (Schwab, 2012). These categories
are based on Gross Domestic Product (GDP) per capita, and the share
of exports from primary goods. Factor-driven economies such as Sri
Lanka are characterized by subsistence farming activities and extraction
businesses, with a significant reliance on unskilled labor and natural
resources. The governments of factor-driven economies generally focus
development efforts and activities to ensure an adequate foundation
to fulfill basic requirements of society. In the case of efficiency-driven
economies, which include economies like South Africa, industrialization
has increased competitiveness and the development of economies of scale,
as well as the emergence of capital-intensive organizations. This phase of
development is reached when basic requirements have been improved, and
there is a growing focus on developing efficiency enhancers (Xavier et al.,
2012).

We examined Sri Lanka as an example of a necessity-based entrepreneurship context as there tends to be more necessity-driven entrepreneurs
than opportunity-driven entrepreneurs in factor-driven economics (Xavier
et al., 2012) and this too is the observation of Sri Lanka by the authors.
Sri Lanka ranks 68th out of 144 countries in terms of global competitiveness, but only 79th for higher education and training, according to World
Economic Forum data (Schwab, 2012). Sri Lanka provided an ideal case
for the research team due to its transitioning economy, readily observable
reliance on necessity entrepreneurship within the country and the access
to appropriate data facilitated by close government links with one of the
research team members.

Research Domain

In this research we collected data by searching Sri Lankan government
websites. Research that engages with policy as communicable material,
that attempts to make political reason more intelligible, is grounded in
the critical field of governmentality and discourse research (Walters and
Haahr, 2005). Our research explores where and how entrepreneurship
education is applied within the context of a transitioning economy by
drawing on government policy documents. The interrogation of this form

of data is located within the interpretive discipline of discourse analysis (Chilton, 2004; Fairclough, 2004; Gee, 2005).

Concept Mapping: Compare, Reflect, Abstract

In this research, we use concept mapping (Alexander, 1964; Trochim and Kane, 2007) and follow James' (1907/1995) guidelines to *compare, reflect* and *abstract* to reveal how Sri Lankan government policy documents position entrepreneurship education as an intervention strategy within the economy. Concept mapping, drawing on the pragmatists' notion of conceptions (Ormerod, 2006; Peirce, 1878), is a network method, where statements are linked to each other based on their similarity, and presented in a visual format (Miles and Huberman, 1994). This method is used as an alternative to the more conventional matrix approach, where data is formatted as categories of statements, such as that used by NVivo (Miles and Huberman, 1994).

Concept mapping is applied by comparing statements and clustering those most similar to each other in a visual network diagram (Miles and Huberman, 1994). Although various social network analysis software tools are available to conduct this type of network method analysis, we used UCINET 6.0 (Borgatti, Everett and Freeman, 2002). The concept map that is constructed presents the clustered statements and allows for the measurement of size, density and relationship between the clusters or concepts in a way that does not confer hierarchy or order of importance. The researcher must be explicit as to the steps taken, from linking similar statements to each other (*compare*), determining the number of clusters (*reflect*), and naming each cluster to best represent each group of statements (*abstract*). This audit trail allows for verification and collaboration, and also allows for the application of creativity, insight and prior experience of the researcher(s). The process undertaken to develop the concept map in this research is described below.

Data Collection

We determined that the most effective way to comprehensively review Sri Lankan government websites was to concentrate on analysing all those listed on the Sri Lankan Government Internet Data Center (GIDC) website (http://www.gidc.gov.lk/). Our goal was to understand current policies as well as training and educational initiatives being carried out by the Sri Lankan government to improve the level of entrepreneurship and enterprising skills in small and medium enterprises. We analyzed the English language version of the websites and verified that these were accurate translations of the Sinhalese versions. This verification was undertaken by one of the authors fluent in Sinhalese.

As GIDC does not support a search function, the first step of the analysis was to carry out a search using the Google search engine on each of the websites listed on the English language version of the GIDC website. The 'AND' function was used to find multiple words on the same website and the 'OR' function was used to support the search using synonyms. The asterisk symbol (*) was used to expand the scope of the search by including words containing parts of a keyword. All the searches were carried out in April 2013.

The order of the keywords used is listed below and the discussion on the methodology is based on these keywords:

1. Enterprise*
2. Entrepreneur*
3. Enterprise* AND Entrepreneur* AND (Training OR Education)
4. Economic Development
5. Microfinance.

Searches 1 and 2 were carried out first in order to better understand the contextual discussions on the subject by the Sri Lankan government. Search 3 directly targeted the proposition of this chapter to understand current policies, training, and educational initiatives on enterprising skills and entrepreneurship. Searches 4 and 5 targeted the proposition of economic development policies in Sri Lanka. Figure 9.1 illustrates the logic of the keyword search process, as well as the number of results returned for each keyword search.

The results from the keyword searches identified above are shown in Table 9.1.

Data Analysis

The above results and their sources were examined in order to assess the quality of the context. We established that very little relevant content was available on Sri Lankan government website pages, but was instead contained in five key policy documents. These documents include Sri Lanka's Micro Enterprise Policy document, National Enterprise Policy document, Small and Medium Enterprise Policy document, Vocational Education and Training Plan for Eastern Province, and Mahinda Chintana: Vision for a New Sri Lanka from the President of Sri Lanka. Statements were extracted from these documents in order to undertake the detailed analysis.

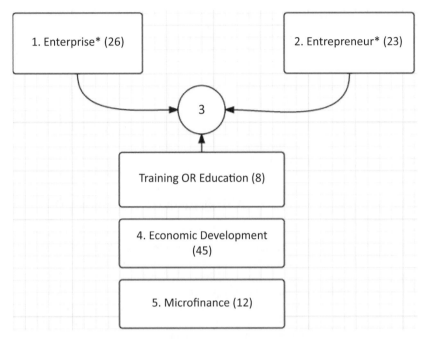

Figure 9.1   Overview of the keyword search process

Once the authors had agreed on the appropriateness and relevance of the collected statements, concept mapping was undertaken to identify the ways in which the Sri Lankan government policy documents position entrepreneurship and enterprise education for necessity entrepreneurs in Sri Lanka. The steps outlined below to link similar statements to each other, was carried out by one researcher; however, due to the presence of the audit trail, the other researchers were able to examine and critique the linking process. All the researchers were involved in the naming step to identify the concepts of entrepreneurship education as presented by the Sri Lankan government.

The 87 collected statements regarding policy and actions by the Sri Lankan government to encourage and support entrepreneurship education were entered into an Excel spreadsheet. A one-way comparison, to compare each statement to every other statement in the list, was undertaken to link similar statements to each other. This corresponds to James' (1907/1995) requirement for comparison. This comparison was undertaken by linking statements with similar keywords; it does not require the researcher to pre-determine any categories, and allows the researcher to be

Table 9.1   Keyword search results

	# of results	% of results	Search keywords and descriptions
1	26	22.8%	**Entrepreneur*** Interpretation of entrepreneurship and future focus on the subject through initiatives including but not limited to awareness building campaigns, educational programs and competitions.
2	23	20.2%	**Enterprise*** Policy focus on supporting the enterprises for developing skills and competencies of enterprises.
3	8	7%	**Enterprise* AND Entrepreneur* AND (Training OR Education)** The initiatives taken to provide awareness and assistance to facilitate the growth of enterprises. This had a sector focus in areas such as agriculture, cottage business development and vocational training.
4	45	39.5%	**Economic Development** Areas of focus through the national policy towards accelerating economic development. This included policy changes towards supporting SMEs, education and training initiatives and infrastructure development initiatives.
5	12	10.5%	**Microfinance** Workshops and schemes building awareness of various microfinance schemes to facilitate small and medium enterprises and industries.

open to unexpected conceptions (Charmaz, 2008). Following this process, statement 1 was linked to statements 2, 10, 18, 28, and 39. Statement 2 was then examined, and linked to statement 8. This linking process was carried out until all statements had been examined and compared to the other statements. A total of 167 linkages were made, and the number of links for each statement ranged from one to six, with an average of 1.9 links per statement.

The links between the statements were first entered into an Excel spreadsheet and then uploaded to UCINET 6.0 (Borgatti et al., 2002). Using the NetDraw function, a three-dimensional network diagram was created with each node representing a statement. The equidistant lines in the network diagram indicate the links between the statements, and, based on the knowledge that networks are inherently inhomogeneous, Girvan-Newman sub-group structure analysis (Girvan and Newman, 2002) was

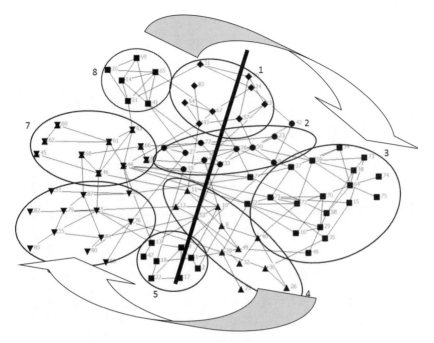

Figure 9.2   Concept clusters and relationships

applied. Starting with two clusters, the researchers went through a process of reflecting upon the statements in each cluster, and increasing the number of clusters until it was determined that new insights were not added by increasing the number of clusters. Based on this reflective process, the researchers agreed that eight clusters provided the most comprehensive and meaningful set of concepts. Drawing from the statements in each cluster, we then abstracted a name for each of these clusters. This is in keeping with James' (1907/1995) concept construction process. The final concept map is presented in Figure 9.2, and shows the final number of clusters along with key relationships discussed in the following section.

The final name for each cluster, as well as statement examples, is listed in Table 9.2.

FINDINGS AND DISCUSSION

According to O'Connor (2013) there are three key sectors for entrepreneurship education; either in the social sector where the aim is to use

Table 9.2 Cluster names and statement examples

Cluster #	Name	Sample statements
1	SME sector capacity and network development objectives	**24:** The Government's Ten Year Plan1 expects to implement policies and programs to reach an economic growth target rate of 8% for six years and higher rates thereafter. **30:** To build better capacity and its distribution to encourage and serve enterprises during their life cycle to compete, improve processes and products, gain more productive technology, assess markets, manage finance, network and cooperate with other enterprises. **31:** To make the network of public and public related enterprise service more effective and work with the private sector to improve quality and to facilitate the growth and distribution of enterprises in the business and enterprise development service sector.
2	Skills, technology and finances (practical)	**4:** Increasing access to microfinance and supporting entrepreneurship are equally important for sustainable development of microenterprises. Hence a comprehensive microenterprises policy has to be formulated to address both the financial and technical issues. **33:** Increase productivity through improved access to technology and skills. **77:** Now the department is taking steps to reorganize its activities towards mainly skill development and technology transfer programs on various fields such as leather, food processing, aluminum fabricating, Batik printing.
3	Educational institutions and infrastructure	**52:** With a view to attracting youth, agricultural entrepreneurship will be promoted through youth vocational training programmes. Encouraging scientific farming with modern technology makes agriculture both intellectually stimulating and economically rewarding. Agro-based small and medium scale industries will be promoted for rural employment generation. **71:** Steps to promote more positive attitudes towards entrepreneurship are already being taken through the introduction of entrepreneurship in secondary schools curricula and various vocational and technical training institutes. This is fundamental to the development of an enterprise culture. **73:** Improving the allocation of basic resources for educational institutions such as adequate staff and basic equipment, improving availability and quality of human resources, leadership development programmes and the promotion of entrepreneurship for these young people will be prioritized.

4	Facilitating processes for micro enterprise transition / Sector transformation	**10:** The overall goal of the New Micro Enterprise Policy is to expand the economic opportunities through sustainable dynamic and compatible microenterprise development and transfer 20% micro-enterprises in the informal sector to formal sector within next three years. **11:** The advocated development approach is transformation of microenterprises from informal sector to the formal sector. It is a challenging task in the management of economic development. Hence innovative policy instruments have to be developed to suit the location specific and sector-specific factors to make the development approach successful. **36:** Facilitate and encourage experimentation and promotion of incubation processes, location policies for aggregating enterprises into enterprise and economic zones for SMEs.
5	Policy and regulations	**2:** In the absence of a National Policy on Micro Enterprises, NEDA is not in a position to undertake the tasks assigned to it in the area of microenterprise development especially the growth of micro-enterprises as envisaged in the National Development Framework. **28:** To provide all enterprises the regulatory and legal environment at natiownal as well as sub national levels for enterprises to begin, operate, grow and transform and where necessary exit and resume activities in more productive ventures. **47:** At present there is no clear definition of SMEs. This position has created confusion in identifying SMEs for various programs. It also creates implementation problems for the national policy.
6	Micro enterprises	**5:** Microenterprises generally defined as very small businesses with five or fewer employees play an important role in the economy of Sri Lanka. Most of these enterprises are developed and managed by self-employed persons and located in non-urban areas. Those enterprises serve mainly the regional markets and add value to the resources available in the nearby areas. **55:** Most of these rural industries are microenterprises conducted by rural entrepreneurs at the cottage level. **87:** The participants were mainly micro or small-time entrepreneurs who have basically learnt their skills on the job with the guidance of skilled craftsmen, without attending any formal training institutions.

Table 9.2 (continued)

Cluster #	Name	Sample statements
7	Self-employment / self-help	**46:** Microenterprises play a major role in the development of local economies, in their self-help efforts to improve competitive conditions such as facilitation of management resources and upgrading management (Vidatha Program by MOST). **63:** Promotion of self: Facilitation for self-employment, and providing entrepreneurship employment training. **68:** It is about your personal abilities to compete in the market place, keep up with new technological skills and remain healthy. It is about developing your entrepreneurial skills, about receiving a fair share of the wealth that you have helped to create and not being discriminated against; it is about having a voice in your workplace and your community.
8	Poverty alleviation	**14:** Enable low-income people to use entrepreneurship as a pathway out of poverty. **41:** The promotion of SMEs sector forms an integral part of poverty alleviation and regional development programs implemented by the Government and non-governmental organizations (NGO). **69:** In the most extreme cases it [microenterprise] is about moving from subsistence to existence. For many, it is the primary route out of poverty.

entrepreneurship education as an economic utility lever to address social problems such as unemployment and poverty; the corporate sector where entrepreneurship education will serve renewal and/or expansion strategies for existing firms to improve the productivity of the market economy; and the knowledge sector where entrepreneurship education will assist individuals with new knowledge and technology to enter new ventures into market economies therefore contributing new businesses toward development of the economy. O'Connor (2013) argues that entrepreneurship education for economic development should be differentiated from the utility and productivity functions. He also argues that entrepreneurship arising from all three sectors contributes to the higher order goal of economic growth.

From this point of view it is interesting to note the structural relationship of the eight clustered concepts. In particular the positioning of Cluster 3 which relates to the education institutions and infrastructure is on the opposite side of the map to the three objective Clusters 6, 7 and 8 of microenterprises, self-employment/self-help and poverty alleviation respectively. There is also an apparent close linkage between skills development and technology transfer that appear conjointly in many statements, suggesting that these two aspects are critical to the development of micro, small and medium enterprises.

This structural relationship suggests that the Sri Lankan government is focused on making the invisible and informal nature of microenterprise visible as a formal microenterprise sector. Between the two opposing extremes are the clusters that represent the government setting about to make the connections between the two halves by providing clear SME sector capacity and network development objectives (Cluster 1), the necessary skills, technology and finances (Cluster 2), facilitating processes for microenterprise transition/sector transformation (Cluster 4), and providing policy and regulation (Cluster 5).

At a high level it would appear that indeed the Sri Lankan government adheres to the theory economic utility and a focus on the social sector with the use of market economics to address the social inequity experienced in the nation. Figure 9.3 outlines a step-wise sequencing approach that has been abstracted from the data by the researchers that represents the key issues and process that a government may take to reach such a policy position. However, a closer examination of the data reveals a much more nuanced and distributed approach with respect to entrepreneurship education across the knowledge and corporate sectors.

Although our keyword search focused on the elements of enterprise, entrepreneurship, economic development (including microfinance, training and education) it is interesting to note the variation contained within

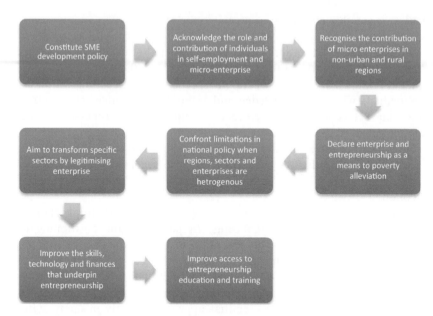

Figure 9.3   Step-wise policy process for entrepreneurship education

the extracted phrases with respect to policy directedness toward particular objectives. The five pillars of SME Policy include 'Entrepreneurship development, enhancement of competitiveness, promotion of regional economy, creation of an enabling business environment and development of micro sectors' (NEDA, 2009, p. 3), which suggests there are different targets for particular programs. However, the Small and Medium Enterprise Policy document also acknowledges, 'At present there is no clear definition of SMEs. This position has created confusion in identifying SMEs for various programs. It also creates implementation problems for the national policy' (NEDA, 2009, p. 6).

Within this context the policies discourse isolated by the keywords highlights policies and programs that are aimed at different purposes: poverty alleviation and employment creation (economic utility objectives in the social sector, provincial and rural communities), competitiveness, product, process and quality improvements (productivity objectives in the corporate sector of established businesses) and enterprise emerging from industry, research and higher education partnerships (economic development objectives in the knowledge sector). With respect to the objective of our research, the policy areas that may be expected to target the necessity-based entrepreneur seems to be in fact distributed across the spectrum of objectives and therefore are not exclusive to economic utility, as is suggested, but also to economic development (our keyword target) and productivity. This scattering of entrepreneurship education and training policy we argue occurs for two reasons. First, the lack of definition and differentiation between types of enterprise and business, and second, the tendency for policy to be framed around the higher order economic growth objective overshadowing a more fine-grained and directed policy approach.

Interestingly, the social sector in terms of aid agencies and non-government and/or non-profit social support agencies in this case are not apparent as a primary site for locating entrepreneurship education policy but instead the policies and programs feature in the rural, non-urban and provincial areas where poverty is harshest. In this way local and provincial government become the instrument of national entrepreneurship education policy and form part of the social support sector.

Referring to the concept map also suggests a distribution of types of entrepreneurship education development programs that start with simple training initiatives close to the poverty sources and working through the system and into formal institutional vocational and higher education. Worth noting is that the vocational and higher education sector as a target site for entrepreneurship education in this Sri Lankan case is not holding the objective of drawing upon a new knowledge pool for the development of industry but rather acts as a training ground of new recruits into entrepreneurship. Targeting the general student population for entrepreneurship education emphasizes a human capital development strategy that is designed to influence job creation and growth of the productivity within firms as students graduate to become active employees and employers. To distinguish between these observed purposes, targeting the knowledge sector for its science and technology with entrepreneurship education would suggest a new industry development approach while embedding entrepreneurship education into the curriculum more generally suggests a different purpose of broader human capital development.

With respect to the overarching research question on how entrepreneurship education is used in policy practice to support the development of necessity-driven entrepreneurs in Sri Lanka, the analysis suggests that indeed an economic utility approach is generally adopted. However, as we dig deeper into the empirical evidence the socially skewed government policy for the necessity-based context also extends into the knowledge and corporate market sectors of the economy. While it is tempting to suggest that this occurs through careful and considered design it would appear much more to be an artifact of the lack of definition and understanding of the relationship between entrepreneurship education and economic objectives. Instead, it is likely that the Sri Lankan government policy makers are grappling with the poverty alleviation and economic development as a composite problem rather than adopting discreet and targeted approaches to each.

Turning attention to the second research question about how the Sri Lankan government understands entrepreneurship education as portrayed through policy documents, and what the focus areas are, the three clusters of microenterprises, self-employment/self-help and poverty alleviation provide a significant response. Predominantly, entrepreneurship education is seen through the lens of these documents as education and training 'for' entrepreneurship. That is, most of the policy push is directed toward establishing and formalizing the microenterprise sector.

However, there is also some push for education that facilitates new business start-up or the transitioning of existing business into more productive areas of an economy and there is some acknowledgement of the need for technology and skill development education and training that could potentially foster new enterprise from the knowledge sector. There is also further evidence of entrepreneurship education being used as a general cultural lever to expand and extend the attitudes and behaviors of the population toward enterprising qualities and characteristics. Disappointingly, the policy documents do not uncover whether these approaches to entrepreneurship education are specifically positioned as education 'for', 'through' or 'about' entrepreneurship. To examine these elements, further research into the practice of entrepreneurship education would be warranted at the institutional levels.

In determining the relationship between entrepreneurship education and policy in a necessity-based context such as Sri Lanka, it raises an important distinction that is awkwardly handled by the terms of 'necessity-' and 'opportunity'-based entrepreneurship. The idea of a necessity entrepreneur is used as a means to differentiate from those who are opportunity motivated. A major implication concluding from the conduct of this research is that the label of opportunity entrepreneurs is misleading. An entrepreneurial opportunity or, put another way an opportunity to become an entrepreneur, is not a motivation but is instead the perceived source of reward and fulfillment of a motivation.

The opportunity is a means to fulfill a motivation whether that motivation is necessity based or otherwise. We argue that the idea of an opportunity-motivated entrepreneur should be replaced by a term such as an autonomy motivation (Benz and Frey, 2008) or an independence-motivated entrepreneur (Block and Koellinger, 2008). This in turn distinguishes two types of motivation at the level of higher and lower order internal human motivation drivers for the entrepreneur.

The necessity motivation, that is predominantly characteristic within a factor-driven economy, is a lower-order motivation that fulfills a basic survival human need while the independence motivation, more frequently observed in wealthier innovation-driven economies, is a higher order human motivation that responds to a self-fulfillment need. In both cases this frees the motivation from the opportunity type and avoids potential confusion when both motivation types can pursue various types of opportunities.

CONCLUSION

Our examination of Sri Lankan government policy documents supports the theoretical proposition that entrepreneurship education in a necessity-based context can be biased toward economic utility. While this policy bias is well intentioned and meaningful for a population the research suggests it is misdirected if economic development more specifically is a national priority. While focusing policy on self-employment and small-scale agricultural or local cultural enterprise may address poverty alleviation needs, prior research (Acs, 2006) suggests it does not necessarily create the scale intensive businesses required to soak up the unemployed into growth oriented and profitable business sectors that supports a nation's development. In fact, creating scale within the established SME or 'corporatized' sector to increase productivity may be more beneficial and this complies with the idea of targeting entrepreneurship education to the corporatized SME sector to prompt market-led growth opportunities.

Targeting the social sector in Sri Lanka also included both local and provincial government, which tends to suggest that localized government agencies can become instruments of social policy for a national government agenda. Local governments are much closer to the source of entrepreneurs and the opportunities that are presented by the local context and are in a far better position to tailor entrepreneurship education programs to achieve outcomes that can be beneficial to the local community.

It was also equally apparent that policy engendering entrepreneurship education also targets the knowledge and corporate sectors of the economy although the clarity of the objectives for entrepreneurship education within these sectors was less defined. The definition of enterprise and entrepreneurship being obscure and vague tends to scatter the targets for policy development, which prompts entrepreneurship education and training initiatives and programs to be developed across multiple sectors. Fortunately, the fact that economic growth can be fuelled to differing degrees by increased entrepreneurial activity from all sectors of the economy at least means initiatives are not entirely wasted but instead they may not be as well coordinated and efficient at delivering any particular outcome. The implication is that much tighter definitions and reasoned targets for entrepreneurship education will be useful for governments to prioritise among sectors and shape the type of entrepreneurial education and training that might be delivered in each sector.

Our analysis also brings into question the way in which distinctions are drawn between necessity and opportunity entrepreneurs. From an economic development and education and training perspective, regardless of the entrepreneur's motivation, it is important that entrepreneurs are encouraged toward opportunities for growth-oriented businesses. This creates the need for a clear distinction between the motivation and the type of opportunity that the entrepreneur may pursue. We argue that while the description of a necessity entrepreneur aptly describes a lower order survival need, the opportunity entrepreneur fails to describe a motivation and instead should be replaced with a term that describes the higher order self-fulfillment need of an opportunity entrepreneur. It is suggested that the term 'independence entrepreneur' or similar would be more appropriate and would assist in separating the entrepreneur's motivation from the type of opportunity that the entrepreneur pursues.

While our research may be informative and revealing with respect to policy making in necessity-based contexts it does still represent the analysis of a single case. This chapter has adopted a proposed framework of analysis for entrepreneurship education as outlined by O'Connor (2013) and suggests that the distinctions between sectors within an economy, the forms of entrepreneurial activity, and the education that is provided within these sectors to generate specific types of activity, are all important for reaching generalized economic purposes at a macro-level. Our analysis to some extent reveals the usefulness of this type of framework, however much further research needs to be done to verify and account for the variations that are theoretically apparent with respect to the empirical veracity of the ideas in practice.

REFERENCES

Acs, Z. (2006). How is entrepreneurship good for economic growth? *Innovations: Technology, Governance, Globalization, 1*(1). Retrieved from http://www.mit-pressjournals.org/doi/pdf/10.1162/itgg.2006.1.1.97.

Acs, Z.J., Desai, S. and Hessels, J. (2008). Entrepreneurship, economic development and institutions. *Small Business Economics, 31*(3), 219–234.

Alexander, C. (1964). *Notes on the synthesis of form.* Cambridge, MA: Harvard University Press.

Benz, M. and Frey, B. (2008). Being independent is a great thing: Subjective evaluations of self-employment and hierarchy. *Economica, 75*(298), 362–383.

Bhola, R., Verheul, I., Grilo, I. and Thurik, A.R. (2006). *Explaining engagement levels of opportunity and necessity entrepreneurs.* Research report H200610. Zoetermeer: EIM Business and Policy Research.

Block, J. and Koellinger, P. (2008). *I can't get no satisfaction – necessity entrepreneurship and procedural utility.* Erasmus Research Institute of Management, ERIM Report Series Research in Management reference no. ERS-2008-051-ORG, Retrieved from http://repub.eur.nl/res/pub/13221/.

Borgatti, S.P., Everett, M.G. and Freeman, L.C. (2002). *Ucinet for Windows: Software for social network analysis.* Harvard, MA: Analytic Technologies.

Caird, S. (1990). What does it mean to be enterprising? *British Journal of Management, 1*(3), 137–145.

Cécora, J. (2000). Entrepreneurs and SMEs in regional economies: Policy issues for sustainable development in a globalizing economy. *International Review of Sociology, 10*(1), 83–101.

Charmaz, K. (2008). Grounded theory as an emergent method. In S.N. Hesse-Biber and P. Leavy (eds), *Handbook of emergent methods.* New York, NY: The Guilford Press.

Chilton, P. (2004). *Analysing political discourse.* London, UK: Routledge.

Fairclough, N. (2004). *Analysing discourse: Textual analysis for social research.* London, UK: Taylor and Francis e-Library.

Gee, P.J. (2005). *An introduction to discourse analysis: Theory and method.* Oxon, UK: Taylor and Francis e-Library.

Girvan, M. and Newman, M.E.J. (2002). Community structure in social and biological networks. *Proceedings of the National Academy of Sciences of the United States of America, 99*, 7821–7826.

Gordon, I., Hamilton, E. and Jack, S. (2010). *A study of the regional economic development impact of a university led entrepreneurship education programme for small business owners.* Lancaster University Management School Working Paper Series 2010/002. http://eprints.lancs.ac.uk/31762/.

Hannon, P.D. (2006). Teaching pigeons to dance: Sense and meaning in entrepreneurship education. *Education + Training, 48*(5), 296–308.

Henry, C., Hill, F. and Leitch, C. (2005). Entrepreneurship education and training: Can entrepreneurship be taught? Part II. *Education + Training, 47*(3), 158–169.

Jaafar, M. and Aziz, A.R.A. (2008). Entrepreneurship education in developing country: Exploration on its necessity in the construction programme. *Journal of Engineering, Design and Technology, 6*(2), 178–189.

James, W. (1907/1995). *Pragmatism.* New York, NY: Dover.

Leffler, E. and Svedberg, G. (2005). Enterprise learning: A challenge to education? *European Educational Research Journal, 4*(3), 219–227.

Martinez, A.C., Levie, J., Kelley, D.J., Sæmundsson, R.J. and Schøtt, T. (2010). *Global entrepreneurship monitor special report: A global perspective on entrepreneurship education and training.* Retrieved from http://www.gemconsortium.org/download/1271392126157/GEM%20Special%20Report%20on%20Ed%20and%20Training.pdf.

Miles, M.B. and Huberman, A.M. (1994). *Qualitative data analysis.* Thousand Oaks, CA: Sage Publications.

Minniti, M., Bygrave, W. and Autio, E. (2006). Global entrepreneurship monitor

2005 executive report. Retrieved from http://www.gemconsortium.org/down load/1157607424015/GEM_2005_Report.pdf.

NEDA (2009). *Small and medium enterprise policy draft*. National Enterprise Development Authority. Retrieved from http://www.neda.lk/index.php?option =com_content&view=article&id=70&Itemid=55&lang=si.

O'Connor, A. (2013). A conceptual framework for entrepreneurship education policy: Meeting government and economic purposes. *Journal of Business Venturing, 28*(4), 546–563.

Oosterbeek, H., Van Praag, M. and Ijsselstein, A. (2010). The impact of entrepreneurship education on entrepreneurship skills and motivation. *European Economic Review, 54*, 442–454.

Ormerod, R. (2006). The history and ideas of pragmatism. *Journal of the Operational Research Society, 57*, 892–909.

Peirce, C.S. (1878). How to make our ideas clear. *Popular Science Monthly, 12*, 286–302.

Peterman, N.E. and Kennedy, J. (2003). Enterprise education: Influencing students' perceptions of entrepreneurship. *Entrepreneurship Theory and Practice, 28*(2), 129–144.

Schwab, K. (2012). *The global competitiveness report 2012–2013: Full data edition*. Geneva, Switzerland: World Economic Forum.

Scott, M., Rosa, P. and Klandt, H. (1998). *Educating entrepreneurs for wealth creation*. In M. Scott, P. Rosa and H. Klandt (eds), *Educating entrepreneurs for wealth creation* (pp. 1–14). Aldershot, UK: Ashgate Publishing.

Shane, S.A. (2008). *The illusions of entrepreneurship*. New Haven, CT: Yale University.

Stevenson, L. and Lundström, A. (2002). *Entrepreneurship policy for the future series*. Beyond the rhetoric: Defining entrepreneurship policy and its best practice. Örebro, Sweden: Swedish Foundation for Small Business Research.

Taylor, M. and Plummer, P. (2003). Promoting local economic growth: the role of entrepreneurship and human capital. *Education + Training, 45*(8/9), 558–563.

Trochim, W.M.K. and Kane, M. (2007). *Concept mapping for planning and evaluation*. Thousand Oaks, CA: Sage Publications.

Van Der Sluis, J., Van Praag, M. and Vijverberg, W. (2003). Entrepreneurship selection and performance: A meta-analysis of the impact of education in industrialized countries. Retrieved from http://www1.fee.uva.nl/scholar/mdw/sluis/ VDSLUISPaper.pdf.

Van Praag, C.M. and Versloot, P.H. (2007). What is the value of entrepreneurship? A review of recent research. *Small Business Economics, 29*, 351–382.

Verheul, I., Wennekers, S., Audretsch, D. and Thurik, R. (2002). *An eclectic theory of entrepreneurship*. Discussion Paper TI2001-030/3, Amsterdam, Netherlands: Tinbergen Institute.

Walters, W. and Haahr, J.H. (2005). *Governing Europe: discourse, governmentality and European integration*. Oxon, UK: Routledge.

Wennekers, S., Van Stel, A., Thurik, R. and Reynolds, P. (2005). Nascent entrepreneurship and the level of economic development. *Small Business Economics, 24*(3), 293–309.

Xavier, S.R., Kelley, D., Kew, J., Herrington, M. and Vorderwülbecke, A. (2012). Global Entrepreneurship Monitor 2012 Global Report.

Conclusion

Jeremi Brewer

In the foreword of this book, Larry Harrison clearly and appropriately explained that this work is not to be considered prescriptive – I have no intention of telling students, scholars, policy makers, development experts, and/or NGO practitioners what they must think or do. Rather, my fundamental objective in dedicating the past 18 months to bring this work to fruition has been to provide a solid foundation to the budding, and often misunderstood, interdisciplinary field of Necessity Entrepreneurship.

I intentionally mention that this field is misunderstood because, not too many years ago, I was a young doctoral student and I found myself trying to explain to a considerable number of professors the following:

1. I was convinced that (a) necessity entrepreneurship was, in fact, a real discipline and (b) necessity entrepreneurs were, in fact, actual human beings trying to earn a living each day.
2. A culture of financial poverty did, in fact, exist among necessity entrepreneurs (especially in developing nations).
3. If this culture of financial poverty were not challenged, and ultimately changed, it would result in chronic underdevelopment.

To my amazement, more than a dozen professors refused to sit on my committee because speaking of a correlation between culture and poverty was a horrendous offense. I then found myself even more puzzled when these good-intending academics were offended when I expressed that what necessity entrepreneurs truly needed was a culture-specific, entrepreneurship education and that capitalism would help alleviate the pains of the hundreds of millions of necessity entrepreneurs around the world. I even had a professor of economics pull out Muhammad Yunus' book *Banker to the Poor: Micro-Lending and the Battle Against World Poverty* and read the following citation to me, verbatim:

'I firmly believe that all human beings have an innate skill. I call it the survival skill. The fact that the poor are alive is clear proof of their ability. They do not need us to teach them how to survive; they already know how to do this. . . . Rather than waste our time teaching them new skills, we try to make maximum use of their existing skills.'

The professor, closing his book, pulled off his glasses and said, sternly: 'starting your academic career by saying that the Nobel Peace Prize recipient is *wrong* is audacious and arrogant. Are you prepared to share that with the world?' I immediately responded, 'I am not saying he is completely wrong, but I am saying that his theory, when used to explain that nearly six billion people on the planet only need access to capital to improve their lives, but no entrepreneurship training, doesn't hold true.' Needless to say, that professor chose not to work with me, either.

This is when I realized that I was going down the *right* path. At the time, I did not even know who Yunus was and I definitely did not want to offend anyone, but I believed differently than what Yunus apparently believed. For me, providing necessity entrepreneurs with capital, but no training, was not the most appropriate way to help them succeed. I also did not believe that 'the poor' (who are usually forced into entrepreneurship) should merely *survive*, but rather, I wanted to help them *thrive*. My premise from that point on was simple: I believed that training necessity entrepreneurs how to change their culture of financial poverty, as well as providing them with basic business principles, was the most appropriate way to help them improve their business practices.

As I gained more experience as a practitioner and started training thousands of necessity entrepreneurs throughout Latin America, Asia, the USA, and Africa, I soon was able to empirically demonstrate that Yunus' theory was not bullet-proof: giving 'the poor' access to capital, but not training them how to use their capital, was simply not a sound solution. In fact, Stephen Gibson's chapter highlights how we created innovative methodologies to help thousands of necessity entrepreneurs start hundreds of income-generating activities and small businesses with no capital at all. To date, just under $750,000 USD has been generated from nothing.

Thus, at its very core, this work is an attempt to provide me, and the many authors found herein, the platform to help nurture the field of Necessity Entrepreneurship. The reader of this work will find that not all of the theoreticians published herein agree that training necessity entrepreneurs is the silver bullet, either. However, this book provides academics and practitioners with the most current thoughts on who necessity entrepreneurs are, andho necessity entrepreneurs are not (see Chapters 1–4), and possible solutions to provide better services to the necessity entrepreneur (see Chapter 5). Lastly, this book discusses the role microenterprise education should play in the development of chronically underdeveloped nations (see Chapters 6–9).

While my thesis remains the same: that necessity entrepreneurs do, in fact, exist and they do, in fact, need specific training to increase their financial potential, I recognize that this book falls short of demonstrating exactly what developed and/or developing nations have done (at the macro level) to train necessity entrepreneurs. Thus, in an effort to provide the field of Necessity Entrepreneurship with quantitative data regarding the role that entrepreneurship education has played at the macro level of developed and developing nations, I have begun working on the second volume of this book series: *Necessity Entrepreneurship: An Institutional Review*. This book will specifically address (1) how necessity entrepreneurs have been and/or are currently being trained and (2) to what degree this microenterprise education implemented in nations has impacted the nation.

Index

Academy for Creating Enterprise
32–8
access
    to family capital 145, 149–52,
    154
    to financial capital 17, 19, 66, 70,
    148
    to financial products and services
    82
    to health care 78, 80, 90, 93–4
    to social and cultural capital 19
Acs, Z. 121, 162, 165
adaptation 46–7
Adventist Development and Relief
    Agency (ADRA) 95
Africa 15, 59, 86, 153–4
African Americans 152–3, 156
age, unemployment and new firm
    creation 44
agricultural cooperatives 87
Ajzen, I. 125–6
Aldrich, H.E. 129–30, 151
Altamiro, E. 76
alumni 36
Amato, P.R. 151
Amish community 151
APROCASSI 87
APROCREDI 87
ARARIWA 85
Asia 59, 153–4
Asian Americans 148, 152–3, 156
Atinchik 85
attitudes (cultural) 25, 27
Au, F. 15–16
awareness 19, 84–5, 164
Aziz, A.R.A. 164

Banco Adopem 86, 90
Bandhan 93, 95
Banfield, E. 156
Bangladesh 66, 86, 98

*Banker to the Poor: Micro-Lending and
the Battle Against World Poverty*
16–17
Banpro 86
barefoot consultants 62–3
Barley, S.R. 148
Bates, T. 148
Becker, G. 155
behaviour-modification learning
    centers 36
behavioural science research 119
beliefs 25
Besanko, D. 3–5
Bhola, R. 164
Bird, B. 126
birth rates 151, 153
Blancaver, J. 36–7
Block, J. 1–2, 164
Bolivia 11–12, 58–9, 63, 87–8, 91, 93,
    95, 98
Bornstein, D. 25
borrowers 30, 59, 70, 80, 91
bottom-up development 58
BRAC 66, 86, 93
Braeutigam, R. 3–5
breadwinners 71
bricolage 127
bridging allowances (FEA) 42
Brigham Young University 31
brokenness *see* poverty
bureaucracy 11
Burkina Faso 95
business
    acumen 80
    education 2, 81, 89
        see also entrepreneurship
        education
    failure 20–29, 41
    focus 26
    outcomes 40, 49, 89, 146, 150
    planning 47, 51

training 14, 24–5, 60, 67, 72, 79, 83, 89
see also microenterprise(s); new business creation
business culture 19–21
business skills 30, 47, 66, 72, 80, 157, 175

Caja de Arequipa 88
Caja los Andes 87
capability (financial) 82–3, 89
CARD 93, 95
Carnegie, A. 31
Carree, M. 105
case studies 35–6
cash advances 74
cash gifts 62–3
CESMACH 87
CFI/Accion survey 83
changeability, entrepreneurial intentions 127–8
charity 31, 64
child entrepreneurs 17–18
child mortality 62
child scribes 72–3
children, maternal investment in 70
China 153–5
client assessment tool (FCAT) 67
Cliff, J.E. 151
coffee cooperatives 87
cohabitation 150
collaboration, child-mother 72
collective service outreach 69
Collins, D. 55
Collins, J. 26–7
COMIXIMUL 94
Community Pharmacy Program 94
community-based training 87
competitive behaviours 120–21
competitive market 80–81
competitiveness 86–8, 104, 107, 109, 112–13, 115, 166, 176
concept mapping 167, 177
Confianza 87
confidence 61, 66–8, 71, 76, 89
Contemporary Microenterprises: Concepts and Cases 13
Cooperativa de Ahorro y Credito Mujeres Unidades (CACMU) 93

Cooperative League of the USA (CLUSA) 87–8
COOPROGESO 94
The Corn Farmers of Motupe 57–8
corporate entrepreneurship 106, 114
corporate sector 162, 175–6, 179
Cowen, T. 30
craft businesses 45–6
CRECER 91, 94–5
Credit with Education 84–5, 89
credit ladder 66, 68–9
cultural barriers 110
cultural typology, economic development 2–3
culture(s)
  counter-productive/dysfunctional 25–9
  of poverty 2, 6–7, 26–8
  of success 19, 28–9
  see also business culture; enterprise culture
'culture matters' thesis 2, 10, 20

Davidsson, P. 120–21, 139
debt 18
delinquency management 85–6
delivery models (educational) 84, 90
dependency 62
Desai, S. 165
destructive entrepreneurship 107
developed countries 1, 104
developing countries
  entrepreneurship in 103–15
    barriers to 109–11, 113, 148
    challenge for 114
    challenge for policy makers 115
    economic development 118, 121
    future of 113–14
    importance of 104, 105–7, 115
    infrastructure support 112–13
    training and education 111–12
    transformation and development 107–9
  government policies 165
  necessity entrepreneurs 108, 118
    failure of 20–21, 23–9
    helping 29–32
    involvement in illegal/immoral transactions 9, 19

Necessity entrepreneurs